Carnegie Learning
Integrated Math I

Student
Skills Practice

Carnegie Learning >

437 Grant St., Suite 918
Pittsburgh, PA 15219
Phone 412.690.2442
Customer Service Phone 877.401.2527
Fax 412.690.2444

www.carnegielearning.com

Acknowledgments

We would like to thank those listed here who helped prepare the *Carnegie Learning Math Series*.

Carnegie Learning Authoring Team
- Sandy Bartle, Senior Academic Officer
- David Dengler, Director, Curriculum Development
- Jen Dilla, Editorial Assistant
- Joshua Fisher, Math Editor
- David "Augie" Rivera, Math Editor
- Lezlee Ross, Curriculum Developer

Contributing Authors
- Jaclyn Snyder
- Dr. Mary Lou Metz

Vendors
- Cenveo Publisher Services
- Mathematical Expressions
- Hess Print Solutions
- Bradford & Bigelow
- Mind Over Media
- Lapiz
- eInstruction

Special Thanks
- Carnegie Learning Managers of School Partnership for content and design review.
- CL Software Development Team for research and content review.
- William S. Hadley for his mentoring leadership and pedagogical pioneering in mathematics education.
- Amy Jones Lewis for content review.

ISBN: 978-1-60972-158-9
Student Skills Practice, Integrated Math I

Printed in the United States of America
2-09/2012 B&B

Name _____ Date _____

A Picture Is Worth a Thousand Words
Understanding Quantities and Their Relationships

Vocabulary

Write a definition for each term in your own words.

1. independent quantity

2. dependent quantity

Problem Set

Determine the independent and dependent quantities in each scenario.

1. Selena is driving to visit her grandmother who lives 325 miles away from Selena's home. She travels an average of 60 miles per hour.

Independent quantity: time (hours)
Dependent quantity: distance (miles)

2. Benjamin works at a printing company. He is making T-shirts for a high school volleyball team. The press he runs can imprint 3 T-shirts per minute with the school's mascot.

3. On her way to work each morning, Sophia purchases a small cup of coffee for $4.25 from the coffee shop.

4. Phillip enjoys rock climbing on the weekends. At some of the less challenging locations he can climb upwards of 12 feet per minute.

5. Jose prefers to walk to work when the weather is nice. He walks the 1.5 miles to work at a speed of about 3 miles per hour.

6. Gavin works for a skydiving company. Customers pay $200 per jump to skydive in tandem skydives with Gavin.

Choose the graph that best models each scenario.

7. Kylie is filling her backyard pool to get ready for the summer. She is using a garden hose to fill the pool at a rate of 14 gallons per minute.

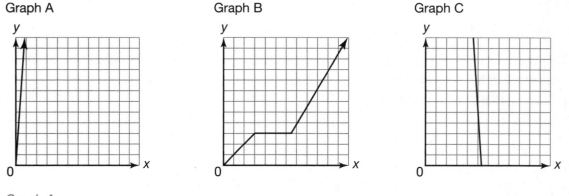

Graph A   Graph B   Graph C

Graph A

8. Hector is training to participate in competitive trampoline. In his best jump, he can reach a maximum height of about 9 meters and can spend about 2 seconds in the air performing tricks.

Graph A   Graph B   Graph C

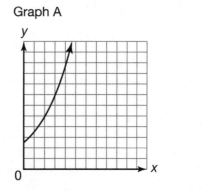
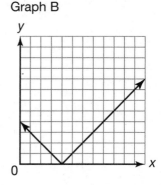
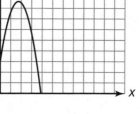

Name _____ Date _____

9. Jasmine is saving for college. She has invested $500 in a mutual fund that is expected to earn an average of 7% annually.

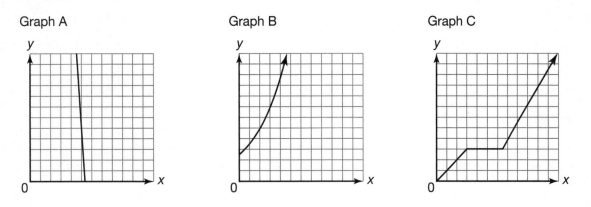

Graph A   Graph B   Graph C

10. Each day Maria starts her walk to school at 7:45 AM. At 7:50 AM she stops at her friend Jenna's house. Jenna is usually late and Maria must wait at least 5 minutes for her to get ready. At 7:55 AM Maria and Jenna leave Jenna's house and arrive at school at 8:10 AM.

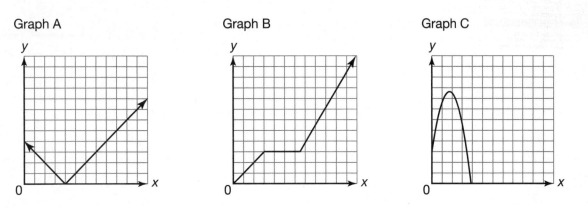

Graph A   Graph B   Graph C

11. Marcus is at the top of an observation tower. He drops an action figure with a parachute attached and watches it descend to the ground.

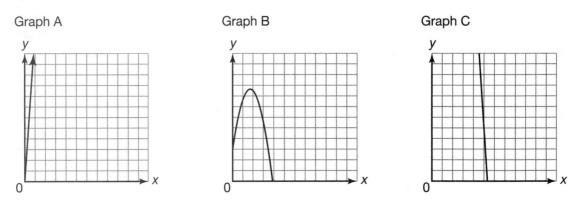

Graph A   Graph B   Graph C

12. Janelle holds a raffle to raise money for a children's hospital. Participants who enter the raffle guess the number of peanuts in a jar. Janelle records the number of peanuts each participant guesses and the number of peanuts their guess is off by.

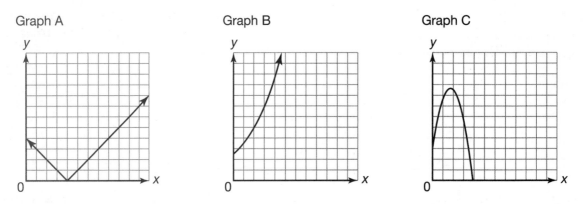

Graph A   Graph B   Graph C

Name _____ Date _____

Label the axes of the graph that models each scenario with the independent and dependent quantities.

13. Madison enjoys bicycling for exercise. Each Saturday she bikes a course she has mapped out around her town. She averages a speed of 12 miles per hour on her journey.

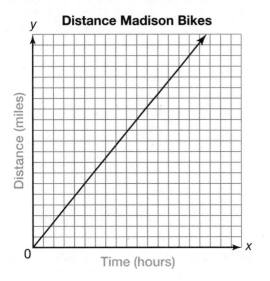

14. Natasha is filling the bathtub with water in order to give her dog Buster a bath. The faucet fills the tub at an average rate of 12 gallons per minute.

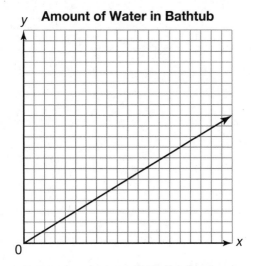

15. Marcus throws a football straight up into the air. After it reaches its maximum height of 20 feet, it descends back to the ground.

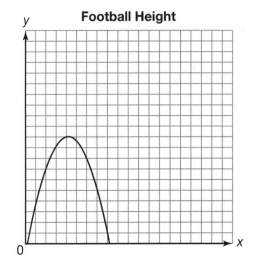

16. Chloe is using a pump to drain her backyard pool to get ready for winter. The pump removes the water at an average rate of 15 gallons per minute.

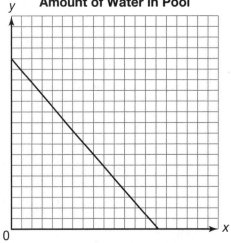

Name _____ Date _____

17. Jermaine is saving money to purchase a used car. He places $850 dollars in a savings account that earns 1.65% interest annually.

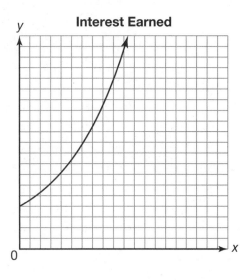

Interest Earned

18. Zachary enjoys hiking. On the first day of his latest hiking trip, he hikes through flat terrain for about 8 miles. On the second day, he hikes through very steep terrain for about 3 miles. On the third day he hikes through some hilly terrain for about 6 miles.

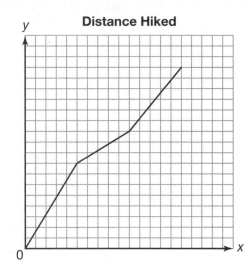

Distance Hiked

Name _____ Date _____

A Sort of Sorts
Analyzing and Sorting Graphs

Vocabulary

Match each definition to its corresponding term.

1. A graph with no breaks in it	**a.** discrete graph
2. The mapping between a set of inputs and a set of outputs	**b.** continuous graph
3. The set of all input values of a relation	**c.** relation
4. The set of all output values of a relation	**d.** function
5. A graph of isolated points	**e.** domain
6. A visual method used to determine whether a relation represented as a graph is a function	**f.** range
7. A relation between a given set of elements for which each input value there exists exactly one output value	**g.** Vertical Line Test

Problem Set

Each pair of graphs has been grouped together. Provide a rationale to explain why these graphs may have been grouped together.

1. Graph A

Graph B

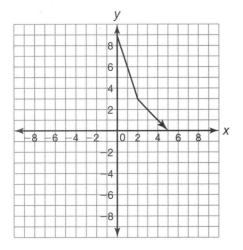 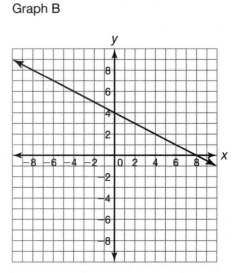

Answers will vary.

Both graphs are always decreasing from left to right. Both graphs are functions. Both graphs are made up of straight lines.

2. Graph A

Graph B

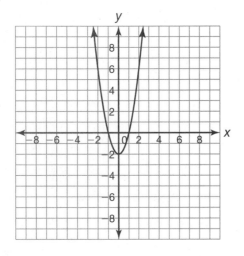 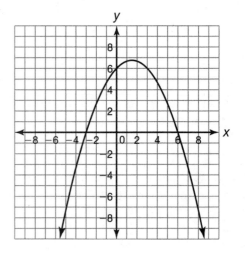

Name _____ Date _____

3. Graph A

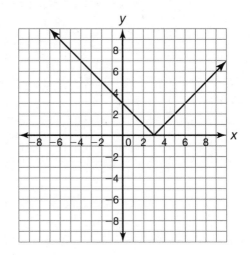

Graph B

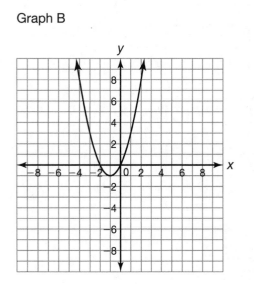

4. Graph A

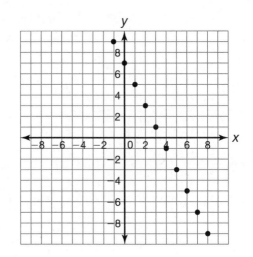

Graph B

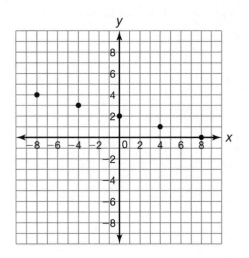

5. Graph A

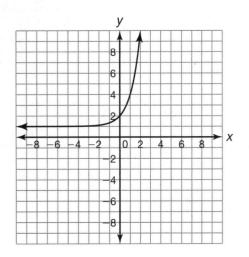

Graph B

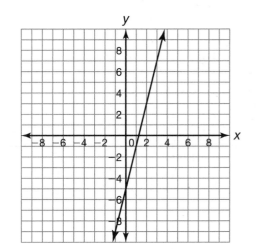

6. Graph A

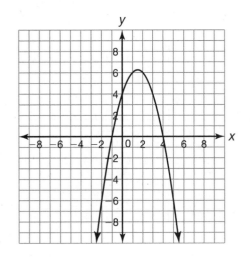

Graph B

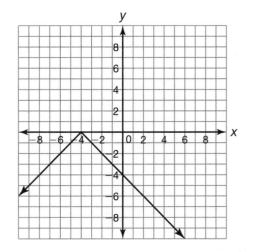

Name _____ Date _____

Determine whether the graph is discrete or continuous.

7.

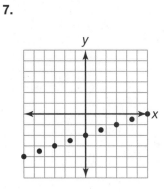

The graph is discrete.

8.

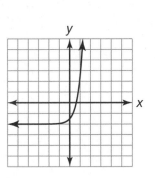

9.

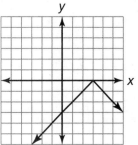

10.

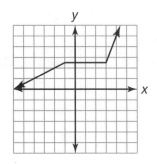

11.

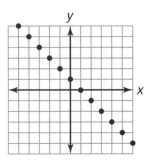

12.

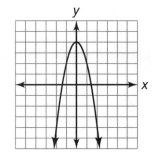

Determine if each graph represents a function by using the Vertical Line Test.

13.

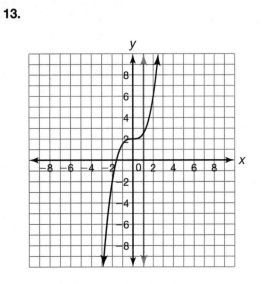

Yes. The graph is a function.

14.

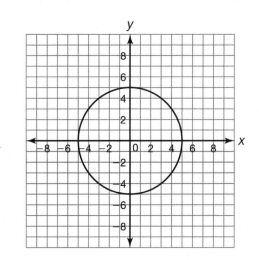

15.

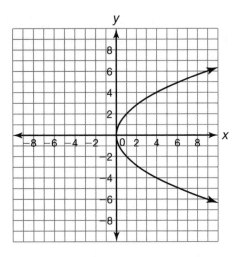

16.

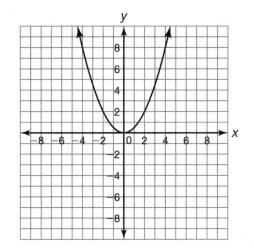

Name _____ Date _____

17.   **18.**

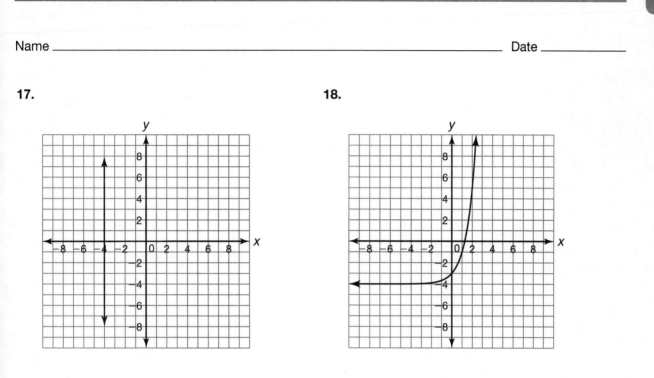

Name _____ Date _____

There Are Many Ways to Represent Functions
Recognizing Algebraic and Graphical Representations of Functions

Vocabulary

Choose the term from the box that best completes each statement.

function notation	increasing function	exponential functions
function family	linear functions	linear absolute value functions
absolute maximum	quadratic functions	constant function
linear piecewise functions	decreasing function	absolute minimum

1. _____ is a way to represent equations algebraically that makes it more efficient to recognize the independent and dependent variables.

2. The family of _____ includes functions of the form $f(x) = a \cdot b^x$, where a and b are real numbers, and b is greater than 0 but is not equal to 1.

3. The family of _____ includes functions that have an equation that changes for different parts, or pieces, of the domain.

4. When both the independent and dependent variables of a function increase across the entire domain, the function is called an _____.

5. A function has an _____ if there is a point on its graph that has a y-coordinate that is greater than the y-coordinates of every other point on the graph.

6. A _____ is a group of functions that share certain characteristics.

7. The family of _____ includes functions of the form $f(x) = a|x + b| + c$, where a, b, and c are real numbers, and a is not equal to 0.

8. When the dependent variable of a function decreases as the independent variable increases across the entire domain, the function is called a _____.

9. The family of _____ includes functions of the form $f(x) = ax^2 + bx + c$, where a, b, and c are real numbers, and a is not equal to 0.

10. The family of _____ includes functions of the form $f(x) = ax + b$, where a and b are real numbers, and a is not equal to 0.

11. If the dependent variable of a function does not change or remains constant over the entire domain, then the function is called a _____.

12. A function has an _____ if there is a point on its graph that has a y-coordinate that is less than the y-coordinates of every other point on the graph.

Problem Set

Rewrite each function using function notation.

1. Rewrite the function $y = 3x - 8$ using function notation so that the dependent quantity, defined as f, is a function of the independent quantity x.

   $f(x) = 3x - 8$

2. Rewrite the function $y = 3x^2 + 6x - 1$ using function notation so that the dependent quantity, defined as C, is a function of the independent quantity x.

3. Rewrite the function $y = 3^x + 8$ using function notation so that the dependent quantity, defined as P, is a function of the independent quantity x.

4. Rewrite the function $I = |n - 2|$ using function notation so that the dependent quantity, defined as L, is a function of the independent quantity n.

5. Rewrite the function $d = -\frac{1}{2}m + 5$ using function notation so that the dependent quantity, defined as A, is a function of the independent quantity m.

6. Rewrite the function $c = 2\pi r^2$ using function notation so that the dependent quantity, defined as C, is a function of the independent quantity r.

Name _____ Date _____

Choose the graph that represents each function. Use your graphing calculator.

7. $f(x) = \frac{2}{3}x + 2$

Graph A   Graph B   Graph C

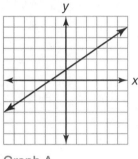   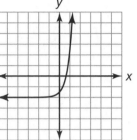   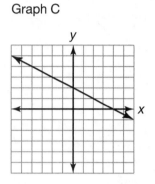

Graph A

8. $f(x) = -x^2 + 4$

Graph A   Graph B   Graph C

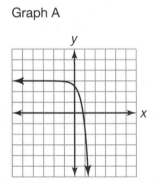   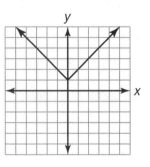   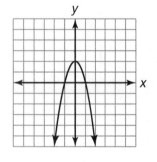

9. $f(x) = 2^x + 5$

Graph A   Graph B   Graph C

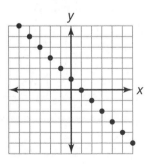   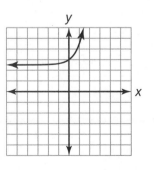   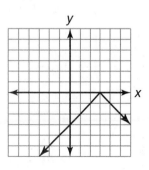

10. $f(x) = |x - 6|$

Graph A

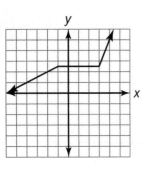

Graph B

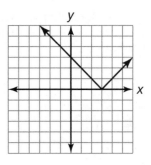

Graph C

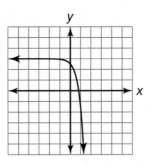

11. $f(x) = 2x - 6$, where x is an integer

Graph A

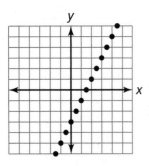

Graph B

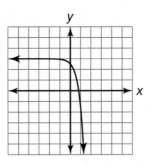

Graph C

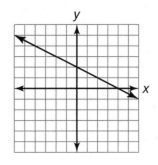

12. $f(x) = -4$

Graph A

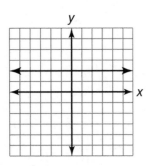

Graph B

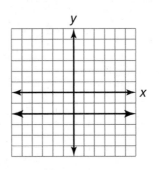

Graph C

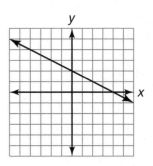

Name _____ Date _____

Determine whether each graph represents an increasing function, a decreasing function, a constant function, or a combination of increasing and decreasing functions.

13.

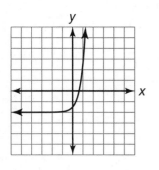

The graph represents an increasing function.

14.

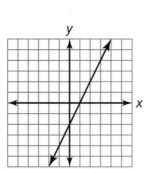

15.

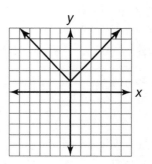

16.

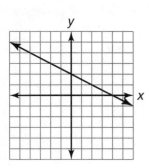

17.

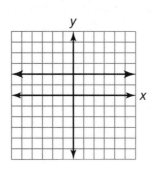

18.

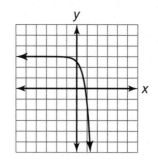

Determine whether each graph represents a function with an absolute minimum, an absolute maximum, or neither.

19.

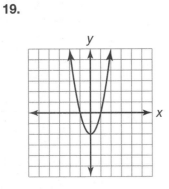

The graph represents a function with an absolute minimum.

20.

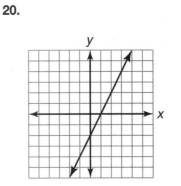

21.

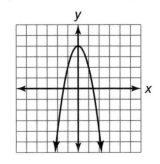

22.

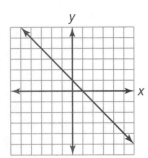

23.

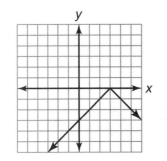

24.

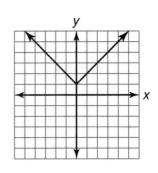

Name _____ Date _____

Determine whether each graph represents a linear function, a quadratic function, an exponential function, a linear absolute value function, a linear piecewise function, or a constant function.

25.

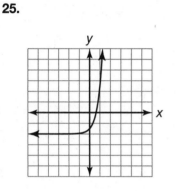

The graph represents an exponential function.

26.

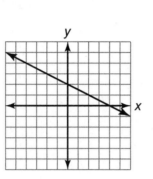

27.

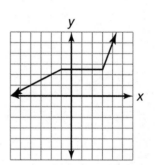

28.

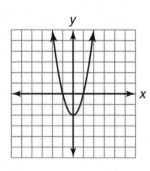

29.

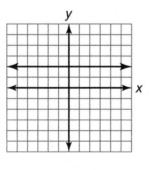

30.

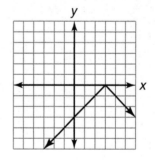

Name _____ Date _____

Function Families for 200, Alex...
Recognizing Functions by Characteristics

Problem Set

Choose the appropriate function family or families to complete each sentence based on the given characteristic(s).

linear functions	quadratic functions
exponential functions	linear absolute value functions

1. The graph of this function family is a straight line. The function family is _____linear functions_____.

2. The graph of this function family has an increasing interval and a decreasing interval. The function family is _____.

3. The graph of this function family has an absolute minimum. The function family is
_____.

4. The graph of this function family in decreasing over the entire domain. The function family is
_____.

5. The graph of this function family forms a V shape. The function family is _____
_____.

6. The graph of this function family has an increasing interval and a decreasing interval and forms a U shape. The function family is _____.

7. The graph of this function family does not have an absolute maximum or absolute minimum and is a smooth curve. The function family is _____.

8. The graph of this function family has an absolute maximum or absolute minimum and is made up straight lines. The function family is _____.

9. The graph of this function family is made up straight lines and does not have an absolute maximum or absolute minimum. The function family is _____.

10. The graph of this function family decreases over the entire domain and is a smooth curve. The function family is _____.

Create an equation and sketch a graph for a function with each set of given characteristics. Use values that are any real numbers between −10 and 10.

11. Create an equation and sketch a graph that:
- is a smooth curve,
- is continuous,
- has a minimum, and
- is quadratic.

Answers will vary.

$f(x) = x^2$

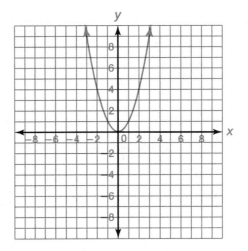

12. Create an equation and sketch a graph that:
- is linear,
- is discrete, and
- is decreasing across the entire domain.

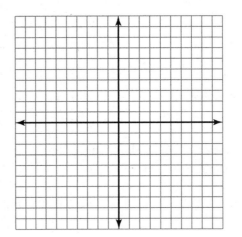

Name _____ Date _____

13. Create an equation and sketch a graph that:
- is a smooth curve,
- is increasing across the entire domain,
- is continuous, and
- is exponential.

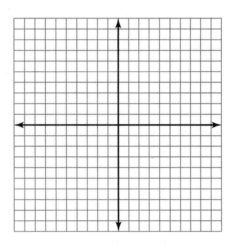

14. Create an equation and sketch a graph that:
- has a maximum,
- is continuous, and
- is a linear absolute value function.

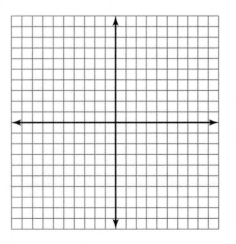

15. Create an equation and sketch a graph that:

  • is linear,

  • is continuous,

  • is neither increasing nor decreasing across the entire domain, and

  • does not pass through the origin.

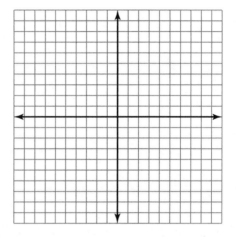

16. Create an equation and sketch a graph that:

  • is discrete,

  • has a maximum,

  • does not pass through the origin, and

  • is quadratic.

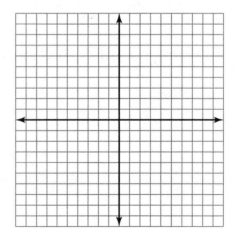

Name _____ Date _____

Choose the function family represented by each graph.

linear function	quadratic function	exponential function
linear absolute value function	linear piecewise function	

17.

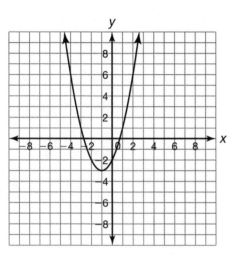

The graph represents a quadratic function.

18.

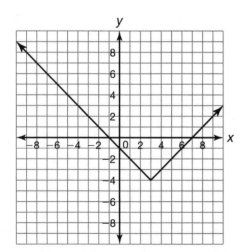

19.

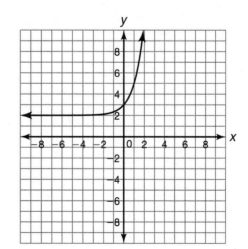

20.

21.

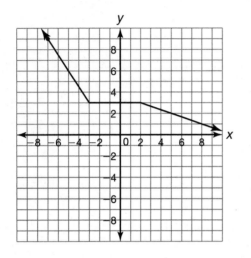

22.

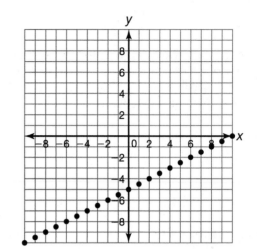

Name _____ Date _____

The Plane!
Modeling Linear Situations

2

Vocabulary

Define each term in your own words.

1. first differences

2. solution

3. intersection point

Problem Set

Identify the independent and dependent quantities in each problem situation. Then write a function to represent the problem situation.

1. Nathan is riding his scooter to school at a rate of 6 miles per hour.

The distance Nathan travels depends on the time. Distance, D, is the dependent quantity and time, t, is the independent quantity.

$D(t) = 6t$

2. Sophia is walking to the mall at a rate of 3 miles per hour.

3. Mario is stuffing envelopes with invitations to the school's Spring Carnival. He stuffs 5 envelopes each minute.

2

4. Shanise plays on the varsity soccer team. She averages 4 goals per game.

5. The football booster club sells hot chocolate during the varsity football games. Each cup of hot chocolate costs $2.

6. The basketball booster club sells t-shirts at the varsity basketball games. Each t-shirt costs $12.

Use each scenario to complete the table of values and calculate the unit rate of change.

7. Miguel is riding his bike to lacrosse practice at a rate of 7 miles per hour.

	Independent Quantity	**Dependent Quantity**
Quantity	Time	Distance
Units	hours	miles
Expression	t	$7t$
	0	0
	0.5	3.5
	1	7
	1.5	10.5
	2	14

(0.5, 3.5) and (1, 7)

$$\frac{7 - 3.5}{1 - 0.5} = \frac{3.5}{0.5}$$
$$= \frac{7}{1}$$

The unit rate of change is 7.

Name _____ Date _____

8. Jada is walking to school at a rate of 2 miles per hour.

	Independent Quantity	Dependent Quantity
Quantity		
Units		
Expression		
	0.25	
	0.5	
	1	
	1.25	
	1.5	

9. Noah is stuffing envelopes with invitations to the school's Harvest Festival. He stuffs 4 envelopes each minute.

	Independent Quantity	Dependent Quantity
Quantity		
Units		
Expression		
	5	
	10	
	15	
	20	
	25	

10. Terell plays on the varsity basketball team. He averages 12 points per game.

	Independent Quantity	Dependent Quantity
Quantity		
Units		
Expression		
	1	
	3	
	5	
	7	
	9	

11. The volleyball boosters sell bags of popcorn during the varsity matches to raise money for new uniforms. Each bag of popcorn costs $3.

	Independent Quantity	Dependent Quantity
Quantity		
Units		
Expression		
	5	
	10	
	15	
	20	
	25	

Name _____ Date _____

12. The football boosters sell hooded sweatshirts to raise money for new equipment. Each sweatshirt costs $18.

	Independent Quantity	Dependent Quantity
Quantity		
Units		
Expression		
	5	
	10	
	20	
	30	
	40	

Identify the input value, the output value, and the rate of change for each function.

13. Belinda is making greeting cards. She makes 4 cards per hour. The function $C(t) = 4t$ represents the total number of cards Belinda makes as a function of time.

The input value is t.

The output value is $4t$.

The rate of change is 4.

14. Owen is riding his bike to his friend's house at a rate of 6 miles per hour. The function $D(t) = 6t$ represents the distance Owen rides as a function of time.

15. Rochelle is shopping for earrings. Each pair of earrings costs $15 dollars. The function $C(e) = 15e$ represents the total cost of the earrings as a function of the number of pairs of earrings Rochelle buys.

16. Lavon is driving to visit a college campus. He is traveling 65 miles per hour. The function $D(t) = 65t$ represents the total distance he travels as a function of time.

17. Kiana is selling coupon books to raise money for her school. Each coupon book cost $35. The function $M(b) = 35b$ represents the total amount of money raised as a function of the number of coupon books sold.

18. Cisco mows lawns in his neighborhood to earn money. He earns $16 for each lawn. The function $A(m) = 16m$ represents the total amount of money earned as a function of the number of lawns mowed.

Name _____ Date _____

Solve each function for the given input value. The function $A(t) = 7t$ represents the total amount of money in dollars Carmen earns babysitting as a function of time in hours.

19. $A(3) =$ _____

$A(3) = 7(3)$

$\quad = 21$

Carmen earns $21 when she babysits for 3 hours.

20. $A(2) =$ _____

21. $A(5) =$ _____

22. $A(4.5) =$ _____

23. $A(3.5) =$ _____

24. $A(6) =$ _____

Use the graph to determine the input value for each given output value. The function $D(t) = 40t$ represents the total distance traveled in miles as a function of time in hours.

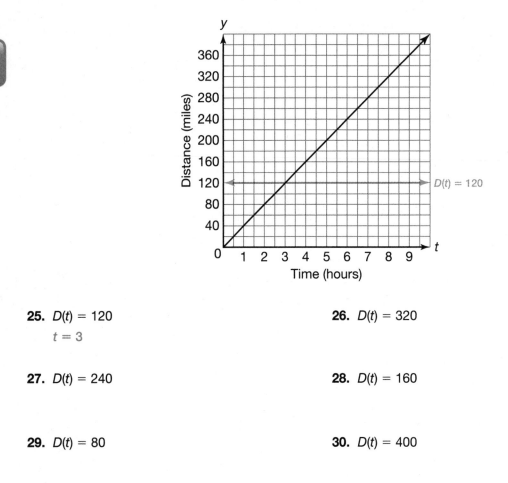

25. $D(t) = 120$

    $t = 3$

26. $D(t) = 320$

27. $D(t) = 240$

28. $D(t) = 160$

29. $D(t) = 80$

30. $D(t) = 400$

Name _____　Date _____

What Goes Up Must Come Down
Analyzing Linear Functions

2

Problem Set

Complete the table to represent each problem situation.

1. A hot air balloon cruising at 1000 feet begins to ascend. It ascends at a rate of 200 feet per minute.

	Independent Quantity	Dependent Quantity
Quantity	Time	Height
Units	minutes	feet
	0	1000
	2	1400
	4	1800
	6	2200
	8	2600
Expression	t	$200t + 1000$

2. A bathtub contains 10 gallons of water. The faucet is turned on and fills the tub at a rate of 5.25 gallons per minute.

	Independent Quantity	Dependent Quantity
Quantity		
Units		
	0	
	1	
	3	
		36.25
		46.75
Expression		

3. A helicopter flying at 4125 feet begins its descent. It descends at a rate of 550 feet per minute.

	Independent Quantity	Dependent Quantity
Quantity		
Units		
	0	
	1	
	2	
		2475
		1925
Expression		

Name _____ Date _____

4. A fish tank filled with 12 gallons of water is drained. The water drains at a rate of 1.5 gallons per minute.

	Independent Quantity	Dependent Quantity
Quantity		
Units		
	0	
	1	
	3	
		4.5
		1.5
Expression		

5. A submarine is traveling at a depth of −300 feet. It begins ascending at a rate of 28 feet per minute.

	Independent Quantity	Dependent Quantity
Quantity		
Units		
	0	
	2	
	4	
		−132
		−76
Expression		

6. A free-diver is diving from the surface of the water at a rate of 15 feet per minute.

	Independent Quantity	Dependent Quantity
Quantity		
Units		
	0	
	1	
	2	
		−45
		−60
Expression		

Identify the input value, the output value, the *y*-intercept, and the rate of change for each function.

7. A hot air balloon at 130 feet begins to ascend. It ascends at a rate of 160.5 feet per minute. The function $f(t) = 160.5t + 130$ represents the height of the balloon as it ascends.

The input value is *t*, time in minutes. The output value is $f(t)$, height in feet.

The *y*-intercept is 130. The rate of change is 160.5.

8. A backyard pool contains 500 gallons of water. It is filled with additional water at a rate of 6 gallons per minute. The function $f(t) = 6t + 500$ represents the volume of water in the pool as it is filled.

9. A submarine is diving from the surface of the water at a rate of 17 feet per minute. The function $f(t) = -17t$ represents the depth of the submarine as it dives.

Name _____ Date _____

10. A helicopter flying at 3505 feet begins its descent. It descends at a rate of 470 feet per minute. The function $f(t) = -470t + 3505$ represents the height of the helicopter as it descends.

11. A bathtub contains 5 gallons of water. The faucet is turned on and water is added to the tub at a rate of 4.25 gallons per minute. The function $f(t) = 4.25t + 5$ represents the volume of water in the bathtub as it is filled.

12. A free-diver is diving from the surface of the water at a rate of 8 feet per minute. The function $f(t) = -8t$ represents the depth of the diver.

Sketch the line for the dependent value to estimate each intersection point.

13. $f(x) = -40x + 1200$ when $f(x) = 720$ **14.** $f(x) = 6x + 15$ when $f(x) = 75$

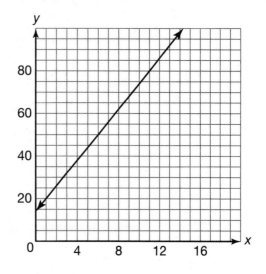

Answers will vary.
$f(x) = 720$ at $x = 12$

15. $f(x) = -2x + 5$ when $f(x) = -7$

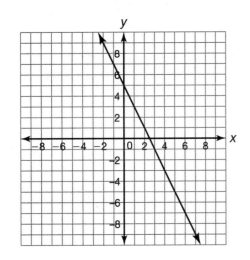

16. $f(x) = 4x - 7$ when $f(x) = 8$

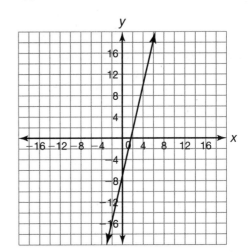

17. $f(x) = -200x + 2400$ when $f(x) = 450$

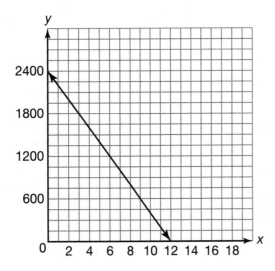

18. $f(x) = 12x + 90$ when $f(x) = 420$

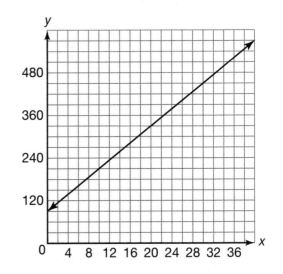

Name _____ Date _____

Substitute and solve for *x* to determine the exact value of each intersection point.

19. $f(x) = -40x + 1200$ when $f(x) = 720$

$f(x) = -40x + 1200$

$720 = -40x + 1200$

$-480 = -40x$

$12 = x$

20. $f(x) = 6x + 15$ when $f(x) = 75$

21. $f(x) = -2x + 5$ when $f(x) = -7$

22. $f(x) = 4x - 7$ when $f(x) = 8$

23. $f(x) = -200x + 2400$ when $f(x) = 450$

24. $f(x) = 12x + 90$ when $f(x) = 420$

Name _____ Date _____

Scouting for Prizes!
Modeling Linear Inequalities

Vocabulary

Define the term in your own words.

1. solve an inequality

Problem Set

Carlos works at an electronics store selling computer equipment. He can earn a bonus if he sells $10,000 worth of computer equipment this month. So far this month, he has sold $4000 worth of computer equipment. He hopes to sell additional laptop computers for $800 each to reach his goal. The function $f(x) = 800x + 4000$ represents Carlos's total sales as a function of the number of laptop computers he sells.

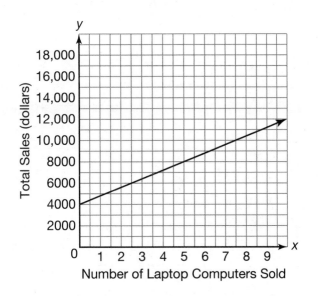

Use the graph to write an equation or inequality to determine the number of laptop computers Carlos would need to sell to earn each amount.

1. at least $10,000

Carlos would need to sell at least
8 laptop computers.

$x \geq 8$

2. less than $7000

3. less than $6000

4. at least $9000

5. more than $12,000

6. exactly $8000

Elena works at the ticket booth of a local playhouse. On the opening night of the play, tickets are $10 each. The playhouse has already sold $500 worth of tickets during a presale. The function $f(x) = 10x + 500$ represents the total sales as a function of tickets sold on opening night.

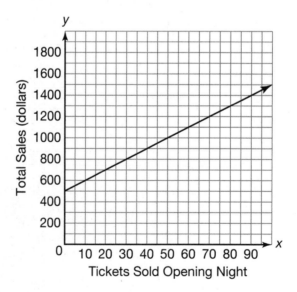

Name _____ Date _____

Use the graph of the function to answer each question. Graph each solution on the number line.

7. How many tickets must Elena sell in order to make at least $1000?

Elena must sell at least 50 tickets. $x \geq 50$

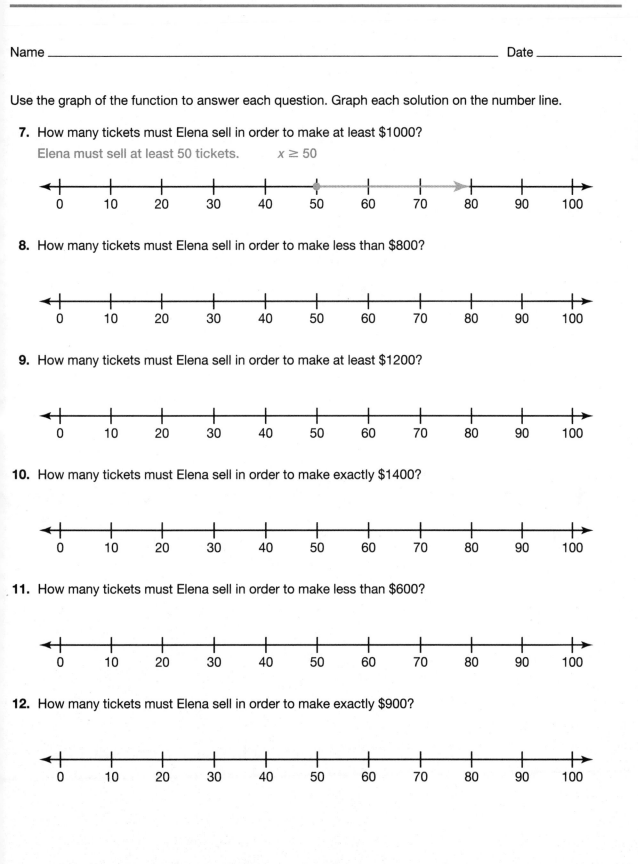

8. How many tickets must Elena sell in order to make less than $800?

9. How many tickets must Elena sell in order to make at least $1200?

10. How many tickets must Elena sell in order to make exactly $1400?

11. How many tickets must Elena sell in order to make less than $600?

12. How many tickets must Elena sell in order to make exactly $900?

Leon plays on the varsity basketball team. So far this season he has scored a total of 52 points. He scores an average of 13 points per game. The function $f(x) = 13x + 52$ represents the total number of points Leon will score this season. Write and solve an inequality to answer each question.

2

13. How many more games must Leon play in order to score at least 117 points?

$f(x) = 13x + 52$

$117 \leq 13x + 52$

$65 \leq 13x$

$5 \leq x$

Leon must play in 5 or more games to score at least 117 points.

14. How many more games must Leon play in order to score fewer than 182 points?

15. How many more games must Leon play in order to score more than 143 points?

Name _____ Date _____

16. How many more games must Leon play in order to score at least 100 points?

17. How many more games must Leon play in order to score fewer than 85 points?

18. How many more games must Leon play in order to score more than 200 points?

Draw an oval on the graph to represent the solution to each question. Write the corresponding inequality statement.

19. A hot air balloon at 4000 feet begins its descent. It descends at a rate of 200 feet per minute. The function $f(x) = -200x + 4000$ represents the height of the balloon as it descends. How many minutes have passed if the balloon is below 3000 feet?

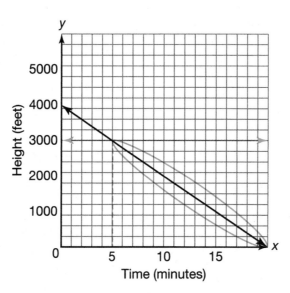

More than 5 minutes have passed if the balloon is below 3000 feet.

$x > 5$

20. A bathtub filled with 55 gallons of water is drained. The water drains at a rate of 5 gallons per minute. The function $f(x) = -5x + 55$ represents the volume of water in the tub as it drains. How many minutes have passed if the tub still has more than 20 gallons of water remaining in it?

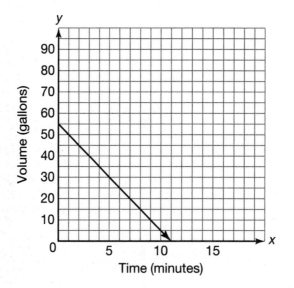

Name _____ Date _____

21. Lea is walking to school at a rate of 250 feet per minute. Her school is 5000 feet from her home. The function $f(x) = 250x$ represents the distance Lea walks. How many minutes have passed if Lea still has more than 2000 feet to walk?

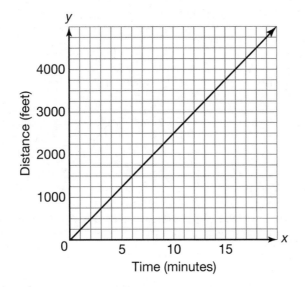

22. Franco is riding his bike to school at a rate of 600 feet per minute. His school is 9000 feet from his home. The function $f(x) = 600x$ represents the distance Franco rides. How many minutes have passed if Franco has less than 3000 feet left to ride?

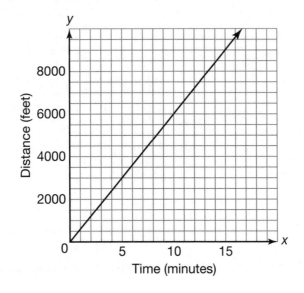

23. A submarine is diving from the surface of the water at a rate of 20 feet per minute. The function
$f(x) = -20x$ represents the depth of the submarine as it dives. How many minutes have passed if
the submarine is at least 160 feet below the surface?

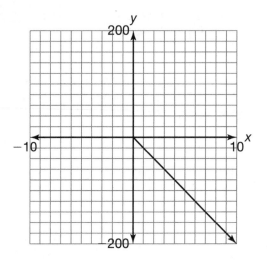

24. A scuba diver is diving from the surface of the water at a rate of 14 feet per minute. The function
$f(x) = -14x$ represents the depth of the diver as he dives. How many minutes have passed if the diver
is less than 42 feet below the surface?

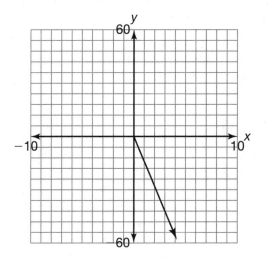

Name _____ Date _____

We're Shipping Out!
Solving and Graphing Compound Inequalities

2

Vocabulary

Match each definition to its corresponding term.

1. compound inequality

a. a solution of a compound inequality in the form $a < x < b$, where a and b are any real numbers

2. solution of a compound inequality

b. an inequality that is formed by the union, "or," or the intersection, "and," of two simple inequalities

3. conjunction

c. the part or parts of the solutions that satisfy both of the inequalities

4. disjunction

d. a solution of a compound inequality in the form $x < a$ or $x > b$, where a and b are any real numbers

Problem Set

Write each compound inequality in compact form.

1. All numbers less than or equal to 22 and greater than -4

$22 \geq x > -4$

2. All numbers less than 55 and greater than 45

3. All numbers greater than or equal to 0 and less than or equal to 6

4. All numbers greater than 10 and less than 1000

5. All numbers less than or equal to 87 and greater than or equal to 83

6. All numbers greater than -1 and less than or equal to 39

Write an inequality for each graph.

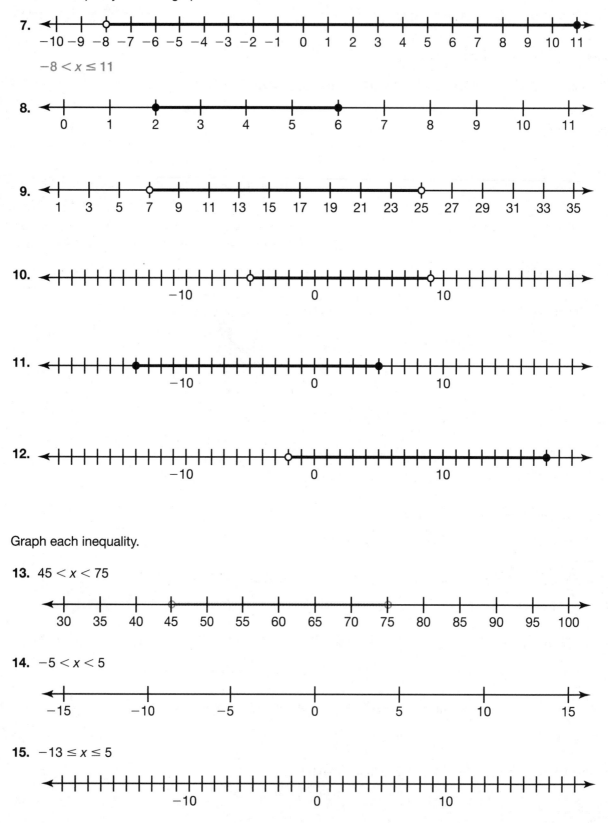

7.

$-8 < x \le 11$

8.

9.

10.

11.

12.

Graph each inequality.

13. $45 < x < 75$

14. $-5 < x < 5$

15. $-13 \le x \le 5$

Name _____ Date _____

16. $-6 \leq x < 19$

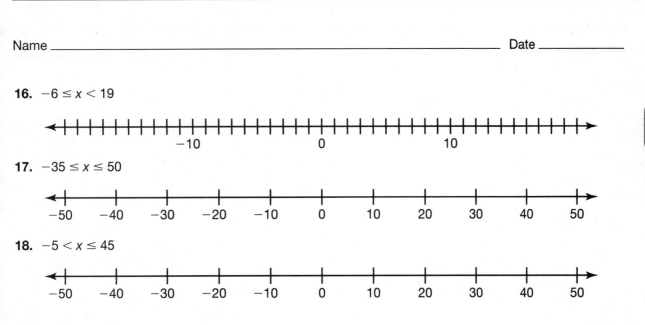

17. $-35 \leq x \leq 50$

18. $-5 < x \leq 45$

Write a compound inequality for each situation.

19. The flowers in the garden are 6 inches or taller *or* shorter than 3 inches.

$x \geq 6$ or $x < 3$

20. People with a driver's license are at least 16 years old *and* no older than 85 years old.

21. Kyle's car gets more than 31 miles per gallon on the highway *or* 26 miles or less per gallon in the city.

22. The number of houses that will be built in the new neighborhood must be at least 14 and no more than 28.

23. At the High and Low Store, they sell high-end items that sell for over $1000 and low-end items that sell for less than $10.

24. The heights of the twenty tallest buildings in New York City range from 229 meters to 381 meters.

Represent the solution to each part of the compound inequality on the number line. Then write the final solution that is represented by each graph.

25. $x > 2$ and $x \leq 7$

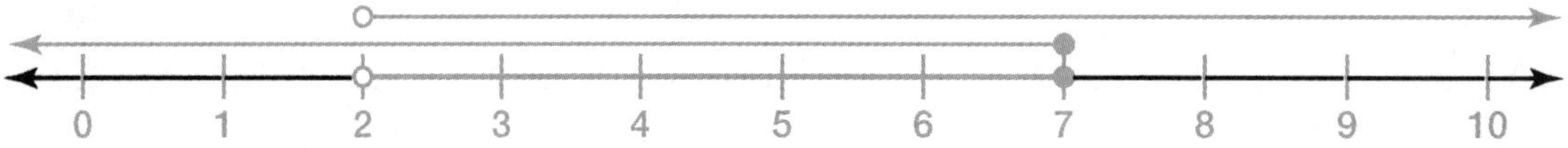

$2 < x \leq 7$

26. $x > 10$ or $x > 6$

27. $x \geq 5$ or $x < 3$

28. $x > 4$ and $x < 3$

29. $x \leq -1$ or $x > 0$

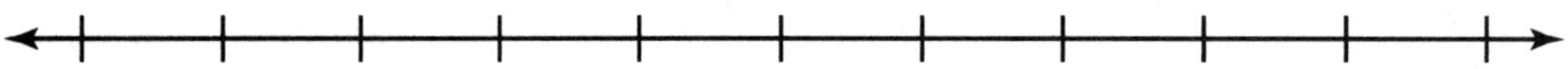

Name _____ Date _____

30. $8 > x \geq -8$

31. $x \leq 9$ and $x \geq 2$

32. $x > -11$ or $x \leq -11$

Solve each compound inequality. Then graph and describe the solution.

33. $-3 < x + 7 \leq 17$

$$-3 < x + 7 \leq 17$$
$$-3 - 7 < x + 7 - 7 \leq 17 - 7$$
$$-10 < x \leq 10$$

Solution: $-10 < x \leq 10$

34. $4 \leq 2x + 2 < 12$

35. $x + 5 > 14$ or $3x < 9$

36. $-5x + 1 \geq 16$ or $x - 6 \leq -8$

Name _____ Date _____

37. $28 \le \frac{7}{8}x < 42$

38. $-2x + 5 \le 9$ or $-x - 13 > -31$

Name _____ Date _____

Play Ball!
Absolute Value Equations and Inequalities

Vocabulary

Define each term in your own words.

1. opposites

2. absolute value

Give an example of each term.

3. linear absolute value equation

4. linear absolute value inequality

Match each equivalent compound inequality to its corresponding absolute value inequality.

5. $|ax + b| < c$

a. $-c < ax + b < c$

6. $|ax + b| \leq c$

b. $ax + b < -c$ or $ax + b > c$

7. $|ax + b| > c$

c. $-c \leq ax + b \leq c$

8. $|ax + b| \geq c$

d. $ax + b \leq -c$ or $ax + b \geq c$

Problem Set

Evaluate each absolute value.

1. $|3| = 3$

2. $|-3| =$

3. $\left|\dfrac{1}{4}\right| =$

4. $\left|-\dfrac{1}{4}\right| =$

5. $|3.7| =$

6. $|-3.7| =$

Determine the number of solutions for each equation. Then calculate the solution.

7. $x = -9$

There is only one solution.

$x = -9$

8. $|x| = -6$

9. $|x| = 4$

10. $|-x| = -8$

11. $|x| = 0$

12. $|-x| = 15$

Solve each linear absolute value equation.

13. $|x + 9| = 2$

$(x + 9) = 2$

$x + 9 - 9 = 2 - 9$

$x = -7$

$-(x + 9) = 2$

$x + 9 = -2$

$x + 9 - 9 = -2 - 9$

$x = -11$

14. $|x + 4| = 10$

15. $|x - 12| = 5$

16. $|2x - 6| = 18$

Name _____ Date _____

17. $|3x + 1| = -9$

18. $|5x + 1| = 14$

Solve each linear absolute value equation.

19. $|x| - 8 = 25$

$$|x| - 8 = 25$$
$$|x| - 8 + 8 = 25 + 8$$
$$|x| = 33 \qquad\qquad -(x) = 33$$
$$x = 33 \qquad\qquad x = -33$$

20. $|x + 3| - 7 = 40$

21. $2|x - 6| = 48$

22. $3|x + 8| = 36$

23. $5|x| + 4 = 79$

24. $2|x| - 5 = 11$

Solve each linear absolute value inequality. Graph the solution on the number line.

25. $|x + 5| < 2$

$(x + 5) < 2$ $-(x + 5) < 2$

$x + 5 - 5 < 2 - 5$ $x + 5 > -2$

$x < -3$ $x + 5 - 5 > -2 - 5$

$x > -7$

Name _____ Date _____

26. $|x - 3| \leq 6$

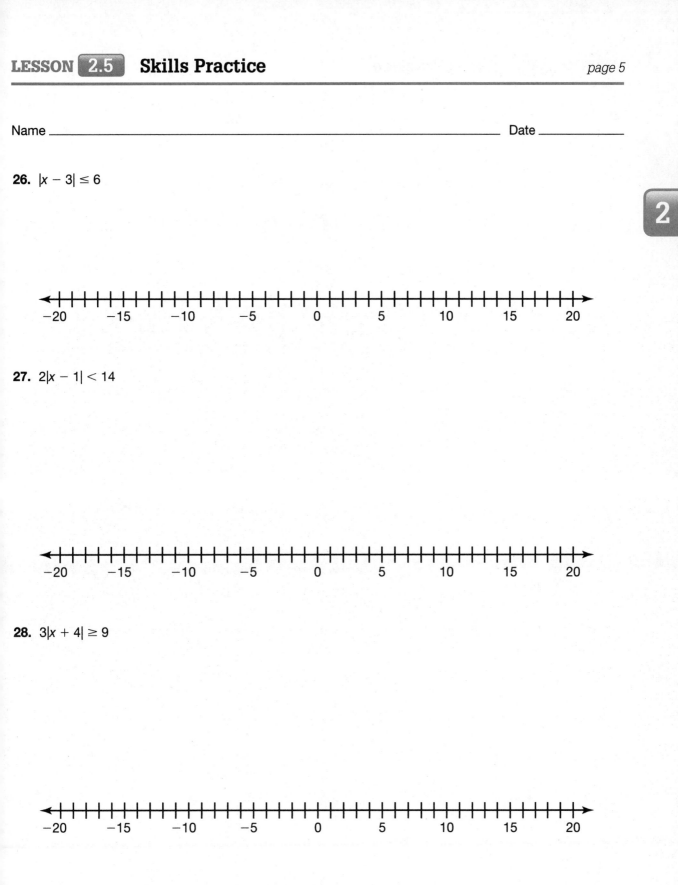

27. $2|x - 1| < 14$

28. $3|x + 4| \geq 9$

29. $2|x - 1| - 8 \leq 10$

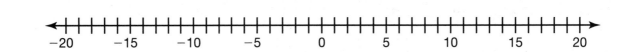

30. $3|x + 2| + 5 \geq 23$

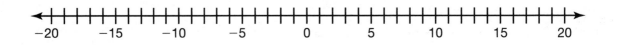

Name _____ Date _____

Graph the function that represents each problem situation.
Draw an oval on the graph to represent the answer.

31. A jewelry company is making 16-inch bead necklaces.
The specifications allow for a difference of 0.5 inch.
The function $f(x) = |x - 16|$ represents the difference
between the necklaces manufactured and the
specifications. Graph the function. What necklace
lengths meet the specifications?

The necklaces can be between 15.5 and 16.5 inches
long to meet the specifications.

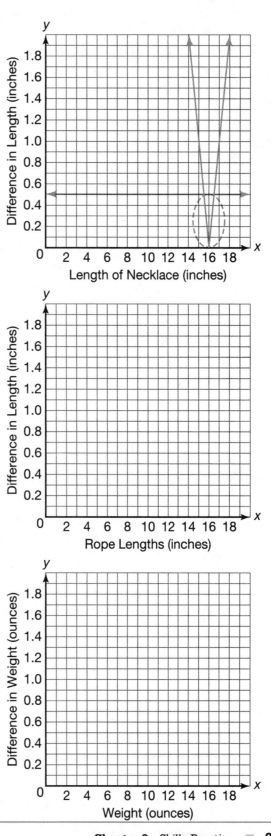

Length of Necklace (inches)

32. Julian is cutting lengths of rope for a class project.
Each rope length should be 10 inches long. The
specifications allow for a difference of 1 inch. The
function $f(x) = |x - 10|$ represents the difference
between the rope lengths cut and the specifications.
Graph the function. What rope lengths meet the
specifications?

Rope Lengths (inches)

33. A snack company is filling bags with pita chips sold
by weight. Each bag should contain 8 ounces of chips.
The specifications allow for a difference of 0.25 ounce.
The function $f(x) = |x - 8|$ represents the difference
between the weight of a bag of chips and the
specifications. Graph the function. What weights meet
the specifications?

Weight (ounces)

34. A cereal company is filling boxes with cereal sold by weight. Each box should contain 32 ounces of cereal. The specifications allow for a difference of 0.5 ounce. The function $f(x) = |x - 32|$ represents the difference between the weight of a box of cereal and the specifications. Graph the function. What weights do not meet the specifications?

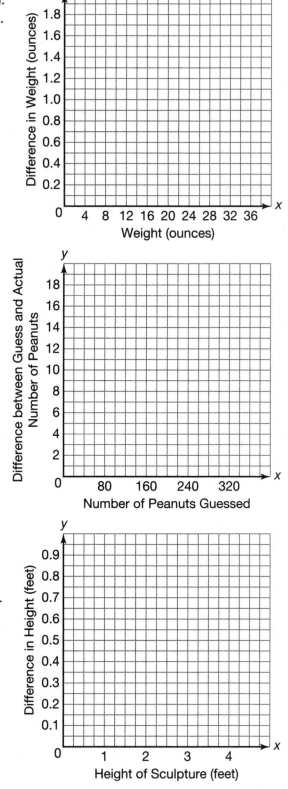

35. Guests at the school harvest festival are asked to guess how many peanuts are in a jar. The jar contains 260 peanuts. All guests within 10 peanuts of the correct answer win a prize. The function $f(x) = |x - 260|$ represents the difference between a guess and the actual number of peanuts in the jar. Graph the function. What possible guesses will not win a prize?

36. The rules of an art contest state that sculptures submitted should be 3 feet high but allow for a difference of 6 inches. The function $f(x) = |x - 3|$ represents the difference between a sculpture that is submitted and the specifications. Graph the function. What heights do not meet the specifications?

Name _____ Date _____

Choose Wisely!
Understanding Non-Linear Graphs and Inequalities

2

Problem Set

Choose the function that represents each problem situation.

1. Tonya is walking to school at a rate of 3 miles per hour.

   A $f(x) = 3x^2$ **B** $f(x) = 3x$ **C** $f(x) = 3^x$

   B $f(x) = 3x$

2. Guests at a craft fair are asked to guess how many beads are in a jar. The jar contains 220 beads. All guests within 10 beads of the correct answer win a prize.

   A $f(x) = |x - 220|$ **B** $f(x) = 220 - x$ **C** $f(x) = 220^x$

3. Mario buys a car for \$25,000. Each year the car loses $\frac{1}{6}$ of its value.

   A $f(x) = 25{,}000 - \frac{1}{6}x$ **B** $f(x) = \frac{1}{6}x^2 + 25{,}000$ **C** $f(x) = 25{,}000\left(\frac{5}{6}\right)^x$

4. A bathtub filled with 50 gallons of water is drained. The water drains at a rate of 5 gallons per minute.

   A $f(x) = 50 - 5x$ **B** $f(x) = 5x^2 - 50$ **C** $f(x) = 50 - 5^x$

5. Rodell throws a football straight up with a speed of 25 feet per second. The acceleration of the ball due to gravity is 32 feet per second.

   A $f(x) = -32x + 25$ **B** $f(x) = -32x^2 + 25x$ **C** $f(x) = |32x - 25|$

6. A pasta company is filling boxes with pasta sold by weight. Each box should contain 16 ounces of pasta. The specifications allow for a difference of 0.5 ounce.

   A $f(x) = 16x - 0.5$ **B** $f(x) = 16x^2 - 0.5x$ **C** $f(x) = |x - 16|$

Graph the function that represents each problem situation. Use the graph to answer the question.

7. A fish tank filled with 20 gallons of water is drained. The water drains at a rate of 4 gallons per minute. The function $f(x) = 20 - 4x$ represents the volume of water in the fish tank as it drains. Graph the function. How many minutes does it take for half of the water to drain from the tank?

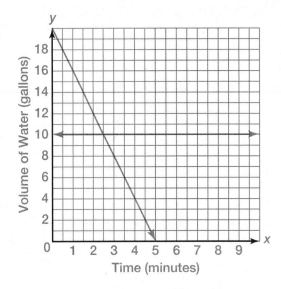

After 2.5 minutes, half of the water in the tank (10 gallons) will be drained.

8. A pasta company is filling boxes with pasta sold by weight. Each box should contain 32 ounces of pasta. The specifications allow for a difference of 1.5 ounces. The function $f(x) = |x - 32|$ represents the difference between the weight of a box of pasta and the specifications. Graph the function. What weights meet the specifications?

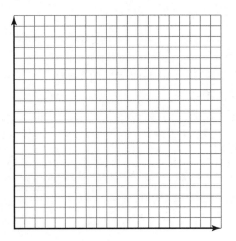

Name _____ Date _____

9. Ronna buys a car for \$20,000. Each year the car loses $\frac{1}{4}$ of its value. The function $f(x) = 20,000\left(\frac{3}{4}\right)^x$ represents the value of the car over time. Graph the function. Ronna wants to eventually sell the car and make at least \$10,000 in the sale. Estimate the number of years Ronna can own the car before she must resell and still make at least \$10,000.

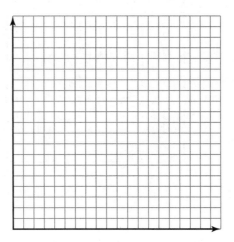

10. Serena is driving to her aunt's house at a rate of 55 miles per hour. The function $f(x) = 55x$ represents the distance Serena travels over time. Graph the function. Estimate how long it will take Serena to get to her aunt's house which is 192 miles away.

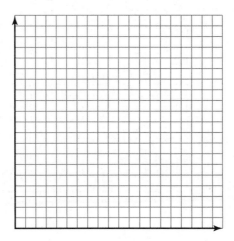

11. Hector throws a softball straight up with a speed of 50 feet per second. The acceleration of the ball due to gravity is 32 feet per second. The function $f(x) = -32x^2 + 50x$ represents the height of the softball as it travels up in the air and back to the ground. Graph the function. Estimate the length of time the softball is in the air.

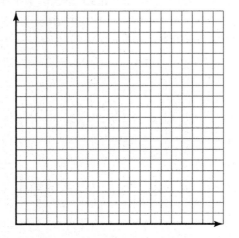

12. Guests at a craft fair are asked to guess how many beads are in a jar. The jar contains 180 beads. All guests within 20 beads of the correct answer win a prize. The function $f(x) = |x - 180|$ represents the difference between a guess and the actual number of beads in the jar. Graph the function. What possible guesses will win a prize?

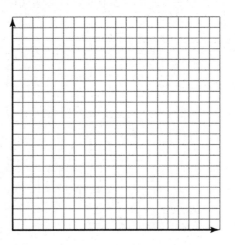

Name _____ Date _____

Is It Getting Hot in Here?
Modeling Data Using Linear Regression

Vocabulary

Choose the term that best completes each sentence.

linear regression	line of best fit	linear regression equation
significant digits	correlation coefficient	

1. The equation that describes a line of best fit is called a _____.

2. Decimal digits that carry meaning contributing to a number's precision are

_____.

3. _____ models the relationship between two variables in a data set by producing a line of best fit.

4. A _____ is a line that best approximates the linear relationship between two variables in a data set.

5. The _____ indicates how closely data points are to forming a straight line.

Problem Set

Use your calculator to determine the linear regression equation and the correlation coefficient for each given set of data. Then use the equation to make the prediction.

1. The table shows the attendance for the varsity football games at Pedro's high school. Predict the attendance for Game 9.

Game	Attendance
1	2000
2	2132
3	2198
4	2301
5	2285
6	2401

$f(x) = 73x + 1963, r \approx 0.9694$

Game 1 is represented by $x = 1$, so Game 9 is represented by $x = 9$.

$f(x) = 73x + 1963$

$f(9) = 73(9) + 1963$

$f(9) = 2620$

The attendance during Game 9 will be 2620 people.

Name _____ Date _____

2. The table shows the attendance for the annual spring concert at Eva's high school for 6 years. Predict the attendance in 2016.

Year	Attendance
2007	789
2008	805
2009	773
2010	852
2011	884
2012	902

3. The table shows the average gas price for 6 months. Predict the average gas price for August.

Month	Price of Gas (dollars)
January	$3.15
February	$3.22
March	$3.19
April	$3.28
May	$3.35
June	$3.32

Name _____ Date _____

4. The table shows monthly record sales of a recording artist over 6 months. Predict the record sales total for December.

Monthly	Record Sales (CDs)
January	60,000
February	54,000
March	58,000
April	46,000
May	43,000
June	30,000

3

5. The table shows the number of miles Kata traveled for work each year for 6 years. Predict the number of miles Kata will travel in 2014.

Year	Miles Traveled
2006	8300
2007	7550
2008	8005
2009	7600
2010	6935
2011	6405

Name _____ Date _____

6. The table shows the number of songs downloaded for a recording artist over 6 months. Predict the number of songs that will be downloaded in November.

Month	Songs Downloaded
January	15,302
February	16,783
March	18,204
April	17,899
May	20,345
June	24,980

3

3

Name _____ Date _____

Tickets for Sale
Standard Form of Linear Equations

Vocabulary

Define each term in your own words.

1. standard form

3

2. slope-intercept form

Problem Set

Define variables and write an expression to represent each situation.

1. A farmer's market sells apples for $0.75 per pound and oranges for $0.89 per pound. Write an expression to represent the total amount the farmer's market can earn selling apples and oranges.

a = pounds of apples

b = pounds of oranges

$0.75a + 0.89b$

2. A photo printing website sells 8 × 10 prints for $4.99 and 3 × 5 prints for $1.99. Write an expression to represent the total amount the website can earn selling 8 × 10 and 3 × 5 prints.

3. A movie theater sells tickets for matinee showings for $7.00 and evening showings for $10.50. Write an expression that represents the total amount the theater can earn selling tickets.

4. A bakery sells muffins for $1.25 each and scones for $1.75 each. Write an expression that represents the total amount the bakery can earn selling muffins and scones.

5. A florist sells daisies for $8.99 a dozen and roses for $15.99 a dozen. Write an expression that represents the total amount the florist can earn selling daisies and roses.

3

6. The hockey booster club is selling winter hats for $12 each and sweatshirts for $26 each. Write an expression that represents the total amount the booster club can earn selling hats and sweatshirts.

Define variables and write an equation to represent each situation.

7. A florist sells carnations for $10.99 a dozen and lilies for $12.99 a dozen. During a weekend sale, the florist's goal is to earn $650. Write an equation that represents the total amount the florist would like to earn selling carnations and lilies during the weekend sale.

c = carnations

f = lilies

$10.99c + 12.99f = 650$

8. A bakery sells bagels for $0.85 each and muffins for $1.10 each. The bakery hopes to earn $400 each day from these sales. Write an equation that represents the total amount the bakery would like to earn selling bagels and muffins each day.

9. A farmer's market sells oranges for $0.79 per pound and peaches for $1.05 per pound. The farmer's market hopes to earn $325 each day from these sales. Write an equation to represent the total amount the farmer's market would like to earn selling oranges and peaches each day.

Name _____ Date _____

10. The high school soccer booster club sells tickets to the varsity matches for $4 for students and $8 for adults. The booster club hopes to earn $200 at each match. Write an equation to represent the total amount the booster club would like to earn from ticket sales at each match.

11. An electronics store sells DVDs for $15.99 and Blu-ray discs for $22.99. The store hopes to earn $2000 each week from these sales. Write an equation to represent the total amount the store would like to earn each week.

3

12. Ling is selling jewelry at a craft fair. She sells earrings for $5 each and bracelets for $7 each. She hopes to earn $300 during the fair. Write an equation to represent the total amount Ling would like to earn during the fair.

The basketball booster club runs the concession stand during a weekend tournament. They sell hamburgers for $2.50 each and hot dogs for $1.50 each. They hope to earn $900 during the tournament. The equation $2.50b + 1.50h = 900$ represents the total amount the booster club hopes to earn. Use this equation to determine each unknown value.

13. If the booster club sells 315 hamburgers during the tournament, how many hot dogs must they sell to reach their goal?

$$2.50b + 1.50h = 900$$
$$2.50(315) + 1.50h = 900$$
$$787.50 + 1.50h = 900$$
$$1.50h = 112.50$$
$$h = 75$$

The booster club must sell 75 hot dogs to reach their goal.

14. If the booster club sells 420 hot dogs during the tournament, how many hamburgers must they sell to reach their goal?

15. If the booster club sells 0 hot dogs during the tournament, how many hamburgers must they sell to reach their goal?

16. If the booster club sells 0 hamburgers during the tournament, how many hot dogs must they sell to reach their goal?

17. If the booster club sells 281 hamburgers during the tournament, how many hot dogs must they sell to reach their goal?

Name _____ Date _____

18. If the booster club sells 168 hot dogs during the tournament, how many hamburgers must they sell to reach their goal?

Determine the x-intercept and the y-intercept of each equation.

19. $20x + 8y = 240$

$$20x + 8y = 240$$
$$20x + 8(0) = 240$$
$$20x = 240$$
$$x = 12$$

$$20x + 8y = 240$$
$$20(0) + 8y = 240$$
$$8y = 240$$
$$y = 30$$

The x-intercept is (12, 0) and the y-intercept is (0, 30).

20. $15x + 3y = 270$

21. $y = 8x + 168$

22. $y = -4x + 52$

23. $14x + 25y = 342$

24. $y = 6x + 291$

Determine the *x*-intercept and *y*-intercept. Then graph each equation.

25. $5x + 6y = 90$ **26.** $12x - 9y = 36$

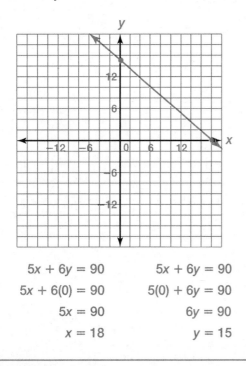

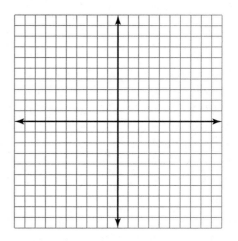

$$5x + 6y = 90 \qquad 5x + 6y = 90$$
$$5x + 6(0) = 90 \qquad 5(0) + 6y = 90$$
$$5x = 90 \qquad 6y = 90$$
$$x = 18 \qquad y = 15$$

Name _____ Date _____

27. $y = 3x - 15$

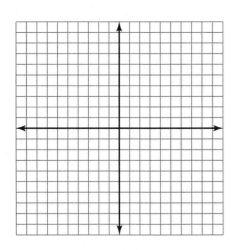

28. $y = -30x + 180$

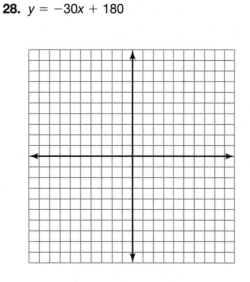

3

29. $6x + 13y = 57$

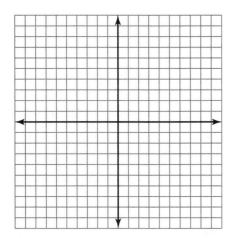

30. $y = 3x - 41$

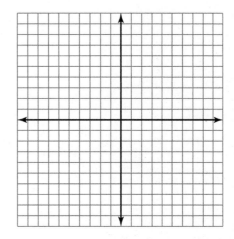

Name _____ Date _____

Cool As A Cucumber or Hot Like A Tamale!
Literal Equations in Standard Form and Slope-Intercept Form

Vocabulary

Define the term in your own words.

1. literal equations

Problem Set

Convert between degrees Fahrenheit and degrees Celsius using the literal equation given. If necessary, round the answer to the nearest hundredth.

$$C = \frac{5}{9}(F - 32)$$

1. 72°F

$$C = \frac{5}{9}(F - 32)$$

$$C = \frac{5}{9}(72 - 32)$$

$$C = \frac{5}{9}(40)$$

$$C \approx 22.22$$

72°F ≈ 22.22°C

2. −11°F

3. 102.6°F

4. 25°C

5. 42°C

6. −3.4°C

Convert each equation from standard form to slope-intercept form.

7. $4x + 6y = 48$

$$4x + 6y = 48$$

$$4x - 4x + 6y = -4x + 48$$

$$\frac{6y}{6} = \frac{-4x + 48}{6}$$

$$y = -\frac{4}{6}x + 8$$

$$y = -\frac{2}{3}x + 8$$

8. $3x - 5y = 25$

9. $-4x + 9y = 45$

10. $6x - 2y = -52$

11. $-x - 8y = 96$

12. $12x + 28y = -84$

Name _____ Date _____

Convert each equation from slope-intercept form to standard form.

13. $y = 5x + 8$

$y = 5x + 8$

$-5x + y = 5x - 5x + 8$

$-5x + y = 8$

14. $y = -4x + 2$

15. $y = \frac{2}{3}x - 6$

16. $y = -\frac{1}{2}x - 3$

17. $y = -5x - 13$

18. $y = \frac{3}{4}x + 10$

Solve each equation for the variable indicated.

19. The formula for the area of a triangle is $A = \frac{1}{2}bh$. Solve the equation for h.

$$A = \frac{1}{2}bh$$

$$(2)A = 2\left(\frac{1}{2}bh\right)$$

$$2A = bh$$

$$\frac{2A}{b} = \frac{bh}{b}$$

$$\frac{2A}{b} = h$$

3

20. The formula for the area of a trapezoid is $A = \frac{1}{2}(b_1 + b_2)h$. Solve the equation for b_1.

21. The formula for the area of a circle is $A = \pi r^2$. Solve the equation for r.

Name _____ Date _____

22. The formula for the volume of a cylinder is $V = \pi r^2 h$. Solve the equation for h.

23. The formula for the volume of a pyramid is $V = \frac{1}{3}lwh$. Solve the equation for w.

24. The formula for the volume of a sphere is $V = \frac{4}{3}\pi r^3$. Solve the equation for r.

Name _____ Date _____

A Growing Business
Combining Linear Equations

Problem Set

Write a linear function in two different ways to represent each problem situation.

1. Mei paints and sells ceramic vases for $35 each. Each month she typically breaks 3 vases in the kiln. Write a linear function that represents the total amount Mei earns each month selling vases taking into account the value of the vases she breaks.

   $f(x) = 35(x - 3)$
   $f(x) = 35x - 105$

2. Isabel makes and sells fruit pies at her bakery for $12.99 each. Each month she gives away 4 pies as samples. Write a linear function that represents the total amount Isabel earns each month selling fruit pies taking into account the value of the pies she gives away as samples.

3. Mattie sells heads of lettuce for $1.99 each from a roadside farmer's market stand. Each week she loses 2 heads of lettuce due to spoilage. Write a linear function that represents the total amount Mattie earns each week selling heads of lettuce taking into account the value of the lettuce she loses due to spoilage.

4. Carlos prints and sells T-shirts for $14.99 each. Each month 5 T-shirts are misprinted and cannot be sold. Write a linear equation that represents the total amount Carlos earns each month selling T-shirts taking into account the value of the T-shirts that cannot be sold.

5. Odell prints and sells posters for $20 each. Each month 1 poster is misprinted and cannot be sold. Write a linear equation that represents the total amount Odell earns each month taking into account the value of the poster that cannot be sold.

6. Emilio builds and sells homemade wooden toys for $40 each. Each month he donates 3 toys to a children's hospital. Write a linear equation that represents the total amount Emilio earns each month selling toys taking into account the toys he donates.

Write a linear function to represent each problem situation.

7. A cereal manufacturer has two production lines. Line A produces a variety of cereal that is sold for $3 per box. Line A typically produces 4 boxes per day that do not meet company standards and cannot be sold. Line B produces a variety of cereal that is sold for $2 per box. Line B typically produces 6 boxes per day that do not meet company standards and cannot be sold. Line A and Line B produce the same total number of boxes each day.

The linear functions $a(x) = 3(x - 4)$ and $b(x) = 2(x - 6)$ represent the total amount each line can produce taking into account the boxes that do not meet company standards and cannot be sold. Write a linear function that represents the total number of boxes the lines can produce combined.

Line A: $\frac{1}{2}x$　　　　　　　　　　　　　　$a(x) = 3\left(\frac{1}{2}x - 4\right)$

Line B: $\frac{1}{2}x$　　　　　　　　　　　　　　$b(x) = 2\left(\frac{1}{2}x - 6\right)$

$c(x) = a(x) + b(x)$

$\quad = 3\left(\frac{1}{2}x - 4\right) + 2\left(\frac{1}{2}x - 6\right)$

$\quad = \frac{3}{2}x - 12 + \frac{2}{2}x - 12$

$\quad = \frac{5}{2}x - 24$

The linear function $c(x) = \frac{5}{2}x - 24$ represents the total number of boxes that Line A and Line B can produce combined.

Name _____ Date _____

8. A pretzel manufacturer has two production lines. Line A produces a variety of pretzel that is sold for $2.40 per bag. Line A typically produces 3 bags per day that do not meet company standards and cannot be sold. Line B produces a variety of pretzel that is sold for $3.60 per bag. Line B typically produces 4 bags per day that do not meet company standards and cannot be sold. Line A produces 3 times as many bags as Line B each day.

The linear functions $a(x) = 2.4(x - 3)$ and $b(x) = 3.6(x - 4)$ represent the total number of bags each line can produce taking into account the bags that do not meet company standards and cannot be. Write a linear function that represents the total number of bags the lines can produce combined.

3

9. Carlos has a roadside stand that sells peaches. He sells his peaches for $1.99 per pound. He typically loses 5 pounds per week to spoilage. Hector also has a roadside stand that sells peaches. He sells his peaches for $2.49 per pound. He typically only loses 1 pound per week to spoilage. Carlos' stand sells twice as many peaches per week as Hector's stand.

The linear functions $c(x) = 1.99(x - 5)$ and $h(x) = 2.49(x - 1)$ represent the total amount each stand can earn taking into account the peaches lost to spoilage. Write a linear function that represents the total amount that Carlos and Hector can earn combined.

10. A lamp manufacturer has two production lines. Line A produces a lamp model that is sold for $24.99 each. Line A typically produces 2 lamps per day that do not meet company standards and cannot be sold. Line B produces a lamp model that is sold for $34.99 each. Line B typically produces 1 lamp per day that does not meet company standards and cannot be sold. Line A produces half as many lamps as Line B each day.

The linear functions $a(x) = 24.99(x - 2)$ and $b(x) = 34.99(x - 1)$ represent the total number of lamps each line can produce taking into account the lamps that do not meet company standards and cannot be sold. Write a linear function that represents the total number of lamps the lines can produce combined.

11. A jean manufacturer has two production lines. Line A produces a style that is sold for $42 each. Line A typically produces 2 pairs per day that do not meet company standards and cannot be sold. Line B produces a style that can be sold for $65 each. Line B typically produces 3 pairs per day that do not meet company standards and cannot be sold. Line A produces three times as many pairs of jeans as Line B each day.

The linear functions $a(x) = 42(x - 2)$ and $b(x) = 65(x - 3)$ represent the total number of pairs of jeans that each line can produce taking into account the jeans that do not meet company standards and cannot be sold. Write a linear function that represents the total number of pairs of jeans the lines can produce combined.

Name _____ Date _____

12. Jada makes and sells handmade puzzles for $32 each. Each month she donates 2 puzzles to a retirement community. Ronna also makes and sells handmade puzzles for $28 each. Each month she donates 2 puzzles to a childcare center. Jada and Ronna make the same number of puzzles each month.

The linear functions $j(x) = 32(x - 2)$ and $r(x) = 28(x - 2)$ represent the total amount each girl can earn taking into account the puzzles that are donated and not sold. Write a linear function that represents the total amount Jada and Ronna can earn combined.

Name _____ Date _____

Is There a Pattern Here?
Recognizing Patterns and Sequences

Vocabulary

Choose the term that best completes each statement.

sequence	term of a sequence	infinite sequence	finite sequence

1. A sequence which terminates is called a(n) _____.

2. A(n) _____ is an individual number, figure, or letter in a sequence.

3. A(n) _____ is a pattern involving an ordered arrangement of numbers, geometric figures, letters, or other objects.

4. A sequence which continues forever is called a(n) _____.

Problem Set

Describe each given pattern. Draw the next two figures in each pattern.

1.

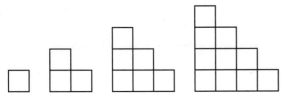

The second figure has 2 more squares than the first, the third figure has 3 more squares than the second, and the fourth figure has 4 more squares than the third.

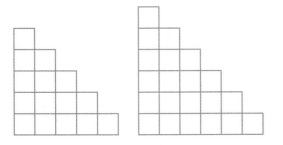

2.

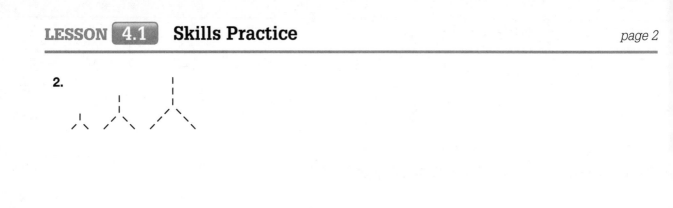

3.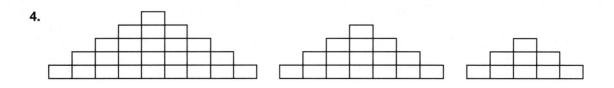

4

4.

5.

Name _____ Date _____

6.

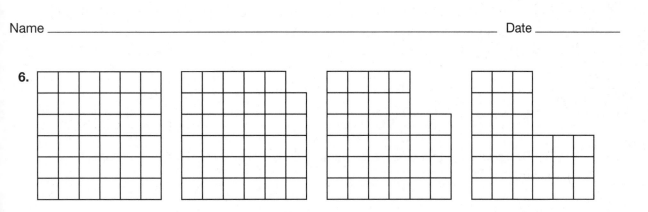

Write a numeric sequence to represent each given pattern or situation.

7. The school cafeteria begins the day with a supply of 1000 chicken nuggets. Each student that passes through the lunch line is given 5 chicken nuggets. Write a numeric sequence to represent the total number of chicken nuggets remaining in the cafeteria's supply after each of the first 6 students pass through the line. Include the number of chicken nuggets the cafeteria started with.

1000, 995, 990, 985, 980, 975, 970

8. Write a numeric sequence to represent the number of squares in each of the first 7 figures of the pattern.

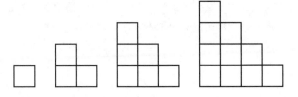

9. Sophia starts a job at a restaurant. She deposits $40 from each paycheck into her savings account. There was no money in the account prior to her first deposit. Write a numeric sequence to represent the amount of money in the savings account after Sophia receives each of her first 6 paychecks.

10. Write a numeric sequence to represent the number of blocks in each of the first 5 figures of the pattern.

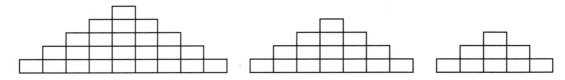

11. Kyle is collecting canned goods for a food drive. On the first day he collects 1 can. On the second day he collects 2 cans. On the third day he collects 4 cans. On each successive day, he collects twice as many cans as he collected the previous day. Write a numeric sequence to represent the total number of cans Kyle has collected by the end of each of the first 7 days of the food drive.

12. Write a numeric sequence to represent the number of line segments in each of the first 7 figures of the pattern.

13. For her 10th birthday, Tameka's grandparents give her a set of 200 stamps. For each birthday after that, they give her a set of 25 stamps to add to her stamp collection. Write a numeric sequence consisting of 7 terms to represent the number of stamps in Tameka's collection after each of her birthdays starting with her 10th birthday.

Name _____ Date _____

14. Write a numeric sequence to represent the number of squares in each of the first 6 figures of the pattern.

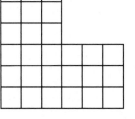

15. Leonardo uses 3 cups of flour in each cake he bakes. He starts the day with 50 cups of flour. Write a numeric sequence to represent the amount of flour remaining after each of the first 7 cakes Leonardo bakes. Include the amount of flour Leonardo started with.

16. Write a numeric sequence to represent the number of triangles in each of the first 7 figures of the pattern.

Name _____ Date _____

The Password Is . . . Operations!
Arithmetic and Geometric Sequences

Vocabulary

Describe each given sequence using the terms arithmetic sequence, common difference, geometric sequence, and common ratio as they apply.

1. 10, 20, 30, 40, . . .

2. 1, 2, 4, 8, . . .

Problem Set

Determine the common difference for each arithmetic sequence.

1. 1, 5, 9, 13, . . .
$d = 5 - 1$
$d = 4$

2. 10, 3, −4, −11, . . .

3. 10.5, 13, 15.5, 18, . . .

4. $\frac{1}{3}, \frac{2}{3}, 1, \frac{4}{3}, \ldots$

5. 95, 91.5, 88, 84.5, . . .

6. 170, 240, 310, 380, . . .

7. 1250, 1190, 1130, 1070, . . .

8. −4.8, −6.0, −7.2, −8.4, . . .

9. $8\frac{1}{2}$, 9, $9\frac{1}{2}$, 10, . . .

10. −28, −13, 2, 17, . . .

Determine the common ratio for each geometric sequence.

11. 5, 10, 20, 40, . . .

$r = 10 \div 5$

$r = 2$

12. 2, 8, 32, 128, . . .

13. 3, −6, 12, −24, . . .

14. 800, 400, 200, 100, . . .

15. 10, −30, 90, −270, . . .

16. 64, −32, 16, −8, . . .

17. 5, 40, 320, 2560, . . .

18. 45, 15, 5, $\frac{5}{3}$, . . .

19. 0.2, −1, 5, −25, . . .

20. 150, 30, 6, 1.2, . . .

Name _____ Date _____

Determine the next 3 terms in each arithmetic sequence.

21. 8, 14, 20, 26, __32__, __38__, __44__, . . .

22. 90, 75, 60, 45, _____, _____, _____, . . .

23. −24, −14, −4, 6, _____, _____, _____, . . .

24. $\frac{3}{5}, \frac{4}{5}, 1, \frac{6}{5}$, _____, _____, _____, . . .

25. 20, 11, 2, −7, _____, _____, _____, . . .

26. 12, 16.5, 21, 25.5, _____, _____, _____, . . .

27. −101, −112, −123, −134, _____, _____, _____, . . .

28. 3.8, 5.1, 6.4, 7.7, _____, _____, _____, . . .

29. −500, −125, 250, 625, _____, _____, _____, . . .

30. 24.5, 20.7, 16.9, 13.1, _____, _____, _____, . . .

Determine the next 3 terms in each geometric sequence.

31. 3, 9, 27, 81, __243__, __729__, __2187__, . . .

32. 512, 256, 128, 64, _____, _____, _____, . . .

33. 5, −10, 20, −40, _____, _____, _____, . . .

34. 3000, 300, 30, 3, _____, _____, _____, . . .

35. 2, −2, 2, −2, _____, _____, _____, . . .

36. 0.2, 1.2, 7.2, 43.2, _____, _____, _____, . . .

37. −8000, 4000, −2000, 1000, _____, _____, _____, . . .

38. 0.1, 0.4, 1.6, 6.4, _____, _____, _____, . . .

39. 156.25, 31.25, 6.25, 1.25, _____, _____, _____, . . .

40. 7, −21, 63, −189, _____, _____, _____, . . .

Determine whether each given sequence is arithmetic, geometric, or neither. For arithmetic and geometric sequences, write the next 3 terms of the sequence.

41. 4, 8, 12, 16, . . .

The sequence is arithmetic. The next 3 terms are 20, 24, and 28.

42. 2, 4, 7, 11, . . .

43. 3, 12, 48, 192, . . .

44. 9, −18, 36, −72, . . .

45. 1.1, 1.11, 1.111, 1.1111, . . .

46. 4, −8, −20, −32, . . .

47. 7.5, 11.6, 15.7, 19.8, . . .

48. 1, −4, 9, −16, . . .

49. 5, −20, 80, −320, . . .

50. 9.8, 5.6, 1.4, −2.8, . . .

Name _____ Date _____

The Power of Algebra Is a Curious Thing
Using Formulas to Determine Terms of a Sequence

Vocabulary

Choose the term that best completes each statement.

| index | explicit formula | recursive formula |

1. A(n) _____ expresses each term of a sequence based on the preceding term of the sequence.

2. The _____ is the position of a term in a sequence.

3. A(n) _____ calculates each term of a sequence using the term's position in the sequence.

Problem Set

Determine each unknown term in the given arithmetic sequence using the explicit formula.

1. Determine the 20th term of the sequence
   1, 4, 7, . . .

   $a_n = a_1 + d(n - 1)$

   $a_{20} = 1 + 3(20 - 1)$

   $a_{20} = 1 + 3(19)$

   $a_{20} = 1 + 57$

   $a_{20} = 58$

2. Determine the 30th term of the sequence
   $-10, -15, -20, . . .$

3. Determine the 25th term of the sequence
   3.3, 4.4, 5.5, . . .

4. Determine the 50th term of the sequence
   100, 92, 84, . . .

5. Determine the 42nd term of the sequence
   12.25, 14.50, 16.75, . . .

6. Determine the 28th term of the sequence
   –242, –251, –260, . . .

7. Determine the 34th term of the sequence
   $-76.2, -70.9, -65.6, . . .$

8. Determine the 60th term of the sequence
   10, 25, 40, . . .

9. Determine the 57th term of the sequence
   672, 660, 648, . . .

10. Determine the 75th term of the sequence
    $-200, -100, 0, . . .$

Determine each unknown term in the given geometric sequence using the explicit formula. Round the answer to the nearest hundredth when necessary.

11. Determine the 10th term of the sequence
    3, 6, 12, . . .

    $g_n = g_1 \cdot r^{n-1}$
    $g_{10} = 3 \cdot 2^{10-1}$
    $g_{10} = 3 \cdot 2^9$
    $g_{10} = 3 \cdot 512$
    $g_{10} = 1536$

12. Determine the 15th term of the sequence
    1, −2, 4, . . .

Name _____ Date _____

13. Determine the 12th term of the sequence
5, 15, 45, . . .

14. Determine the 16th term of the sequence
9, 18, 36, . . .

15. Determine the 20th term of the sequence
0.125, −0.250, 0.500, . . .

16. Determine the 18th term of the sequence
3, 9, 27, . . .

17. Determine the 14th term of the sequence
−4, 8, −16, . . .

18. Determine the 10th term of the sequence
0.1, 0.5, 2.5, . . .

19. Determine the 12th term of the sequence
4, 5, 6.25, . . .

20. Determine the 10th term of the sequence
5, −25, 125, . . .

Determine whether each sequence is arithmetic or geometric. Then, use the appropriate recursive formula to determine the unknown term(s) in the sequence.

21. 4, 8, 16, 32, _____64_____, . . .

The sequence is geometric.

$g_n = g_{n-1} \cdot r$

$g_5 = g_4 \cdot 2$

$g_5 = 32 \cdot 2$

$g_5 = 64$

22. 16, 30, 44, 58, _____, . . .

23. 2, −6, 18, _____, 162, _____, . . .

24. 7.3, 9.4, 11.5, _____, 15.7, _____, . . .

25. 320, 410, 500, _____, _____, . . .

Name _____ Date _____

26. 7, 21, 63, _____, 567, _____, . . .

27. −68, −83, −98, _____, _____, _____, . . .

28. −5, 20, −80, _____, _____, _____, . . .

4

Determine the unknown term in each arithmetic sequence using a graphing calculator.

29. Determine the 20th term of the sequence
30, 70, 110, . . .

$a_{20} = 790$

30. Determine the 25th term of the sequence
−25, −50, −75, . . .

31. Determine the 30th term of the sequence
16, 24, 32, . . .

32. Determine the 35th term of the sequence
120, 104, 88, . . .

33. Determine the 30th term of the sequence 350, 700, 1050, . . .

34. Determine the 22nd term of the sequence 0, −45, −90, . . .

35. Determine the 24th term of the sequence 6.8, 9.5, 12.2, . . .

36. Determine the 36th term of the sequence 189, 200, 211, . . .

37. Determine the 20th term of the sequence 2500, 3100, 3700, . . .

38. Determine the 50th term of the sequence −97, −94, −91, . . .

4

Name _____ Date _____

Thank Goodness Descartes Didn't Drink Some Warm Milk!
Graphs of Sequences

Problem Set

Complete the table for each given sequence then graph each sequence on the coordinate plane.

1. $a_n = 15 + 3(n - 1)$

Term Number (n)	Value of Term (a_n)
1	15
2	18
3	21
4	24
5	27
6	30
7	33
8	36
9	39
10	42

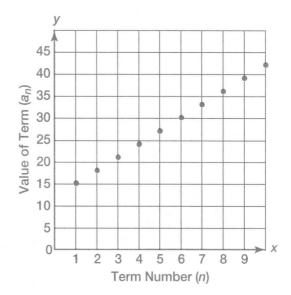

2. $g_n = 3 \cdot 2^{n-1}$

Term Number (n)	Value of Term (g_n)
1	
2	
3	
4	
5	
6	
7	
8	
9	
10	

3. $a_n = 50 + (-8)(n - 1)$

Term Number (n)	Value of Term (a_n)
1	
2	
3	
4	
5	
6	
7	
8	
9	
10	

4. $g_n = 3 \cdot (-2)^{n-1}$

Term Number (n)	Value of Term (g_n)
1	
2	
3	
4	
5	
6	
7	
8	
9	
10	

Name _____ Date _____

5. $a_n = -24 + 6(n - 1)$

Term Number (n)	Value of Term (a_n)
1	
2	
3	
4	
5	
6	
7	
8	
9	
10	

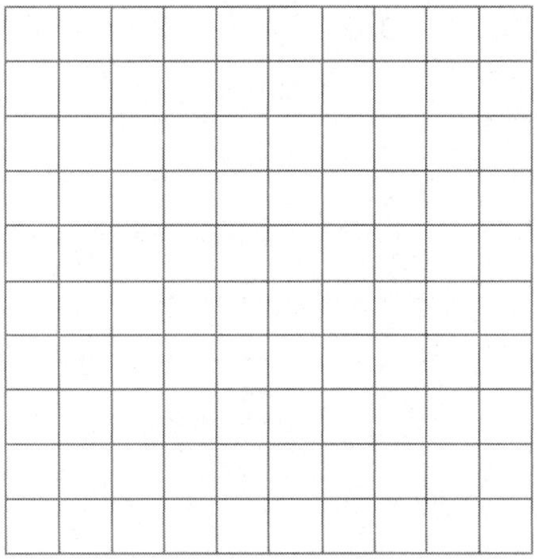

4

6. $g_n = -1 \cdot 2^{n-1}$

Term Number (n)	Value of Term (g_n)
1	
2	
3	
4	
5	
6	
7	
8	
9	
10	

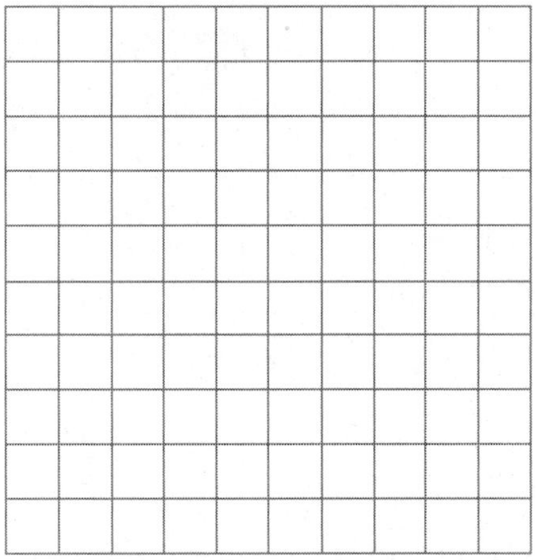

7. $a_n = 75 + 25(n - 1)$

Term Number (*n*)	Value of Term (*a_n*)
1	
2	
3	
4	
5	
6	
7	
8	
9	
10	

8. $g_n = 32{,}000 \cdot (0.5)^{n-1}$

Term Number (*n*)	Value of Term (*g_n*)
1	
2	
3	
4	
5	
6	
7	
8	
9	
10	

Name _____ Date _____

9. $a_n = 400 + (-80)(n - 1)$

Term Number (n)	Value of Term (a_n)
1	
2	
3	
4	
5	
6	
7	
8	
9	
10	

4

10. $g_n = 2 \cdot (-3)^{n-1}$

Term Number (n)	Value of Term (g_n)
1	
2	
3	
4	
5	
6	
7	
8	
9	
10	

4

Name _____ Date _____

Well, Maybe It *Is* a Function!
Sequences and Functions

Problem Set

Write each arithmetic sequence as a linear function. Graph the function for all integers, *n*, such that $1 \le n \le 10$.

1. $a_n = 16 + 5(n - 1)$

$a_n = 16 + 5(n - 1)$

$f(n) = 16 + 5(n - 1)$

$f(n) = 16 + 5n - 5$

$f(n) = 5n + 16 - 5$

$f(n) = 5n + 11$

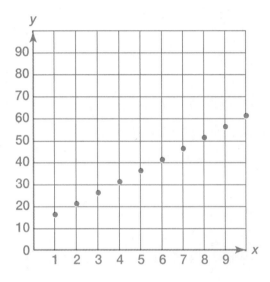

2. $a_n = -50 + 15(n - 1)$

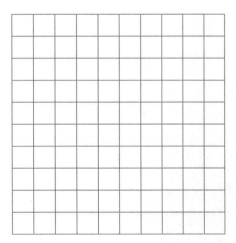

3. $a_n = 100 + (-20)(n - 1)$

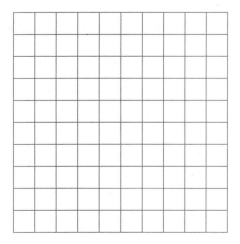

4. $a_n = -9 + (-7)(n - 1)$

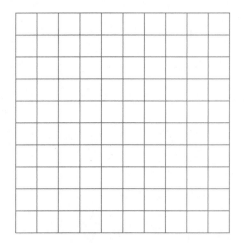

5. $a_n = 550 + (-50)(n - 1)$

Name _____ Date _____

6. $a_n = 3 + \left(-\frac{3}{5}\right)(n - 1)$

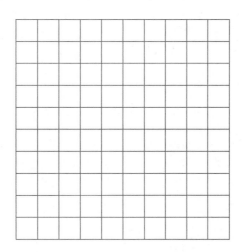

Write each geometric sequence as an exponential function. Graph the function for all integers, n, such that $1 \le n \le 10$.

7. $g_n = 5 \cdot 2^{n-1}$

$g_n = 5 \cdot 2^{n-1}$

$f(n) = 5 \cdot 2^{n-1}$

$f(n) = 5 \cdot 2^n \cdot 2^{-1}$

$f(n) = 5 \cdot 2^{-1} \cdot 2^n$

$f(n) = 5 \cdot \frac{1}{2} \cdot 2^n$

$f(n) = \frac{5}{2} \cdot 2^n$

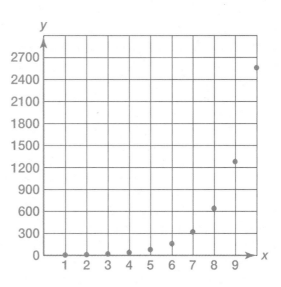

8. $g_n = -3 \cdot 3^{n-1}$

9. $g_n = 20 \cdot 2.5^{n-1}$

10. $g_n = 900 \cdot 0.9^{n-1}$

Name _____ Date _____

11. $g_n = -0.5 \cdot 2^{n-1}$

12. $g_n = 1250 \cdot 1.25^{n-1}$

4

4

Name _____ Date _____

Go for the Curve!
Comparing Linear and Exponential Functions

Vocabulary

Describe each type of account as simple interest or compound interest based on the scenario given. Explain your reasoning.

1. Andrew deposits $300 into an account that earns 2% interest each year. After the first year, Andrew has $306 in the account. After the second year, Andrew has $312 in the account, and after the third year, Andrew has $318 in the account.

2. Marilyn deposits $600 in an account that earns 1.5% interest each year. After the first year, Marilyn has $609 in the account. After the second year, Marilyn has $618.14 in the account, and after the third year, Marilyn has $627.41 in the account.

Problem Set

Write a function to represent each problem situation.

1. Nami deposits $500 into a simple interest account. The interest rate for the account is 3%. Write a function that represents the balance in the account as a function of time t.

   $P(t) = P_0 + (P_0 \cdot r)t$
   $P(t) = 500 + (500 \cdot 0.03)t$
   $P(t) = 500 + 15t$

2. Carmen deposits $1000 into a simple interest account. The interest rate for the account is 4%. Write a function that represents the balance in the account as a function of time t.

5

3. Emilio deposits $250 into a simple interest account. The interest rate for the account is 2.5%. Write a function that represents the balance in the account as a function of time t.

4. Vance deposits $1500 into a simple interest account. The interest rate for the account is 5.5%. Write a function that represents the balance in the account as a function of time t.

5. Perry deposits $175 into a simple interest account. The interest rate for the account is 4.25%. Write a function that represents the balance in the account as a function of time t.

6. Julian deposits $5000 into a simple interest account. The interest rate for the account is 2.75%. Write a function that represents the balance in the account as a function of time t.

5

Sherwin deposits $500 into a simple interest account. The interest rate for the account is 3.75%. The function $P(t) = 500 + 18.75t$ represents the balance in the account as a function of time. Determine the account balance after each given number of years.

7. 3 years

$P(t) = 500 + 18.75t$

$P(3) = 500 + 18.75(3)$

$P(3) = 556.25$

In 3 years, the account balance will be $556.25.

8. 2 years

9. 10 years

10. 15 years

Name _____ Date _____

11. 50 years

12. 75 years

Hector deposits $400 into a simple interest account. The interest rate for the account is 5.25%. The function $P(t) = 400 + 21t$ represents the balance in the account as a function of time. Determine the number of years it will take for the account balance to reach each given amount.

13. $505

$P(t) = 400 + 21t$

$505 = 400 + 21t$

$105 = 21t$

$5 = t$

It will take 5 years for the account balance to reach $505.

14. $610

15. $1450

16. $2500

17. double the original deposit

18. triple the original deposit

5

Write a function to represent each problem situation.

19. Ronna deposits $500 into a compound interest account. The interest rate for the account is 4%.

$P(t) = P_0 \cdot (1 + r)^t$

$P(t) = 500 \cdot (1 + 0.04)^t$

$P(t) = 500 \cdot 1.04$

20. Leon deposits $250 into a compound interest account. The interest rate for the account is 6%.

21. Chen deposits $1200 into a compound interest account. The interest rate for the account is 3.5%.

22. Serena deposits $2700 into a compound interest account. The interest rate for the account is 4.25%.

23. Shen deposits $300 into a compound interest account. The interest rate for the account is 1.75%.

24. Lea deposits $450 into a compound interest account. The interest rate for the account is 5.5%.

Name _____ Date _____

Cisco deposits $500 into a compound interest account. The interest rate for the account is 3.25%. The function $P(t) = 500 \cdot 1.0325^t$ represents the balance in the account as a function of time. Determine the account balance after each given number of years.

25. 2 years

$P(t) = 500 \cdot 1.0325^t$

$P(2) = 500 \cdot 1.0325^2$

$P(2) \approx 533.03$

In 2 years, the account balance will be $533.03.

26. 4 years

27. 15 years

28. 20 years

29. 50 years

30. 65 years

5

Mario deposits $1000 into a compound interest account. The interest rate for the account is 5%. The function $P(t) = 1000 \cdot 1.05^t$ represents the balance in the account as a function of time. Use a graphing calculator to estimate the number of years it will take for the account balance to reach each given amount.

31. $1500

It will take about 8.3 years for the account balance to reach $1500.

32. $4000

33. $6000

34. $10,000

35. double the original amount

36. triple the original amount

Use the simple and compound interest formula to complete each table. Round to the nearest cent.

37. Teresa has $300 to deposit into an account. The interest rate available for the account is 4%.

Quantity	Time	Simple Interest Balance	Compound Interest Balance
Units	years	dollars	dollars
Expression	t	$300 + 12t$	$300 \cdot 1.04^t$
	0	300.00	300.00
	2	324.00	324.48
	6	372.00	379.60
	10	420.00	444.07

38. Ye has $700 to deposit into an account. The interest rate available for the account is 6%.

Quantity	Time	Simple Interest Balance	Compound Interest Balance
Units			
Expression			
	0		
	3		
	10		
	20		

Name _____ Date _____

39. Pablo has $1100 to deposit into an account. The interest rate available for the account is 3.5%.

Quantity	Time	Simple Interest Balance	Compound Interest Balance
Units			
Expression			
	0		
	5		
	10		
	30		

40. Ty has $525 to deposit into an account. The interest rate available for the account is 2.5%.

Quantity	Time	Simple Interest Balance	Compound Interest Balance
Units			
Expression			
	0		
	10		
	20		
	50		

5

41. Xavier has $2300 to deposit into an account. The interest rate available for the account is 3.75%.

Quantity	Time	Simple Interest Balance	Compound Interest Balance
Units			
Expression			
	0		
	2		
	5		
	15		

42. Denisa has $100 to deposit into an account. The interest rate available for the account is 6.25%.

Quantity	Time	Simple Interest Balance	Compound Interest Balance
Units			
Expression			
	0		
	5		
	15		
	30		

Name _____ Date _____

Downtown and Uptown
Graphs of Exponential Functions

Vocabulary

Define the term in your own words.

1. horizontal asymptote

Problem Set

Write a function that represents each population as a function of time.

1. Blueville has a population of 7000. Its population is increasing at a rate of 1.4%.

$P(t) = P_0 \cdot (1 + r)^t$

$P(t) = 7000 \cdot (1 + 0.014)^t$

$P(t) = 7000 \cdot 1.014^t$

2. Youngstown has a population of 12,000. Its population is increasing at a rate of 1.2%.

3. Greenville has a population of 8000. Its population is decreasing at a rate of 1.75%.

4. North Park has a population of 14,000. Its population is decreasing at a rate of 3.1%.

5. West Lake has a population of 9500. Its population is increasing at a rate of 2.8%.

6. Springfield has a population of 11,500. Its population is decreasing at a rate of 1.25%.

Waynesburg has a population of 16,000. Its population is increasing at a rate of 1.5%. The function $P(t) = 16,000 \cdot 1.015^t$ represents the population as a function of time. Determine the population after each given number of years. Round your answer to the nearest whole number.

7. 1 year

$P(t) = 16,000 \cdot 1.015^t$

$P(1) = 16,000 \cdot 1.015^1$

$P(1) = 16,240$

The population after 1 year will be 16,240.

8. 3 years

9. 5 years

10. 10 years

11. 20 years

12. 50 years

Name _____ Date _____

Morristown has a population of 18,000. Its population is decreasing at a rate of 1.2%. The function, $P(t) = 18{,}000 \cdot 0.988^t$ represents the population as a function of time. Use a graphing calculator to estimate the number of years it will take for the population to reach each given amount.

13. 17,000

It will take about 4.7 years for the population to reach 17,000.

14. 15,000

15. half

16. one-third

17. 0

18. 10,000

Complete each table and graph the function. Identify the *x*-intercept, *y*-intercept, asymptote, domain, range, and interval(s) of increase or decrease for the function.

19. $f(x) = 2^x$

x	f(x)
−2	$\frac{1}{4}$
−1	$\frac{1}{2}$
0	1
1	2
2	4

x-intercept: none

y-intercept: (0, 1)

asymptote: $y = 0$

domain: all real numbers

range: $y > 0$

interval(s) of increase or decrease: increasing over the entire domain

20. $f(x) = 4^x$

x	f(x)
−2	
−1	
0	
1	
2	

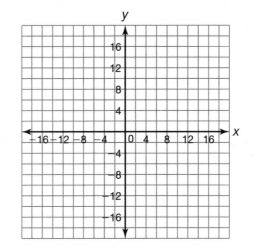

21. $f(x) = \frac{1}{3}^x$

x	f(x)
−2	
−1	
0	
1	
2	

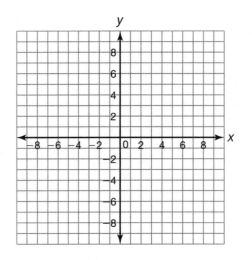

Name _____ Date _____

22. $f(x) = \dfrac{1}{4}^x$

x	f(x)
−2	
−1	
0	
1	
2	

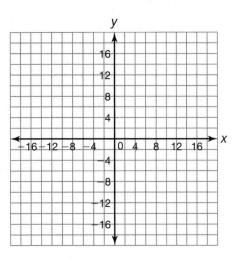

23. $f(x) = -2 \cdot 2^x$

x	f(x)
−2	
−1	
0	
1	
2	

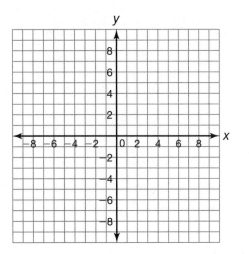

24. $f(x) = -2 \cdot \dfrac{1}{2}^{x}$

x	f(x)
−2	
−1	
0	
1	
2	

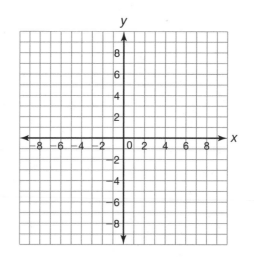

Name _____ Date _____

Let the Transformations Begin!
Translations of Linear and Exponential Functions

Vocabulary

Match each definition to its corresponding term.

1. the mapping, or movement, of all the points of a figure in a plane according to a common operation

   A basic function

2. a type of transformation that shifts the entire graph left or right

   B transformation

3. a function that can be described as the simplest function of its type

   C vertical translation

4. a type of transformation that shifts the entire graph up or down

   D coordinate notation

5. the variable on which a function operates

   E argument of a function

6. notation that uses ordered pairs to describe a transformation on a coordinate plane

   F horizontal translation

Problem Set

Rewrite each function $g(x)$ in terms of the basic function $f(x)$.

1. $f(x) = x$

   $g(x) = x + 4$

   $g(x) = f(x) + 4$

2. $f(x) = x$

   $g(x) = x - 7$

3. $f(x) = x$

   $g(x) = x - 8$

4. $f(x) = 3^x$

   $g(x) = 3^x + 1$

5. $f(x) = 3^x$

   $g(x) = 3^x + 2$

6. $f(x) = 4^x$

   $g(x) = 4^x - 6$

Represent each vertical translation, $g(x)$, using coordinate notation.

7. $f(x) = x$

$g(x) = x + 8$

$(x, y) \rightarrow (x, y + 8)$

8. $f(x) = x$

$g(x) = x + 9$

9. $f(x) = x$

$g(x) = x - 4$

10. $f(x) = 4^x$

$g(x) = 4^x - 1$

11. $f(x) = 4^x$

$g(x) = 4^x + 6$

12. $f(x) = 3^x$

$g(x) = 3^x - 5$

Rewrite each function $g(x)$ in terms of the basic function $f(x)$.

13. $f(x) = 3^x$

$g(x) = 3^{(x + 1)}$

$g(x) = 3^{(x + 1)} = f(x + 1)$

14. $f(x) = 3^x$

$g(x) = 3^{(x + 5)}$

15. $f(x) = 2^x$

$g(x) = 2^{(x - 1)}$

16. $f(x) = 2^x$

$g(x) = 2^{(x - 9)}$

17. $f(x) = 2x$

$g(x) = 2(x - 3)$

18. $f(x) = 2x$

$g(x) = 2(x + 4)$

Represent each horizontal translation, $g(x)$, using coordinate notation.

19. $f(x) = 3^x$

$g(x) = 3^{(x - 2)}$

$(x, y) \rightarrow (x + 2, y)$

20. $f(x) = 3^x$

$g(x) = 3^{(x + 2)}$

21. $f(x) = 4^x$

$g(x) = 4^{(x + 1)}$

22. $f(x) = 4^x$

$g(x) = 4^{(x - 3)}$

23. $f(x) = 3x$

$g(x) = 3(x - 1)$

24. $f(x) = 3x$

$g(x) = 3(x + 1)$

Name _____ Date _____

Describe each graph in relation to its basic function.

25. Compare $f(x) = (x) + b$ when $b < 0$ to the basic function $h(x) = x$.
The graph of $f(x)$ is b units below the graph of $h(x)$.

26. Compare $f(x) = b^{x-c}$ when $c > 0$ to the basic function $h(x) = b^x$.

27. Compare $f(x) = (x - b)$ when $b > 0$ to the basic function $h(x) = x$.

28. Compare $f(x) = b^{x-c}$ when $c < 0$ to the basic function $h(x) = b^x$.

29. Compare $f(x) = b^x + k$ when $k > 0$ to the basic function $h(x) = b^x$.

30. Compare $f(x) = (x - b)$ when $b < 0$ to the basic function $h(x) = x$.

Each coordinate plane shows the graph of $f(x)$. Sketch the graph of $g(x)$.

31. $g(x) = f(x) + 2$

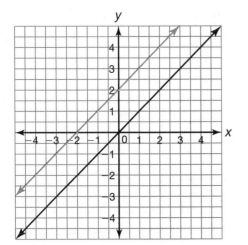

32. $g(x) = f(x) + 4$

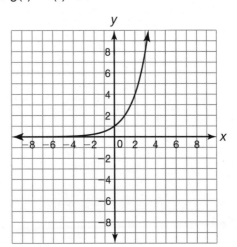

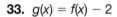
33. $g(x) = f(x) - 2$

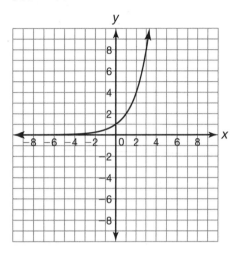

34. $g(x) = f(x - 3)$

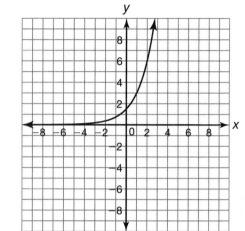

35. $g(x) = f(x + 3)$

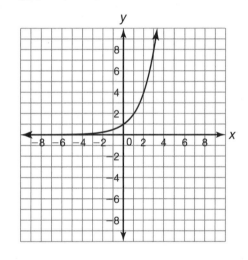

36. $g(x) = f(x - 4)$

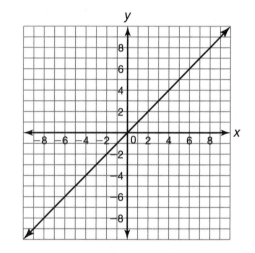

37. $g(x) = f(x) + 5$

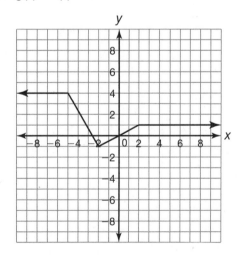

38. $g(x) = f(x + 5)$

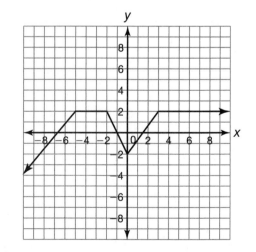

Name _____ Date _____

Write the equation of the function given each translation.

39. $f(x) = x$

Vertical translation up 2 units

$g(x) = x + 2$

40. $f(x) = x$

Vertical translation down 5 units

41. $f(x) = 3^x$

Horizontal translation right 4 units

42. $f(x) = 2^x$

Horizontal translation left 6 units

43. $f(x) = 3^x$

Vertical translation down 5 units

44. $f(x) = 4x$

Horizontal translation right 3 units

Each graph shows the function $g(x)$ as a translation of the function $f(x)$. Write the equation of $g(x)$.

45.

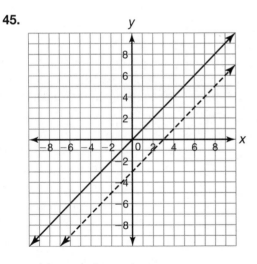

$g(x) = x - 3$

46.

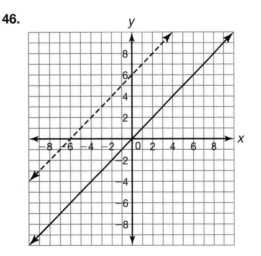

47.

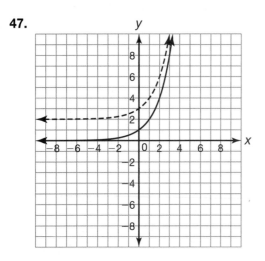

48.

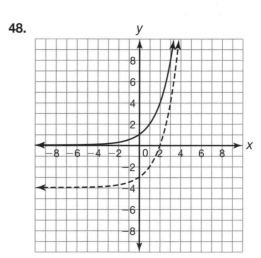

49.

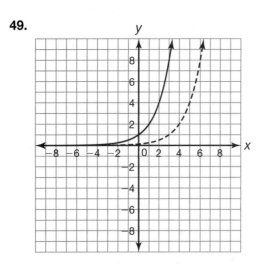

50.

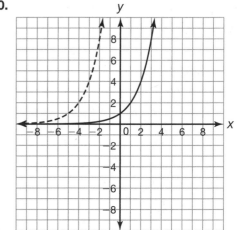

Name _____ Date _____

Take Some Time to Reflect
Reflections of Linear and Exponential Functions

Vocabulary

Define each term in your own words.

1. reflection

2. line of reflection

Problem Set

Rewrite each function $g(x)$ in terms of the basic function $f(x)$.

1. $f(x) = 3^x$

    $g(x) = -(3^x)$

    $g(x) = -f(x)$

2. $f(x) = 3^x$

    $g(x) = 3^{-x}$

3. $f(x) = 4^x$

    $g(x) = -(4^x)$

4. $f(x) = 4^x$

    $g(x) = 4^{-x}$

5. $f(x) = 2^x + 4$

    $g(x) = 2^{-x} + 4$

6. $f(x) = 2^x - 1$

    $g(x) = -(2^x - 1)$

Represent each reflection using coordinate notation. Identify whether $g(x)$ is a reflection about a horizontal line of reflection or a vertical line of reflection.

7. $f(x) = 2^x$

$g(x) = -(2^x)$

$(x, y) \rightarrow (x, -y)$

$g(x)$ is a horizontal reflection about $y = 0$.

8. $f(x) = 2^x$

$g(x) = 2^{-x}$

9. $f(x) = 5x$

$g(x) = -(5x)$

10. $f(x) = 5x$

$g(x) = 5(-x)$

11. $f(x) = 3^x + 7$

$g(x) = 3^{-x} + 7$

12. $f(x) = 4^x - 3$

$g(x) = -(4^x - 3)$

Each coordinate plane shows the graph of $f(x)$. Sketch the graph of $g(x)$.

13. $g(x) = -f(x)$

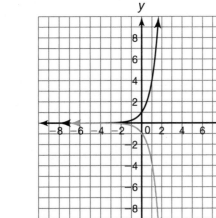

14. $g(x) = f(-x)$

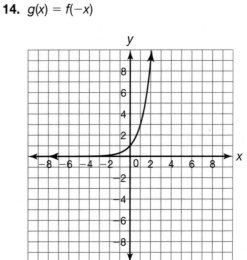

Name _____ Date _____

15. $g(x) = f(-x)$

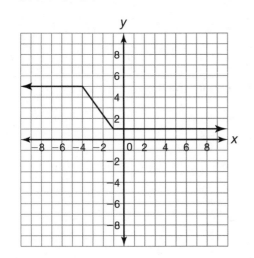

16. $g(x) = -f(x)$

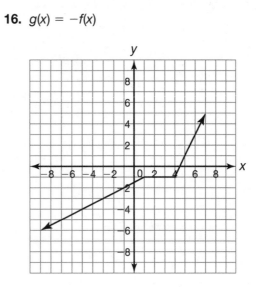

17. $g(x) = -f(x)$

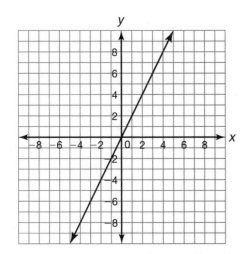

18. $g(x) = f(-x)$

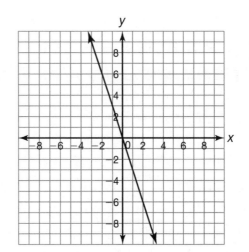

Write a function, $g(x)$, to describe each reflection of $f(x)$.

19. $f(x) = 3^x$

Reflection about the horizontal line $y = 0$.

$g(x) = -3^x$

20. $f(x) = 4^x$

Reflection about the vertical line $x = 0$.

21. $f(x) = -12x$

Reflection about the vertical line $x = 0$.

22. $f(x) = 7x$

Reflection about the horizontal line $y = 0$.

23. $f(x) = 2^x + 9$

Reflection about the horizontal line $y = 0$.

24. $f(x) = -8^x + 1$

Reflection about the vertical line $x = 0$.

Write an equation for $g(x)$ given each transformation. Sketch the graph of $g(x)$.

25. $f(x) = 5^x$

$g(x)$ is a reflection of $f(x)$ over the line $y = 0$.

$g(x) = -5^x$

26. $f(x) = 5^x$

$g(x)$ is a reflection of $f(x)$ over the line $x = 0$.

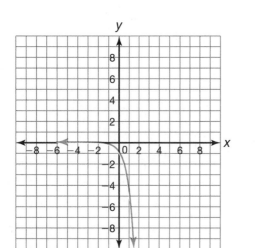

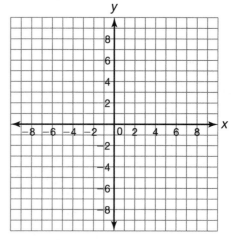

Name _____ Date _____

27. $f(x) = 3^x$

g(x) is a translation of f(x) up 2 units.

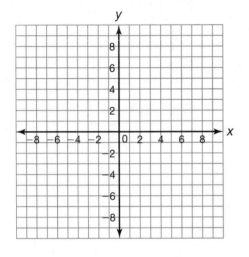

28. $f(x) = 4^x$

g(x) is a translation of f(x) right 3 units.

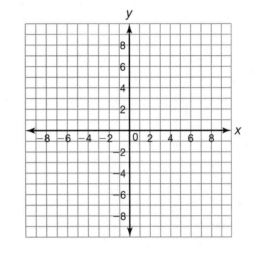

29. $f(x) = 4^x$

g(x) is a translation of f(x) down 4 units.

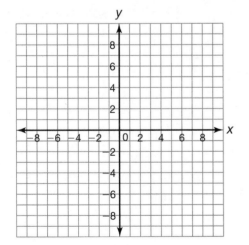

30. $f(x) = 3^x$

g(x) is a translation of f(x) left 5 units.

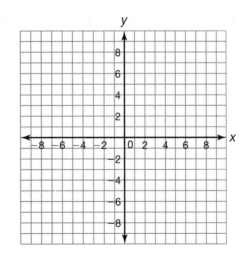

Identify the transformation required to transform *f(x)* to *g(x)* as shown in each graph.

31.

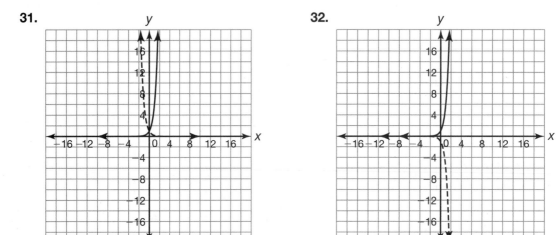

g(x) is a reflection of *f(x)* over the line *x* = 0.

32.

33.

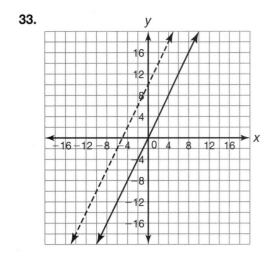

34.

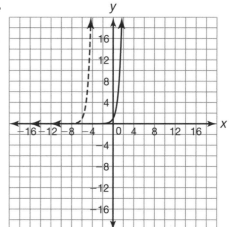

Name _____ Date _____

35.

36.

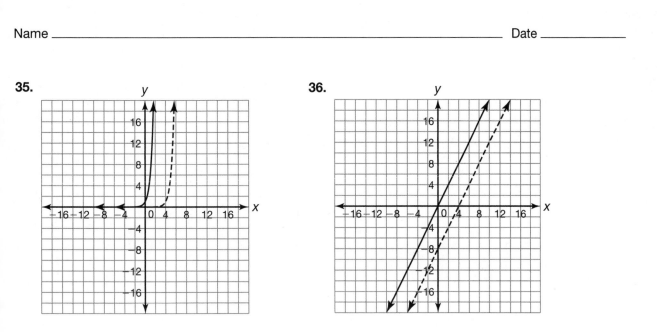

Identify the transformation required to transform each $f(x)$ to $g(x)$.

37. $f(x) = 8^x$

$g(x) = -(8^x)$

$g(x)$ is a reflection of $f(x)$ over the line $y = 0$.

38. $f(x) = 9^x$

$g(x) = 9^{-x}$

39. $f(x) = 8^x$

$g(x) = 8^x - 5$

40. $f(x) = 3^x$

$g(x) = 3^{x-1}$

41. $f(x) = 10x$

$g(x) = 10x + 2$

42. $f(x) = -12x$

$g(x) = -12(x + 1)$

5

Name _____ Date _____

Radical! Because It's Cliché!
Properties of Rational Exponents

Vocabulary

Match each definition to its corresponding term.

1. the number a in the expression $\sqrt[n]{a}$ **A** cube root

2. the number b when $b^3 = a$ **B** index

3. the exponent $\frac{1}{n}$ in the expression $a^{\frac{1}{n}}$ **C** nth root

4. the number n in the expression $\sqrt[n]{a}$ **D** radicand

5. the number b when $b^n = a$ **E** rational exponent

Problem Set

Write each expression as a single power.

1. $\dfrac{10^5}{10^8}$ **2.** $\dfrac{10^0}{10^4}$

$\dfrac{10^5}{10^8} = 10^{5-8} = 10^{-3}$

3. $\dfrac{10^2}{10^5}$ **4.** $\dfrac{x^4}{x^9}$

5. $\dfrac{5^3}{5^{10}}$ **6.** $\dfrac{y^2}{y^8}$

Evaluate each expression.

7. $\sqrt[3]{216} =$

$\sqrt[3]{216} = 6$

8. $\sqrt[3]{64} =$

9. $\sqrt[3]{-125} =$

10. $\sqrt[3]{-343} =$

11. $\sqrt[3]{729} =$

12. $\sqrt[3]{-8} =$

Evaluate each expression.

13. $\sqrt[5]{32} =$

$\sqrt[5]{32} = 2$

14. $\sqrt[4]{625} =$

15. $\sqrt[6]{729} =$

16. $\sqrt[5]{-1024} =$

17. $\sqrt[7]{-128} =$

18. $\sqrt[5]{-243} =$

Write each radical as a power.

19. $\sqrt[4]{15}$

$\sqrt[4]{15} = 15^{\frac{1}{4}}$

20. $\sqrt[3]{5}$

21. $\sqrt[4]{31}$

22. $\sqrt[3]{x}$

23. $\sqrt[6]{y}$

24. $\sqrt{z}$

Name _____ Date _____

Write each power as a radical.

25. $12^{\frac{1}{3}}$

$$12^{\frac{1}{3}} = \sqrt[3]{12}$$

26. $7^{\frac{1}{5}}$

27. $18^{\frac{1}{4}}$

28. $a^{\frac{1}{2}}$

29. $d^{\frac{1}{5}}$

30. $c^{\frac{1}{6}}$

Write each expression in radical form.

31. $5^{\frac{2}{3}}$

$$5^{\frac{2}{3}} = \sqrt[3]{5^2}$$

32. $8^{\frac{2}{5}}$

33. $18^{\frac{3}{4}}$

34. $x^{\frac{3}{5}}$

35. $y^{\frac{4}{3}}$

36. $m^{\frac{5}{2}}$

5

Write each expression in rational exponent form.

37. $\sqrt[4]{6^3}$

$\sqrt[4]{6^3} = 6^{\frac{3}{4}}$

38. $\sqrt[5]{8^4}$

39. $\sqrt[3]{12^2}$

40. $\sqrt{n^5}$

41. $\sqrt[4]{p^7}$

42. $\sqrt[5]{m^3}$

Name _____ Date _____

Checkmate!
Solving Exponential Functions

Problem Set

Complete each table. Write a function that represents the data in the table and explain how you determined your expression.

1.

x	f(x)	Expression
0	1	3^0
1	3	3^1
2	9	3^2
3	27	3^3
4	81	3^4
5	243	3^5
x	3^x	-----

The exponents of the expressions in the third column equal x. So, $f(x) = 3x$.

2.

x	f(x)	Expression
0	5	$4^0 + 5$
1	9	
2	21	
3	69	
4	261	
5	1029	
x		-----

3.

x	f(x)	Expression
0	−1	-2^0
1	−2	
2	−4	
3		
4		
5		
x		-----

4.

x	f(x)	Expression
−2	$-\dfrac{1}{2}$	-2^{-1}
−1	−1	
0	−2	
1		
2		
3		
x		-----

5.

x	f(x)	Expression
0	$-\dfrac{1}{25}$	-5^{-2}
1	$-\dfrac{1}{5}$	
2	−1	
3		
4		
5		
x		-----

6.

x	f(x)	Expression
0	16	2^4
1	8	
2	4	
3		
4		
5		
x		-----

Name _____ Date _____

Graph each function.

7. $f(x) = 3^x$

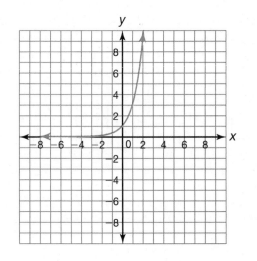

8. $f(x) = 8^{-x}$

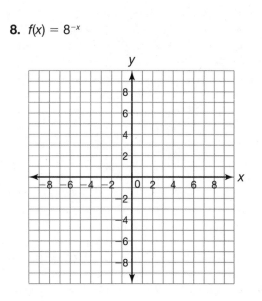

9. $f(x) = 5 \cdot 2^{-x}$

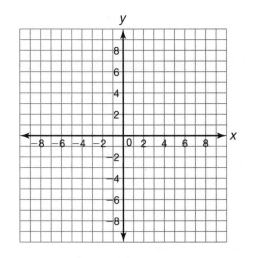

10. $f(x) = 2 \cdot 3^x$

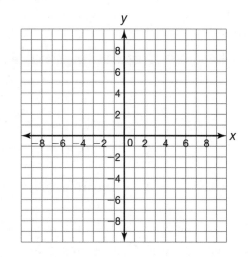

11. $f(x) = -4^x$

12. $f(x) = -3^{x+2}$

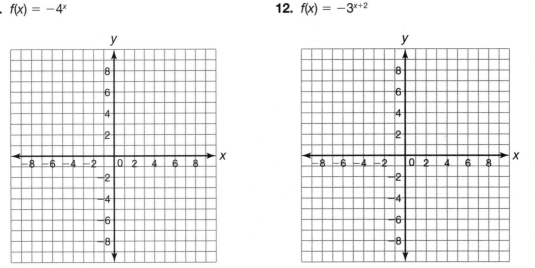

Use the intersection feature of your graphing calculator to answer each question.

13. For the function $f(x) = 6^{x-1}$ determine the value of x for which $f(x) = 7776$.

For the function $f(x) = 6^{x-1}$, $f(x) = 7776$ when $x = 6$.

14. For the function $f(x) = -4^{x+2}$ determine the value of x for which $f(x) = -4096$.

15. For the function $f(x) = 5^{-x+1}$ determine the value of x for which $f(x) = 625$.

16. For the function $f(x) = 2^{x+4}$ determine the values of x for which $f(x) < 128$.

17. For the function $f(x) = -3^{x+1}$ determine the values of x for which $f(x) > -9$.

18. For the function $f(x) = 5^{x+2}$ determine the values of x for which $f(x) = 15{,}625$.

Name _____ Date _____

Solve each exponential equation for *x*.

19. $4^x = 256$

$4^x = 256$

$4^4 = 256$

$x = 4$

20. $6^{3x} = 216$

21. $2^{5-x} = \dfrac{1}{16}$

22. $3^{-2x} = \dfrac{1}{729}$

23. $4^{x+3} = 4$

24. $\dfrac{1}{5^{x+4}} = 625$

25. $-6^{x-2} = \dfrac{1}{-1296}$

26. $\dfrac{1}{2^{x-6}} = \dfrac{1}{4}$

For each pair of expressions, determine whether the second expression is an equivalent form of the first expression.

27. 2^{s-1} $\frac{1}{2}(2)^2$

$2^{-1} \cdot 2^s$

2^{s-1}

28. 3^{x+1} $\frac{1}{3}(3)^x$

29. 2^{2x+1} $2(4)^x$

30. 5^{2x-1} $\frac{1}{5}(10)^x$

31. $4(64)^x$ 4^{3x+1}

32. $\frac{1}{2}\left(\frac{1}{8}\right)^x$ 2^{-3x-1}

Write the exponential function represented by the table of values.

33.

x	y
0	2
1	1
2	$\frac{1}{2}$
3	$\frac{1}{4}$

$f(x) = a \cdot b^x$

$f(x) = 2 \cdot b^x$

$1 = 2 \cdot b^1$

$\frac{1}{2} = b$

$f(x) = 2\left(\frac{1}{2}\right)^x$

34.

x	y
0	1
2	25
4	625
6	15625

Name _____ Date _____

35.

x	y
0	1
1	$\frac{3}{4}$
2	$\frac{9}{16}$
3	$\frac{27}{64}$

36.

x	y
0	-1
2	-4
4	-16
6	-64

37.

x	y
0	3
3	$\frac{1}{9}$
6	$\frac{1}{243}$
9	$\frac{1}{6561}$

38.

x	y
0	-2
1	$-\frac{1}{2}$
2	$-\frac{1}{8}$
3	$-\frac{1}{32}$

5

5

Name _____ Date _____

Prepping for the Robot Challenge
Solving Linear Systems Graphically and Algebraically

Vocabulary

Match each term to its corresponding definition.

1. a process of solving a system of equations by substituting a variable in one equation with an equivalent expression

    a. system of linear equations

2. systems with no solutions

    b. break-even point

3. the point when the cost and the income are equal

    c. substitution method

4. systems with one or many solutions

    d. consistent systems

5. two or more linear equations that define a relationship between quantities

    e. inconsistent systems

6

Problem Set

Write a system of linear equations to represent each problem situation. Define each variable. Then, graph the system of equations and estimate the break-even point. Explain what the break-even point represents with respect to the given problem situation.

1. Eric sells model cars from a booth at a local flea market. He purchases each model car from a distributor for $12, and the flea market charges him a booth fee of $50. Eric sells each model car for $20.

   Eric's income can be modeled by the equation $y = 20x$, where y represents the income (in dollars) and x represents the number of model cars he sells.

   Eric's expenses can be modeled by the equation $y = 12x + 50$, where y represents the expenses (in dollars) and x represents the number of model cars he purchases from the distributor.

   $$\begin{cases} y = 20x \\ y = 12x + 50 \end{cases}$$

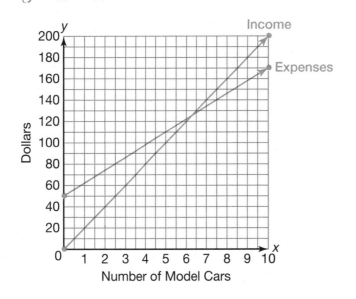

   The break-even point is between 6 and 7 model cars. Eric must sell more than 6 model cars to make a profit.

Name _____ Date _____

2. Ramona sets up a lemonade stand in front of her house. Each cup of lemonade costs Ramona $0.30 to make, and she spends $6 on the advertising signs she puts up around her neighborhood. She sells each cup of lemonade for $1.50.

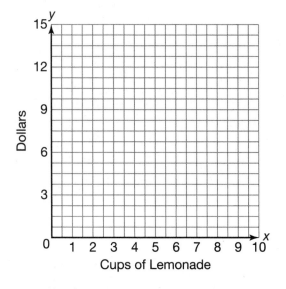

3. Chen starts his own lawn mowing business. He initially spends $180 on a new lawnmower. For each yard he mows, he receives $20 and spends $4 on gas.

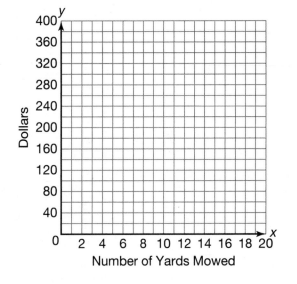

Name _____ Date _____

4. Olivia is building birdhouses to raise money for a trip to Hawaii. She spends a total of $30 on the tools needed to build the houses. The material to build each birdhouse costs $3.25. Olivia sells each birdhouse for $10.

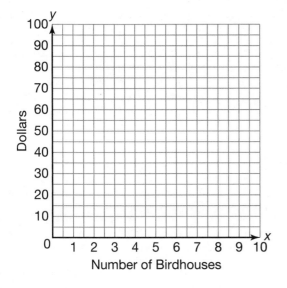

Number of Birdhouses

5. The Spanish Club is selling boxes of fruit as a fundraiser. The fruit company charges the Spanish Club $7.50 for each box of fruit and a shipping and handling fee of $100 for the entire order. The Spanish Club sells each box of fruit for $15.

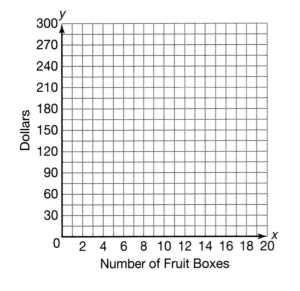

Name _____ Date _____

6. Jerome sells flowers for $12 per bouquet through his Internet flower site. Each bouquet costs him $5.70 to make. Jerome also paid a one-time fee of $150 for an Internet marketing firm to advertise his company.

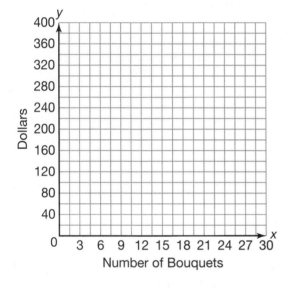

Transform both equations in each system of equations so that each coefficient is an integer.

7. $\begin{cases} \dfrac{1}{2}x + \dfrac{3}{2}y = 4 \\ \dfrac{2}{3}x - \dfrac{1}{3}y = 7 \end{cases}$

8. $\begin{cases} -\dfrac{1}{3}x + \dfrac{1}{2}y = 5 \\ \dfrac{3}{4}x - \dfrac{1}{4}y = 10 \end{cases}$

$\dfrac{1}{2}x + \dfrac{3}{2}y = 4 \qquad \dfrac{2}{3}x - \dfrac{1}{3}y = 7$

$2\left(\dfrac{1}{2}x + \dfrac{3}{2}y = 4\right) \quad 3\left(\dfrac{2}{3}x - \dfrac{1}{3}y = 7\right)$

$x + 3y = 8 \qquad\quad 2x - y = 21$

9. $\begin{cases} \dfrac{5}{4}x - 3 = \dfrac{1}{6}y \\ \dfrac{2}{5}x + \dfrac{1}{5}y = \dfrac{9}{5} \end{cases}$

10. $\begin{cases} 0.5x + 1.2y = 2 \\ 3.3x - 0.7y = 3 \end{cases}$

11. $\begin{cases} 0.2x - 0.4y = 2 \\ -0.1x - 0.5y = 1.1 \end{cases}$

12. $\begin{cases} 0.3y = 2 - 0.8x \\ 1.1x = 3y - 0.4 \end{cases}$

Name _____ Date _____

Solve each system of equations by substitution. Determine whether the system is consistent or inconsistent.

13. $\begin{cases} y = 2x - 3 \\ x = 4 \end{cases}$

$y = 2(4) - 3$

$y = 8 - 3$

$y = 5$

The solution is (4, 5).

The system is consistent.

14. $\begin{cases} 2x + y = 9 \\ y = 5x + 2 \end{cases}$

15. $\begin{cases} y = 3x - 2 \\ y - 3x = 4 \end{cases}$

16. $\begin{cases} \dfrac{1}{2}x + \dfrac{3}{2}y = -7 \\ \dfrac{1}{3}y = 2x - 10 \end{cases}$

6

17. $\begin{cases} 0.8x - 0.2y = 1.5 \\ 0.1x + 1.2y = 0.8 \end{cases}$

18. $\begin{cases} 0.3y = 0.6x + 0.3 \\ 1.2x + 0.6 = 0.6y \end{cases}$

6

Name _____ Date _____

There's Another Way?
Using Linear Combinations to Solve a Linear System

Vocabulary

Define the term in your own words.

1. linear combinations method

Problem Set

Write a system of equations to represent each problem situation. Solve the system of equations using the linear combinations method.

1. The high school marching band is selling fruit baskets as a fundraiser. They sell a large basket containing 10 apples and 15 oranges for $20. They sell a small basket containing 5 apples and 6 oranges for $8.50. How much is the marching band charging for each apple and each orange?

Let x represent the amount charged for each apple. Let y represent the amount charged for each orange.

$$\begin{cases} 10x + 15y = 20 \\ 5x + 6y = 8.50 \end{cases} \qquad \begin{aligned} 10x + 15y &= 20 \\ -2(5x + 6y &= 8.50) \end{aligned}$$

$$\begin{aligned} 10x + 15y &= 20 \\ \underline{-10x - 12y} &= \underline{-17} \\ 3y &= 3 \\ y &= 1 \end{aligned}$$

$$\begin{aligned} 10x + 15(1) &= 20 \\ 10x + 15 &= 20 \\ 10x &= 5 \\ x &= 0.5 \end{aligned}$$

The solution is (0.5, 1). The band charges $0.50 for each apple and $1.00 for each orange.

2. Asna works on a shipping dock at a tire manufacturing plant. She loads a pallet with 4 Mudslinger tires and 6 Roadripper tires. The tires on the pallet weigh 212 pounds. She loads a second pallet with 7 Mudslinger tires and 2 Roadripper tires. The tires on the second pallet weigh 184 pounds. How much does each Mudslinger tire and each Roadripper tire weigh?

3. The Pizza Barn sells one customer 3 large pepperoni pizzas and 2 orders of breadsticks for $30. They sell another customer 4 large pepperoni pizzas and 3 orders of breadsticks for $41. How much does the Pizza Barn charge for each pepperoni pizza and each order of breadsticks?

6

Name _____ Date _____

4. Nancy and Warren are making large pots of chicken noodle soup. Nancy opens 4 large cans and 6 small cans of soup and pours them into her pot. Her pot contains 115 ounces of soup. Warren opens 3 large cans and 5 small cans of soup. His pot contains 91 ounces of soup. How many ounces of soup does each large can and each small can contain?

5. Taylor and Natsumi are making block towers out of large and small blocks. They are stacking the blocks on top of each other in a single column. Taylor uses 4 large blocks and 2 small blocks to make a tower 63.8 inches tall. Natsumi uses 9 large blocks and 4 small blocks to make a tower 139.8 inches tall. How tall is each large block and each small block?

6

6. Dave has 2 buckets that he uses to fill the water troughs on his horse farm. He wants to determine how many ounces each bucket holds. On Tuesday, he fills an empty 2000 ounce water trough with 7 large buckets and 5 small buckets of water. On Thursday, he fills the same empty water trough with 4 large buckets and 10 small buckets of water. How many ounces does each bucket hold?

Solve each system of equations using the linear combinations method.

7. $\begin{cases} 3x + 5y = 8 \\ 2x - 5y = 22 \end{cases}$

$3x + 5y = 8$

$\underline{2x - 5y = 22}$

$\quad 5x = 30$

$\quad\; x = 6$

$3(6) + 5y = 8$

$18 + 5y = 8$

$\quad 5y = -10$

$\quad\; y = -2$

The solution is $(6, -2)$.

8. $\begin{cases} 4x - y = 2 \\ 2x + 2y = 26 \end{cases}$

Name _____ Date _____

9. $\begin{cases} 10x - 6y = -6 \\ 5x - 5y = 5 \end{cases}$

10. $\begin{cases} 2x - 4y = 4 \\ -3x + 10y = 14 \end{cases}$

11. $\begin{cases} 3x + 2y = 14 \\ 4x + 5y = 35 \end{cases}$

12. $\begin{cases} x + 6y = 11 \\ 2x - 12y = 10 \end{cases}$

6

13. $\begin{cases} 1.5x + 1.2y = 0.6 \\ 0.8x - 0.2y = 2 \end{cases}$

14. $\begin{cases} \dfrac{3}{4}x + \dfrac{1}{2}y = -\dfrac{3}{4} \\ \dfrac{2}{3}x + \dfrac{2}{3}y = \dfrac{2}{3} \end{cases}$

Name _____ Date _____

What's For Lunch?
Solving More Systems

Problem Set

Write a system of equations to represent each problem situation. Solve the system of equations using any method. Then, answer any associated questions.

1. Jason and Jerry are competing at a weightlifting competition. They are both lifting barbells containing 200 pounds of plates (weights). Jason's barbell has 4 large and 10 small plates on it. Jerry's barbell has 6 large and 5 small plates on it. How much does each large plate and each small plate weigh?

   Let x represent the weight (in pounds) of a large plate. Let y represent the weight (in pounds) of a small plate.

   $$\begin{cases} 4x + 10y = 200 \\ 6x + 5y = 200 \end{cases}$$

   One possible solution path:
   Linear Combinations Method:

   $$4x + 10y = 200$$
   $$-2(6x + 5y = 200)$$

   $$\begin{array}{r} 4x + 10y = 200 \\ \underline{-12x - 10y = -400} \\ -8x = -200 \\ x = 25 \end{array}$$

   $$4(25) + 10y = 200$$
   $$100 + 10y = 200$$
   $$10y = 100$$
   $$y = 10$$

   The solution is (25, 10). Each large plate weighs 25 pounds. Each small plate weighs 10 pounds.

6

2. Rachel needs to print some of her digital photos. She is trying to choose between Lightning Fast Foto and Snappy Shots. Lightning Fast Foto charges a base fee of $5 plus an additional $0.20 per photo. Snappy Shots charges a base fee of $7 plus an additional $0.10 per photo. Determine the number of photos for which both stores will charge the same amount. Explain which store Rachel should choose depending on the number of photos she needs to print.

6

Name _____ Date _____

3. Raja is trying to decide which ice cream shop is the better buy. Cold & Creamy Sundaes charges $2.50 per sundae plus an additional $0.25 for each topping. Colder & Creamier Sundaes charges $1.50 per sundae plus an additional $0.50 for each topping. Determine the number of toppings for which both vendors charge the same amount. Explain which vendor is the better buy depending on the number of toppings Raja chooses.

4. Marcus is selling t-shirts at the State Fair. He brings 200 shirts to sell. He has long-sleeve and short-sleeved T-shirts for sale. On the first day of the fair, he sells $\frac{1}{2}$ of his long-sleeved T-shirts and $\frac{1}{3}$ of his short-sleeved T-shirts for a total of 80 T-shirts sold. How many of each type of T-shirt did Marcus bring to the fair?

Name _____ Date _____

5. Alicia has a booth at the flea market where she sells purses and wallets. All of her purses are the same price and all of her wallets are the same price. The first hour of the day, she sells 10 purses and 6 wallets for a total of $193. The second hour, she sells 8 purses and 10 wallets for a total of $183. How much does Alicia charge for each purse and each wallet?

6. Weston wants to buy a one-year membership to a golf course. Rolling Hills Golf Course charges a base fee of $200 and an additional $15 per round of golf. Majestic View Golf Course charges a base fee of $350 and an additional $10 per round of golf. Determine the number of rounds of golf for which both golf courses charge the same amount. Explain which golf course Weston should become a member at depending on the number of rounds he intends to play.

Name _____ Date _____

Which Is the Best Method?
Using Graphing, Substitution, and Linear Combinations

Problem Set

Write a system of equations to represent each problem situation. Solve the system of equations using any method and answer any associated questions.

1. Jun received two different job offers to become a real estate sales agent. Dream Homes offered Jun a base salary of $20,000 per year plus a 2% commission on all real estate sold. Amazing Homes offered Jun a base salary of $25,000 per year plus a 1% commission on all real estate sold. Determine the amount of real estate sales in dollars for which both real estate companies will pay Jun the same amount. Explain which offer Jun should accept based on the amount of real estate sales he expects to have.

   Let x represent the amount of Jun's real estate sales in dollars. Let y represent the yearly income when Jun has x dollars in real estate sales.

   $\begin{cases} y = 0.02x + 20{,}000 \\ y = 0.01x + 25{,}000 \end{cases}$ Dream Homes
   Amazing Homes

   One possible solution path:

   Substitution Method:

   $0.02x + 20{,}000 = 0.01x + 25{,}000$ $\qquad$ $y = 0.02(500{,}000) + 20{,}000$
   $0.01x + 20{,}000 = 25{,}000$ $\qquad\qquad$ $y = 10{,}000 + 20{,}000$
   $\qquad\quad 0.01x = 5000$ $\qquad\qquad\qquad$ $y = 30{,}000$
   $\qquad\qquad\quad x = 500{,}000$

   The solution is (500,000, 30,000). Both real estate companies will pay Jun $30,000 per year for $500,000 in real estate sales. If Jun expects to sell less than $500,000 of real estate per year, then he should accept the offer from Amazing Homes. If Jun expects to sell more than $500,000 of real estate per year, then he should accept the offer from Dream Homes.

6

2. Stella is trying to choose between two rental car companies. Speedy Trip Rental Cars charges a base fee of $24 plus an additional fee of $0.05 per mile. Wheels Deals Rental Cars charges a base fee of $30 plus an additional fee of $0.03 per mile. Determine the amount of miles driven for which both rental car companies charge the same amount. Explain which company Stella should use based on the number of miles she expects to drive.

6

Name _____ Date _____

3. Renee has two job offers to be a door-to-door food processor salesperson. Pro Process Processors offers her a base salary of $15,000 per year plus an additional $25 for each processor she sells. Puree Processors offers her a base salary of $18,000 per year plus an additional $21 for each processor she sells. Determine the number of food processors Renee would have to sell for both companies to pay her the same amount. Explain which job offer Renee should accept based on the number of food processors she expects to sell.

4. Alex needs to rent a bulldozer. Smith's Equipment Rentals rents bulldozers for a delivery fee of $600 plus an additional $37.50 per day. Robinson's Equipment Rentals rents bulldozers for a delivery fee of $400 plus an additional $62.50 per day. Determine the number of rental days for which both rental companies charge the same amount. Explain which company Alex should choose based on the number of days he expects to rent a bulldozer.

6

Name _____ Date _____

5. Serena has job offers from two car dealerships. Classic Cars offers her a base salary of $22,000 per year plus an additional 1% commission on all sales she makes. Sweet Rides offers her a base salary of $13,000 per year plus an additional 2.5% commission on all sales she makes. Determine the amount of car sales in dollars for which both dealerships will pay Serena the same amount. Explain which offer Serena should accept based on the amount of car sales she expects to have.

6. Dominique is trying to choose a satellite Internet service provider. Reliable Satellite charges customers a monthly fee of $26 plus an additional $0.30 per hour of online time. Super Satellite charges customers a monthly fee of $18 plus an additional $0.50 per hour of online time. Determine the number of hours of online time for which both providers charge the same amount. Explain which provider Dominique should choose based on the number of hours she expects to spend online each month.

Name _____ Date _____

The Playoffs
Graphing Inequalities

Vocabulary

Define the term in your own words

1. half-plane

Problem Set

Write a linear inequality in two variables to represent each problem situation.

1. Tanya is baking zucchini muffins and pumpkin muffins for a school event. She needs at least 500 muffins for the event.

   $x + y \geq 500$

2. Hiro needs to buy new pens and pencils for school. Pencils cost \$1 each and pens cost \$2.50 each. He has \$10 to spend.

3. Patti makes decorative flower pots. It costs her \$20 to purchase the materials for each pot. She wants to charge more than \$6 per hour of labor plus her materials cost for each pot.

4. Jose and Devon are working on a construction job together. Devon can put in 4 times as many hours per week as Jose. Together they must work at least 80 hours per week.

5. The Foxes are playing the Titans. The Titans have been scoring 28 or more points per game this season. Between 7-point touchdowns and 3-point field goals, the Foxes need to score more than the Titan's lowest score to have a hope of winning the game.

6. Jack made twice his fundraising goal, which was less than the total that Cameron raised. Cameron raised $14 more than 5 times her goal.

Tell whether the graph of each linear inequality will have a dashed line or a solid line. Explain your reasoning.

7. $x - 3y \leq 32$

The line will be solid because the symbol is $\leq$.

8. $8y + 7x > 15$

9. $y < 14x + 9$

10. $-5.2y - 8.3x \leq -28.6$

11. $\frac{2}{3}x + \frac{4}{9}y \geq 3$

12. $y - 17 > x + 8$

13. $185x + 274y \geq 65$

14. $36 < 9y - 2x$

For each inequality, use the test point (0, 0) to determine which half-plane should be shaded.

15. $5x + 7y > -13$

$5(0) + 7(0) > -13$

$0 > -13$

The half-plane that includes (0, 0) should be shaded because the inequality is true for that point.

16. $y - 30 \leq 9x$

17. $-8y > 6x + 12$

18. $46 \geq -5y + 10x$

7

Name _____ Date _____

19. $31.9x + 63.7y < -44.5$

20. $y - \dfrac{5}{6} > \dfrac{1}{2}x + \dfrac{1}{3}$

Graph each linear inequality.

21. $y < 4x + 2$

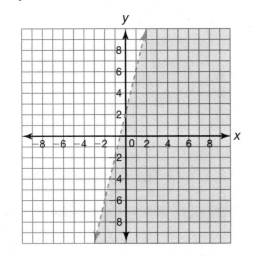

22. $y \geq 10 - x$

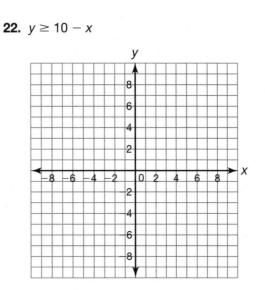

23. $y \geq \dfrac{1}{2}x - 3$

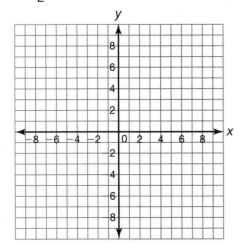

24. $-x + y > 1$

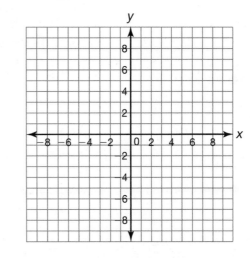

7

25. $3x - 4y \geq 8$

26. $\frac{3}{8}y - \frac{1}{4}x < \frac{3}{4}$

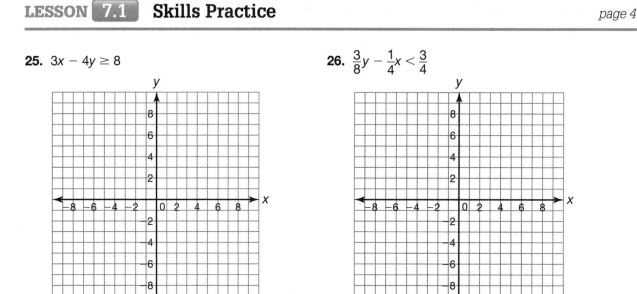

Graph each inequality and determine if the ordered pair is a solution for the problem situation.

27. Marcus has 50 tokens to spend at the school carnival. The Ferris wheel costs 7 tokens and the carousel costs 5 tokens. The inequality $7x + 5y \leq 50$ represents the possible ways Marcus could use his tokens on the two rides. Is the ordered pair (6, 3) a solution for the problem situation?

No. The ordered pair (6, 3) is not a solution to the inequality. It is not in the shaded half-plane.

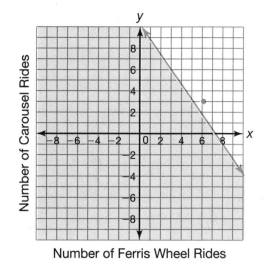

28. Sophia has $2 to buy oranges and apples. Oranges cost $0.45 each and apples cost $0.25 each. The inequality $0.45x + 0.25y \leq 2$ represents the possible ways Sophia could spend her $2. Is the ordered pair (2, 3) a solution for the problem situation?

Name _____ Date _____

29. Noah plays football. His team's goal is to score at least 15 points per game. A touchdown is worth 6 points and a field goal is worth 3 points. Noah's league does not allow teams to try for the extra point after a touchdown. The inequality $6x + 3y \geq 15$ represents the possible ways Noah's team could score points to reach their goal. Is the ordered pair $(6, -1)$ a solution for the problem situation?

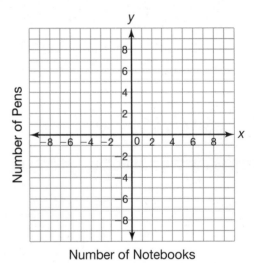

30. Lea has $5 to buy notebooks and pens. Notebooks cost $1.25 each and pens cost $0.75 each. The inequality $1.25x + 0.75y \leq 5$ represents the possible ways Lea could spend her $5. Is the ordered pair $(5, 2)$ a solution for the problem situation?

7

31. Leon has $10 to buy squash and carrots. Squash cost $1.50 each and carrots cost $2.75 per bunch. The inequality $1.50x + 2.75y \leq 10$ represents the possible ways Leon could spend his $10. Is the ordered pair $(-2, 4)$ a solution for the problem situation?

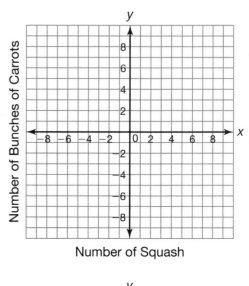

32. Olivia makes and sells muffins and scones at a school bake sale. She sells muffins for $0.50 each and scones for $0.80 each. She hopes to raise at least $20. The inequality $0.50x + 0.80y \geq 20$ represents the possible ways Olivia could reach her goal. Is the ordered pair $(20, 32)$ a solution for the problem situation?

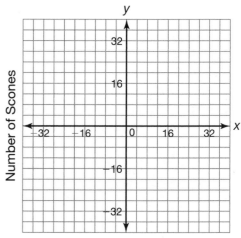

7

Name _____ Date _____

Working the System
Systems of Linear Inequalities

Vocabulary

Define each term in your own words.

1. constraints

2. solution of a system of linear inequalities

Problem Set

Write a system of linear inequalities that represents each problem situation. Remember to define your variables.

1. Jamal runs the bouncy house at a festival. The bouncy house can hold a maximum of 1200 pounds at one time. He estimates that adults weigh approximately 200 pounds and children under 16 weigh approximately 100 pounds. For 1 four-minute session of bounce time, Jamal charges adults $3 each and children $2 each. Jamal hopes to charge at least $24 for each session.

x = the number of adults

y = the number of children

$$\begin{cases} 3x + 2y \geq 24 \\ 200x + 100y \leq 1200 \end{cases}$$

2. Carlos works at a movie theater selling tickets. The theater has 300 seats and charges $7.50 for adults and $5.50 for children. The theater expects to make at least $2000 for each showing.

3. The maximum capacity for an average passenger elevator is 15 people and 3000 pounds. It is estimated that adults weigh approximately 200 pounds and children under 16 weigh approximately 100 pounds.

4. Pablo's pickup truck can carry a maximum of 1000 pounds. He is loading his truck with 20-pound bags of cement and 80-pound bags of cement. He hopes to load at least 10 bags of cement into his truck.

5. Eiko is drawing caricatures at a fair for 8 hours. She can complete a small drawing in 15 minutes and charges $10 for the drawing. She can complete a larger drawing in 45 minutes and charges $25 for the drawing. Eiko hopes to make at least $200 at the fair.

6. Sofia is making flower arrangements to sell in her shop. She can complete a small arrangement in 30 minutes that sells for $20. She can complete a larger arrangement in 1 hour that sells for $50. Sofia hopes to make at least $350 during her 8-hour workday.

7

Name _____ Date _____

Determine whether each given point is a solution to the system of linear inequalities.

7. $\begin{cases} 2x - y > 4 \\ -x + y \le 7 \end{cases}$

Point: $(-2, -10)$

$$2x - y > 4 \qquad\qquad\qquad -x + y \le 7$$
$$2(-2) - (-10) > 4 \qquad\qquad -(-2) + (-10) \le 4$$
$$-4 + 10 > 4 \qquad\qquad\qquad 2 - 10 \le 7$$
$$6 > 4 \;\checkmark \qquad\qquad\qquad -8 \le 7 \;\checkmark$$

Yes. The point $(-2, -10)$ is a solution to the system of inequalities.

8. $\begin{cases} x + 5y < -1 \\ 2y \ge -3x - 2 \end{cases}$

Point: $(0, -1)$

9. $\begin{cases} 4x + y < 21 \\ \frac{1}{2}x \le 36 - 5y \end{cases}$

Point: $(3, 7)$

7

10. $\begin{cases} 5x + 3y > 6 \\ -2x + 2y < 20 \end{cases}$

Point: $(-2, 6)$

11. $\begin{cases} 15x + 25y \geq 300 \\ 20x + 30y \leq 480 \end{cases}$

Point: $(14, 8)$

12. $\begin{cases} -2.1x + 7y \geq -49.5 \\ -y \leq -6.3x + 78 \end{cases}$

Point: $(10, -8)$

Graph each system of linear inequalities and identify two solutions.

13. $\begin{cases} y - 3x < 5 \\ y + x > 3 \end{cases}$

Answers will vary.

$(2, 3)$ and $(6, 0)$

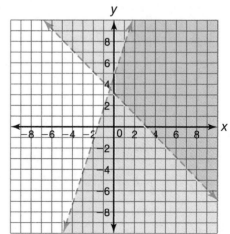

Name _____ Date _____

14. $\begin{cases} y > 2x + 3 \\ y < 2x - 5 \end{cases}$

15. $\begin{cases} y \le -\dfrac{2}{3}x + 3 \\ y \ge 3x - 4 \end{cases}$

16. $\begin{cases} y < -\dfrac{1}{2}x + 6 \\ y < 2x + 1 \end{cases}$

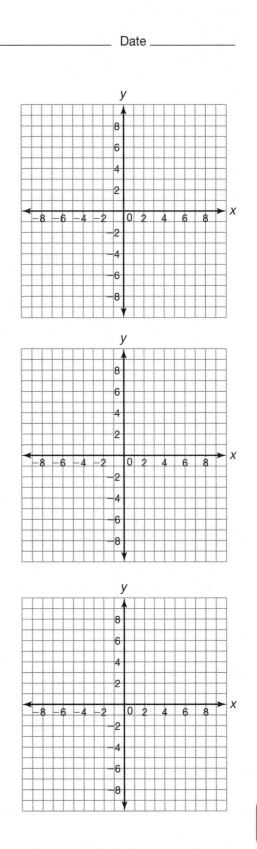

7

17. $\begin{cases} y \geq -\dfrac{1}{3}x + 4 \\ y \geq 2x + 5 \end{cases}$

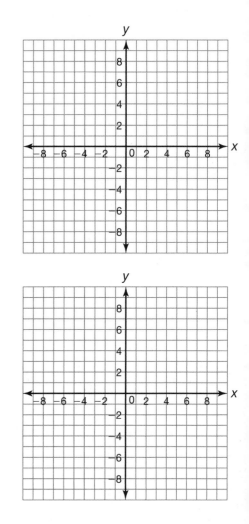

18. $\begin{cases} y > -4x + 8 \\ y < -4x - 2 \end{cases}$

7

Name _____ Date _____

Our Biggest Sale of the Season!
Systems with More Than Two Linear Inequalities

Problem Set

Write a system of linear inequalities that represents each problem situation. Remember to define your variables.

1. Ronna is shopping for a winter coat. The regular price of a winter coat is between $65 and $180. The store is running a special promotion where all coats are up to 35% off the regular price. Write a system of linear inequalities that represents the amount Ronna could spend.

   Let r represent the regular price.

   Let s represent the amount Ronna could spend.

   $$\begin{cases} r \geq 65 \\ r \leq 180 \\ s \leq 0.65r \end{cases}$$

2. Stephen is shopping for a snowboard. The regular price of a snowboard is between $120 and $425. The store is running a special promotion where all snowboards are between 25% and 75% off the regular price. Write a system of linear inequalities that represents the amount Stephen could spend.

3. Ling is shopping for a gold necklace. The regular price of a necklace is between $55 and $325. The store is running a special promotion where all necklaces are between 20% and 40% off the regular price. Write a system of linear inequalities that represents the amount Ling could spend.

7

4. Mario is shopping for a watch. The regular price of a watch is between $45 and $120. The store is running a special promotion where all watches are at least 25% off the regular price. Write a system of linear inequalities that represents the amount Mario could spend.

5. A company manufactures at most 20 mattresses each day. The company produces a twin size mattress and a queen size mattress. Its daily production goal is to produce at least 5 of each type of mattress. Write a system of linear inequalities that represents the number of each type of mattress that can be produced.

6. A company manufactures at most 200 tires each day. The company produces an all-weather tire and a snow tire. Its daily production goal is to produce at least 75 of each type of tire. Write a system of linear inequalities that represents the number of each type of tire that can be produced.

Name _____ Date _____

Graph the solution set for each system of linear inequalities. Label all points of intersection of the boundary lines. Then determine a point that satisfies all of the linear inequalities in the system.

7. $\begin{cases} y \leq 4 \\ 2x - y \leq 10 \\ y > -x - 4 \end{cases}$

8. $\begin{cases} y \geq -2 \\ y \leq 4 \\ x + 1 > y \\ x - 1 < y \end{cases}$

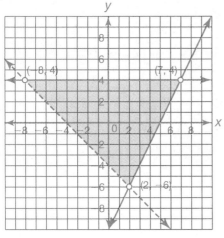

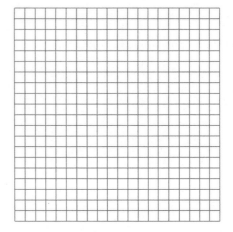

Answers will vary.

A solution to the system of inequalities would be (0, 0).

9. $\begin{cases} y \le 2 + x \\ y > x - 1 \\ 2x + y \ge -3 \\ -x + 1 > y \end{cases}$

10. $\begin{cases} y > -2 \\ y \le x + 1 \\ -x \le y + 3 \\ y \le -x + 1 \\ y \le 0 \end{cases}$

11. $\begin{cases} y > -2 \\ y \le 5 \\ x \ge -3 \\ x \le 1 \\ y > 3x + 1 \end{cases}$

12. $\begin{cases} y \le 3x + 2 \\ y < 4 - x \\ -2x + 3y \le 2 \\ 3y \ge 2x - 8 \end{cases}$

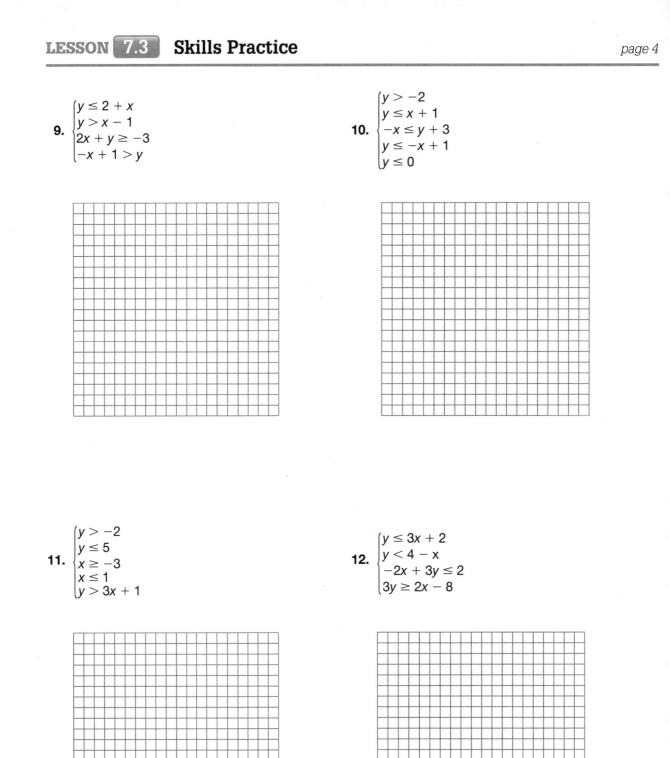

Name _____ Date _____

Analyze the solution set for the system of linear inequalities to answer each question.

Pedro is shopping for a surfboard. The regular price of a surfboard is between $200 and $400. The store is running a special promotion where all surfboards are between 20% and 60% off the regular price. The system of linear inequalities represents the amount Pedro can save.

Let *r* represent the regular price.

Let *s* represent the amount Pedro can save.

$$\begin{cases} r \geq 200 \\ r \leq 400 \\ s \leq 0.60r \\ s \geq 0.20r \end{cases}$$

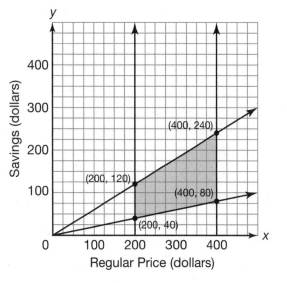

13. What is the most that Pedro can save?

The most Pedro can save is $240 represented by the point (400, 240).

14. What is the least that Pedro can save?

15. What is the most that Pedro will pay for the most expensive surfboard?

7

16. What is the most that Pedro will pay for the least expensive surfboard?

17. What is the least that Pedro will pay for the most expensive surfboard?

18. What is the least that Pedro will pay for the least expensive surfboard?

7

Name _____ Date _____

Take It to the Max . . . or Min
Linear Programming

Vocabulary

Define the term in your own words.

1. linear programming

Problem Set

Write a system of linear inequalities to represent each problem situation. Remember to define your variables.

1. A company is manufacturing two different models of lamps, a table lamp and a floor lamp. A table lamp takes 1 hour to make and a floor lamp takes 2 hours to make. The company has 9 employees working 8-hour days. The total manufacturing capacity is 40 lamps per day.

Let t represent the number of table lamps.

Let f represent the number of floor lamps.

9 employees $\times$ 8 hours per day = 72 work hours per day

$$\begin{cases} t \geq 0 \\ f \geq 0 \\ t + f \leq 40 \\ t + 2f \leq 72 \end{cases}$$

2. A company is manufacturing calculators. A financial calculator costs $65 to make and a graphing calculator costs $105 to make. The budget available for materials is $2500 per day. The manufacturing capacity is 20 calculators per day.

3. A company is manufacturing computers. A tablet computer costs $300 to make and a laptop computer costs $600 to make. The budget available for materials is $20,000 per day. The manufacturing capacity is 50 computers per day.

4. A furniture company is manufacturing sofas and loveseats. A loveseat takes 5 hours and $650 to make. A sofa takes 8 hours and $950 to make. The company has 30 employees working 8-hour days. The daily operating budget is $25,000 per day for materials to make at most 40 pieces of furniture.

5. An electronics company is manufacturing headphones. In-ear headphones take 2 hours and $65 to make. Around-ear headphones take 3 hours and $85 to make. The company has 14 employees working 12-hour days. The daily operating budget is $5000 per day for materials to make at most 65 pairs of headphones.

6. A company is manufacturing golf clubs. A putter takes 2 hours and $80 to make. A driver takes 2 hours and $120 to make. The company has 6 employees working 12 hour days. The daily operating budget is $3000 per day for materials. The company wants to make at least 10 of each kind of club per day.

Name _____ Date _____

Graph the solution set for each system of linear inequalities. Label all points of intersection of the boundary lines.

7. $\begin{cases} y \geq 0 \\ x \geq 0 \\ 3x + y \leq 18 \\ x + 3y \leq 30 \end{cases}$

8. $\begin{cases} y \geq 0 \\ x \geq 0 \\ x + y \leq 20 \\ 4x + 9y \leq 135 \end{cases}$

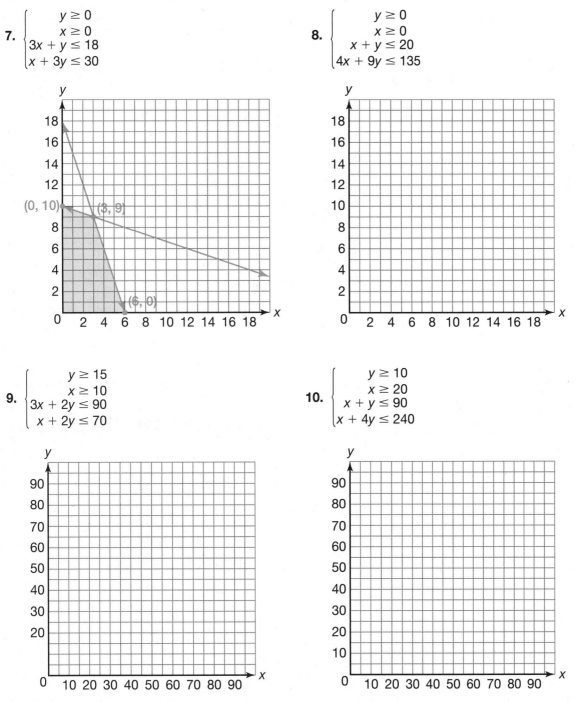

9. $\begin{cases} y \geq 15 \\ x \geq 10 \\ 3x + 2y \leq 90 \\ x + 2y \leq 70 \end{cases}$

10. $\begin{cases} y \geq 10 \\ x \geq 20 \\ x + y \leq 90 \\ x + 4y \leq 240 \end{cases}$

11. $\begin{cases} y \geq 0 \\ x \geq 0 \\ x + y \leq 26 \\ x + 4y \leq 80 \end{cases}$

12. $\begin{cases} y \geq 14 \\ x \geq 10 \\ x + 5y \leq 130 \\ 2x + 5y \leq 150 \end{cases}$

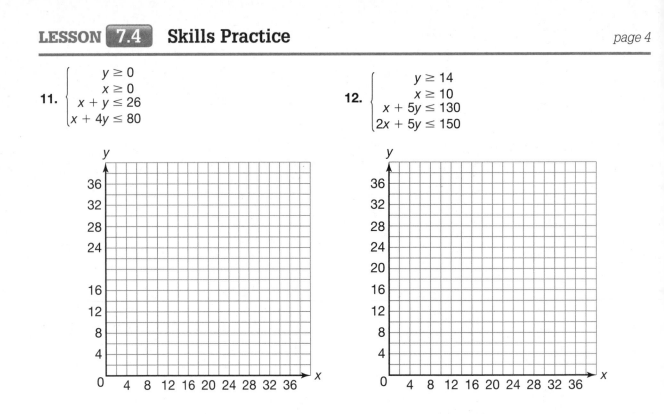

Analyze the solution set for the system of linear inequalities to answer each question.

An electronics company is manufacturing electronic book readers. A basic model takes 4 hours and $40 to make. A touch screen model takes 6 hours and $120 to make. The company has 10 employees working 12-hour days. The daily operating budget is $1920 per day for materials. The company would like at least 3 basic models and 8 touch screen models produced per day. The system of linear inequalities represents the problem situation. The graph shows the solution set for the system of linear inequalities.

Let x represent the number of basic models.

Let y represent the number of touch screen models.

$\begin{cases} y \geq 8 \\ x \geq 3 \\ 4x + 6y \leq 120 \\ 40x + 120y \leq 1920 \end{cases}$

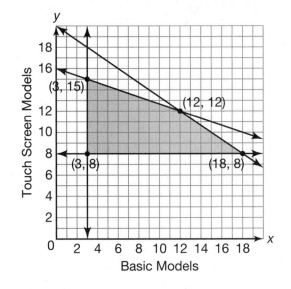

Name _____ Date _____

13. How many of each model should the company produce to minimize their daily cost?

$C(x, y) = 40x + 120y$

$C(3, 8) = 40(3) + 120(8) = 1080$

$C(18, 8) = 40(18) + 120(8) = 1680$

$C(3, 15) = 40(3) + 120(15) = 1920$

$C(12, 12) = 40(12) + 120(12) = 1920$

The minimum daily cost is $1080. To minimize their daily cost, the company should produce 3 basic models and 8 touch screen models.

14. How many of each model should the company produce to maximize the number of work hours utilized per day?

15. The company earns $30 for each basic model sold and $50 for each touch screen model sold. How many of each model should the company produce to maximize their profit?

16. How many of each model would have to be produced to maximize the company's daily cost?

17. How many of each model would have to be produced to minimize the number of work hours utilized per day?

18. During a special promotion, the company earns $20 for each basic model sold and $30 for each touch screen model sold. How many of each model should the company produce to maximize their profit?

Name _____ Date _____

Start Your Day the Right Way
Graphically Representing Data

Vocabulary

Choose the term that best completes each statement.

dot plot	five number summary	data distribution
symmetric	discrete data	skewed left
histogram	skewed right	frequency
box-and-whisker plot	bin	continuous

1. A(n) _____ is a graphical way to display quantitative data using vertical bars.

2. A data distribution is _____ if the peak of the data is to the left side of the graph with only a few data points to the right side of the graph.

3. _____ are data that have only a finite number of values or data that can be "counted."

4. A(n) _____ displays the data distribution based on a five number summary.

5. The overall shape of a graph which shows the way in which data are spread out or clustered together is called the _____.

6. _____ are data which can take any numerical value within a range.

7. A data distribution is _____ if the peak of the data is to the right side of the graph with only a few data points to the left side of the graph.

8. A(n) _____ is a graph that shows how discrete data are distributed using a number line.

9. For a set of data, the _____ consists of the minimum value, the first quartile, the median, the third quartile, and the maximum value.

10. A data distribution is _____ if the peak of the data is in the middle of the graph. The left and right sides of the graph are nearly mirror images of each other.

11. The number of data values included in a given bin of a data set is called _____.

12. The bar width in a histogram that represents an interval of data is often referred to as a _____.

Problem Set

Construct the graphical display for each given data set. Describe the distribution of the data.

1. Construct a dot plot to display the scores on a recent math quiz. The data are 12, 14, 8, 13, 12, 14, 5, 13, 14, 3, 15, 15, 10, 13, 12, 0, 14, 11, 14, 13, and 10.

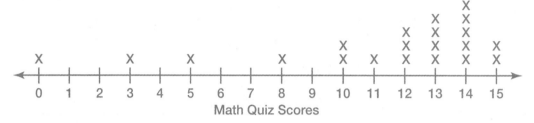

The data are skewed left.

2. Construct a dot plot to display the number of canned goods donated by each student during a charity event. The data are 15, 18, 18, 22, 13, 15, 19, 17, 18, 17, 16, 10, 17, 20, 19, 25, 17, 18, 19, and 16.

3. Construct a dot plot to display the number of items purchased by a number of randomly chosen customers at a toy store. The data are 2, 4, 3, 7, 12, 3, 1, 5, 6, 3, 4, 2, 4, 3, 7, 14, 10, 3, 5, and 9.

Name _____ Date _____

4. Construct a box-and-whisker plot to display the number of pets owned by a number of randomly chosen students. The data are 2, 0, 5, 1, 2, 1, 0, 8, 4, 3, 9, 1, 2, 3, and 1.

5. Construct a box-and-whisker plot to display the scores on a recent science test. The data are 90, 95, 100, 70, 85, 65, 90, 80, 65, 70, 75, 80, 85, 80, 60, 80, 75, and 85.

6. Construct a box-and-whisker plot to display the number of miles from school that a number of randomly chosen students live. The data are 5, 10, 15, 12, 1, 14, 9, 15, 3, 10, 12, 15, 8, 14, 13, and 2.

7. Construct a histogram to display the circumferences of the pumpkins in the Jeffiers' family pumpkin crop. The data are 22.1, 35.6, 15.8, 36.9, 40.0, 28.5, 38.4, 20.4, 25.8, 34.1, 39.9, 42.2, 24.3, 22.7, 19.8, 27.9, 22.2, 34.3, 40.4, 20.6, 38.2, and 18.1. Use $10 \leq x < 20$ as the first interval.

8. Construct a histogram to display the scores on a recent English quiz. The data are 18, 45, 20, 32, 9, 35, 49, 28, 25, 19, 5, 30, 22, 24, and 14. Use $0 \leq x < 10$ as the first interval.

Name _____ Date _____

Analyze the given dot plot which displays the number of home runs by each of the girls on the softball team this season. Use the dot plot to answer each question.

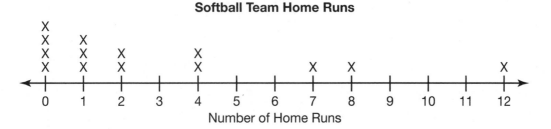

Softball Team Home Runs

Number of Home Runs

9. Describe the distribution of the data in the dot plot and explain what it means in terms of the problem situation.

The data are skewed right, because a majority of the data values are on the left of the plot and only a few of the data values are on the right of the plot. This means that a majority of the players on the softball team hit a small number of home runs, while only a few players on the team hit a large number of home runs.

10. How many players are on the softball team?

11. How many players hit more than 2 home runs?

12. How many players hit at least 1 home run?

13. How many players hit more than 1 and fewer than 9 home runs?

14. How many players scored more than 12 home runs?

Analyze the given box-and-whisker plot which displays the heights of 40 randomly chosen adults. Use the box-and-whisker plot to answer each question.

Heights of 40 Randomly Chosen Adults

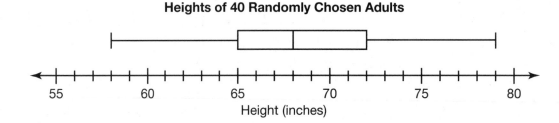

Height (inches)

15. What is the height range of the middle 50 percent of the surveyed adults?

The middle 50 percent of the surveyed adults are at least 65 inches and at most 72 inches tall.

16. How many of the surveyed adults are exactly 68 inches tall?

17. What percent of the surveyed adults are 68 inches tall or shorter?

18. What is the height of the tallest adult surveyed?

19. How many of the surveyed adults are at least 58 inches tall?

20. Describe the distribution of the data in the box-and-whisker plot and explain what it means in terms of the problem situation.

Name _____ Date _____

Analyze the given histogram which displays the ACT composite score of several randomly chosen students. Use the histogram to answer each question.

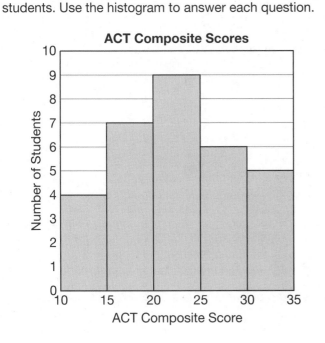

ACT Composite Scores

Number of Students (y-axis: 0–10)

ACT Composite Score (x-axis: 10, 15, 20, 25, 30, 35)

21. How many students are represented by the histogram?

There are a total of 31 students represented by the histogram.

22. Describe the distribution of the data in the histogram and explain what it means in terms of the problem situation.

23. How many of the students had an ACT composite score of exactly 25?

24. How many of the students had an ACT composite score of at least 20?

25. How many of the students had an ACT composite score less than 30?

26. How many more students had an ACT composite score between 15 and 20 than had a composite score between 30 and 35?

Name _____ Date _____

Which Measure Is Better?
Determining the Best Measure of Center for a Data Set

Vocabulary

Define each term in your own words.

1. statistics

2. measure of central tendency

Problem Set

Create a dot plot of each given data set. Calculate the mean and median. Determine which measure of center best describes each data set.

1. The data are 1, 3, 2, 0, 7, 2, 1, 10, 1, 12, 1, 2, 0, 3, and 4.

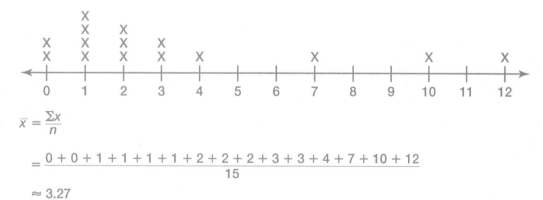

$$\bar{x} = \frac{\Sigma x}{n}$$

$$= \frac{0 + 0 + 1 + 1 + 1 + 1 + 2 + 2 + 2 + 3 + 3 + 4 + 7 + 10 + 12}{15}$$

$$\approx 3.27$$

The mean is approximately 3.27 and the median is 2. The median is the best measure of center because the data are skewed right.

2. The data are 7, 2, 9, 9, 10, 12, 17, 10, 6, 11, 9, 10, 8, 11, and 8.

3. The data are 4, 0, 13, 15, 14, 10, 13, 8, 13, 12, 11, 13, 14, 1, 15, 13, 14, 12, 10, and 7.

4. The data are 50, 50, 40, 70, 60, 50, 20, 50, 80, 40, 60, 40, and 50.

Name _____ Date _____

5. The data are 40, 45, 48, 49, 50, 49, 47, 50, 49, 42, 49, 50, 48, 50, and 47.

6. The data are 13, 12, 12, 11, 17, 10, 11, 12, 14, 20, 15, 12, 18, 13, 12, 17, 14, and 11.

Determine which measure of center best describes the data in each given data display. Then determine the mean and median, if possible. If it is not possible, explain why not.

7.

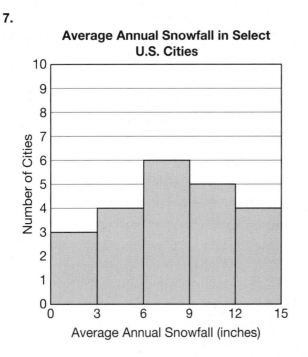

Average Annual Snowfall in Select U.S. Cities

Number of Cities

Average Annual Snowfall (inches)

The mean is the best measure of center to describe the data because the data are symmetric. The mean and median cannot be determined because the data values are not given.

8.

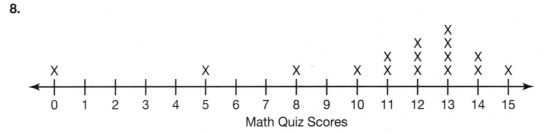

Math Quiz Scores

Name _____ Date _____

9.

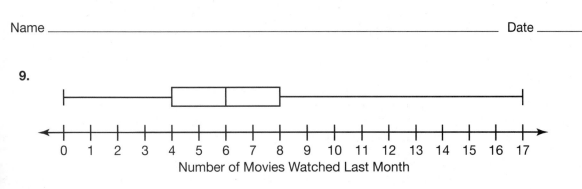

Number of Movies Watched Last Month

10.

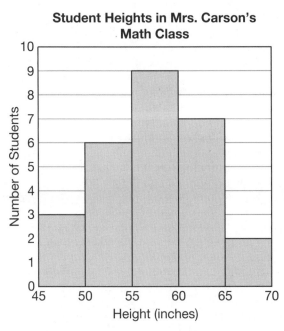

Student Heights in Mrs. Carson's Math Class

11.

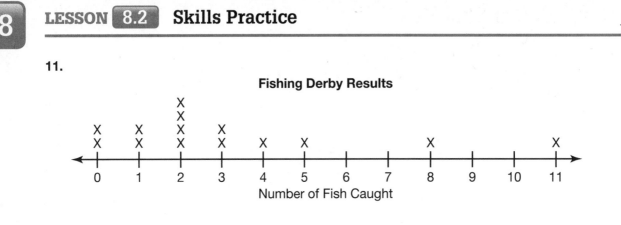

12.

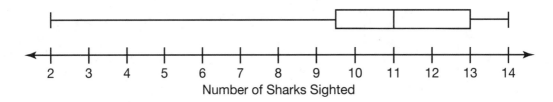

Name _____ Date _____

You Are Too Far Away!
Calculating IQR and Identifying Outliers

Vocabulary

Match each definition to its corresponding term.

1. interquartile range (IQR)

    a. A value calculated using the formula Q1 − (IQR · 1.5).

2. outlier

    b. A value calculated by subtracting Q1 from Q3.

3. lower fence

    c. A value calculated using the formula Q3 + (IQR · 1.5).

4. upper fence

    d. A data value that is significantly greater than or less than the other values in a data set.

Problem Set

Calculate the IQR of each given data set. Determine whether there are any outliers in each set and list them.

1. The data are 4, 4, 5, 5, 8, 9, 10, 10, 12, 12, 16, 20, and 30.

   Q1 = 5, Q3 = 14

   IQR = Q3 − Q1

        = 14 − 5

        = 9

   Lower Fence: Upper Fence:

   Q1 − (IQR · 1.5) = 5 − (9 · 1.5)   Q3 + (IQR · 1.5) = 14 + (9 · 1.5)

                   = 5 − 13.5   = 14 + 13.5

                   = − 8.5   = 27.5

   The value 30 is an outlier because it is greater than the upper fence.

2. The data are 0, 3, 10, 16, 16, 18, 20, 21, 22, 24, 25, 25, 27, 30, 35, and 41.

Name _____ Date _____

3. The data are 9, 15, 26, 30, 32, 32, 35, 36, 38, 40, 40, 45, and 59.

4. The data are 18, 25, 30, 32, 33, 33, 35, 38, 39, 40, 42, 43, 44, 48, and 55.

5. The data are 22, 19, 20, 20, 21, 25, 10, 8, 18, 28, 32, 24, and 25.

6. The data are 60, 55, 70, 80, 20, 60, 105, 65, 75, 100, 55, 15, 115, 65, 70, 45, and 60.

Name _____ Date _____

Calculate the IQR of the data set represented in each box-and-whisker plot and determine whether there are any outliers in each data set.

7.

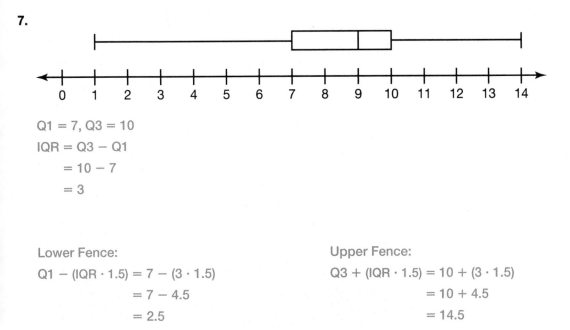

$Q1 = 7$, $Q3 = 10$

$IQR = Q3 - Q1$

$\quad = 10 - 7$

$\quad = 3$

Lower Fence:

$Q1 - (IQR \cdot 1.5) = 7 - (3 \cdot 1.5)$

$\quad = 7 - 4.5$

$\quad = 2.5$

Upper Fence:

$Q3 + (IQR \cdot 1.5) = 10 + (3 \cdot 1.5)$

$\quad = 10 + 4.5$

$\quad = 14.5$

There is at least 1 outlier less than the lower fence because the minimum value of the data set is 1.

8.

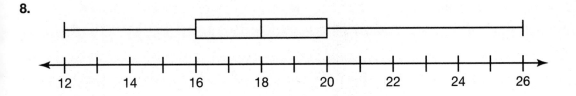

9.

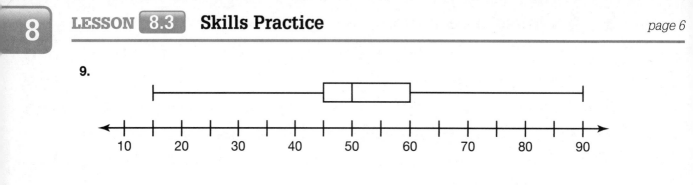

10.

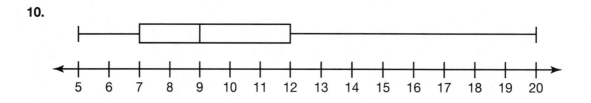

Name _____ Date _____

11.

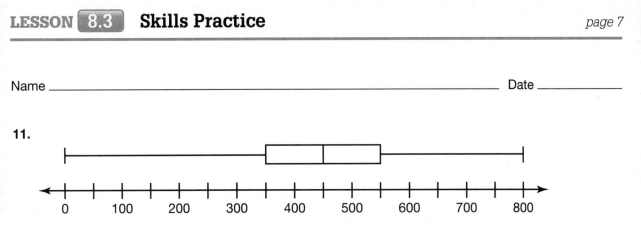

12.

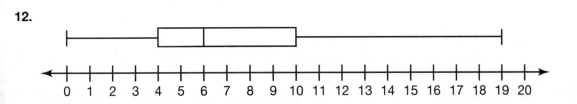

Name _____ Date _____

Whose Scores Are Better?
Calculating and Interpreting Standard Deviation

Vocabulary

Define each term in your own words.

1. standard deviation

2. normal distribution

Problem Set

Calculate the mean and the standard deviation of each data set without the use of a calculator.

1. The data are 0, 3, 6, 7, and 9.

$$\bar{x} = \frac{0 + 3 + 6 + 7 + 9}{5}$$

$$= \frac{25}{5}$$

$$= 5$$

$$\sigma = \sqrt{\frac{25 + 4 + 1 + 4 + 16}{5}}$$

$$= \sqrt{\frac{50}{5}}$$

$$= \sqrt{10}$$

$$\approx 3.16$$

$(x_1 - \bar{x})^2 = (0 - 5)^2 = 25$
$(x_2 - \bar{x})^2 = (3 - 5)^2 = 4$
$(x_3 - \bar{x})^2 = (6 - 5)^2 = 1$
$(x_4 - \bar{x})^2 = (7 - 5)^2 = 4$
$(x_5 - \bar{x})^2 = (9 - 5)^2 = 16$

The mean is 5. The standard deviation is approximately 3.16.

2. The data are 6, 8, 9, 10, 10, and 11.

3. The data are 1, 5, 10, 15, 16, 20, and 24.

Name _____ Date _____

4. The data are 13, 14, 15, 15, 16, 16, 17, and 18.

5. The data are represented by a dot plot.

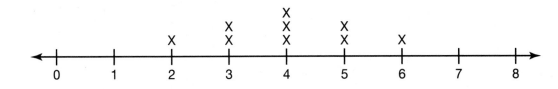

6. The data are represented by a dot plot.

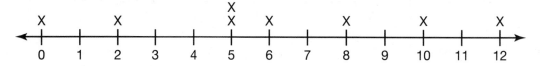

Calculate the mean and the standard deviation of each given data set using a graphing calculator.

7. The data are 1, 3, 4, 6, 6, 8, 9, 10, and 12.

The mean is approximately 6.56. The standard deviation is approximately 3.34.

8. The data are 18, 20, 24, 25, 26, 26, 28, 30, 32, and 35.

9. The data are 102, 103, 103, 104, 104, 104, 105, 105, 106, 106, and 107.

10. The data are 3.5, 4, 5.5, 6, 6, 7, 7.5, 8, 9.5, and 10.5.

Name _____ Date _____

11. The data are represented by a dot plot.

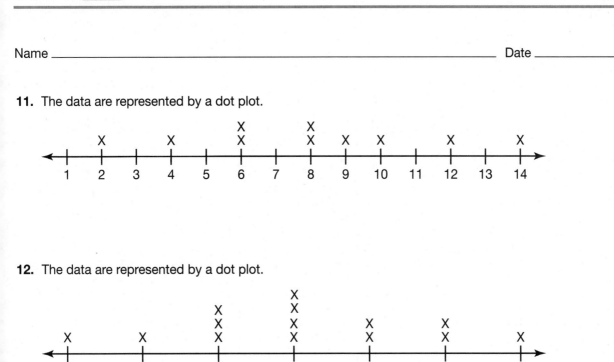

12. The data are represented by a dot plot.

Name _____ Date _____

Putting the Pieces Together
Analyzing and Interpreting Data

Vocabulary

For each problem situation, identify whether a stem-and-leaf plot or a side-by-side stem-and-leaf plot would be appropriate. Explain your choice for each.

1. For a history project, Roberto is comparing the ages of the U.S. Presidents at inauguration and at death.

2. During the Summer Olympic Games, Karen keeps track of the number of gold medals won by the various countries participating.

Problem Set

Construct a box-and-whisker plot of each given data set and include any outliers. Calculate the most appropriate measure of center and spread for each data set based on the data distribution.

1. The data are 0, 2, 3, 4, 4, 5, 5, 5, 6, 6, 8, and 9.

The most appropriate measure of center is the mean, and the most appropriate measure of spread is the standard deviation because the data are symmetric.
The mean is 4.75 and the standard deviation is approximately 2.35.

2. The data are 1, 6, 9, 12, 14, 15, 17, 17, 17, 18, 18, 18, 19, and 20.

3. The data are 50, 53, 57, 58, 58, 59, 59, 60, 60, 60, 61, 61, 62, 63, and 67.

4. The data are 20, 20, 20, 21, 21, 21, 22, 22, 23, 24, 25, 28, and 30.

5. The data are 80, 85, 90, 30, 70, 90, 95, 10, 100, 70, 80, 55, 50, 95, 65, and 90.

6. The data are 7, 11, 10, 13, 0, 3, 10, 9, 17, 11, 10, 20, 9, 8, and 12.

Name _____ Date _____

Two data sets are given in a side-by-side stem-and-leaf plot. Calculate the most appropriate measure of center and spread for each set based on the data distribution.

7.

Data Set 1		Data Set 2
8 7 5 3	0	3 4 6 9
8 4	1	1 4 5
2	2	5
0	3	2

Key: 2|5 = 25

For each data set, the most appropriate measure of center is the median and the most appropriate measure of spread is the IQR, because the data are skewed right.
For Data Set 1, the median is 11 and the IQR is 14.
For Data Set 2, the median is 11 and the IQR is 15.

8.

Data Set 1		Data Set 2
9 8 7	1	8 9
8 7 5 5 3	2	0 2 4 4 6 9
2 1 0	3	1 3

Key: 2|0 = 20

9.

Data Set 1		Data Set 2
9 9	5	9
7 5 1	6	5 8
8 6 2	7	0 4
2 0	8	1 1 5 7

Key: 6|5 = 65

10.

Data Set 1		Data Set 2
	0	9
9	1	4
8 3	2	2 5
9 5 1	3	3 6
5 5 4 3 2 0	4	0 0 1 1 1 2

Key: 1|4 = 14

Name _____ Date _____

11.

	Data Set 1		Data Set 2
9 9 9 8 8 8	3	7 9
8 6 5 2	4	0 3 4 5 8
5 1	5	2 5 5 6 6
0	6	1 2

Key: 4|0 = 40

12.

	Data Set 1		Data Set 2
7 5 3 3 2 1	10	1 1 3 5 8 8 9
8 5 2	11	1 3 5
9 4	12	5
2	13	3
0	14	

Key: 12|5 = 125

Name _____ Date _____

9

Like a Glove
Least Squares Regression

Vocabulary

Write a definition for each term.

1. least squares regression line

2. interpolation

3. extrapolation

Problem Set

Determine the least squares regression line for each set of points. Round your answer to the nearest hundredth.

1. (3, 4), (7, 6) and (−2, −4)

$n = 3$

$\Sigma x = 3 + 7 + (-2)$

$\quad = 8$

$\Sigma y = 4 + 6 + (-4)$

$\quad = 6$

$\Sigma x^2 = 3^2 + 7^2 + (-2)^2$

$\quad = 9 + 49 + 4$

$\quad = 62$

$\Sigma xy = (3 \cdot 4) + (7 \cdot 6) + (-2 \cdot -4)$

$\quad = 12 + 42 + 8$

$\quad = 62$

$(\Sigma x)^2 = 8^2$

$\quad = 64$

$a = \dfrac{n\Sigma xy - (\Sigma x)(\Sigma y)}{n\Sigma x^2 - (\Sigma x)^2}$

$\quad = \dfrac{(3)(62) - (8)(6)}{(3)(62) - (64)}$

$\quad = \dfrac{186 - 48}{186 - 64} = \dfrac{138}{122}$

$a \approx 1.13$

$b = \dfrac{(\Sigma y)(\Sigma x^2) - (\Sigma x)(\Sigma xy)}{n\Sigma x^2 - (\Sigma x)^2}$

$\quad = \dfrac{(6)(62) - (8)(62)}{(3)(62) - (64)}$

$\quad = \dfrac{372 - 496}{186 - 64} = \dfrac{-124}{122}$

$b \approx -1.02$

The least squares regression line for the points is $y = 1.13x - 1.02$.

2. (−7, 1), (3, 8) and (9, 7)

Name _____ Date _____

3. (−3, 6), (−2, −1) and (6, −4)

4. (−8, 7), (−5, 3), (3, 6) and (9, 0)

5. $(-7, -1), (-5, -9), (3, 3)$ and $(6, 9)$

6. $(-8, 6), (-8, -2), (-6, -9)$ and $(-5, -4)$

Name _____ Date _____

While in high school, Clayton started his own T-shirt printing business. The table shows the number of T-shirts Clayton has sold each year since starting his business in 2006.

Year	2006	2007	2008	2009	2010	2011	2012
Number of T-shirts	50	75	175	125	250	350	375

The linear regression equation representing the data shown in the table is $y = 57.14x + 28.57$, where x represents the number of years since 2006 and y represents the number of T-shirts sold. Use the regression equation to predict the number of T-shirts Clayton sold during each given year. Then compare the prediction to the actual number of T-shirts or determine if the prediction is reasonable based on the problem situation.

7. 2008

For 2008, $x = 2$.

$y = 57.14x + 28.57$

$y = 57.14(2) + 28.57$

$y = 114.28 + 28.57$

$y = 142.85$

The total number of T-shirts sold in 2008 should be about 143. The actual number of T-shirts sold was 175, so the predicted value is fairly close to the actual value.

8. 2010

9

9. 2012

10. 2014

11. 2020

12. 2000

Name _____ Date _____

Gotta Keep It Correlatin'
Correlation

Problem Set

Determine whether the points in each scatter plot have a positive correlation, a negative correlation, or no correlation. Then determine which *r*-value is most accurate.

1.

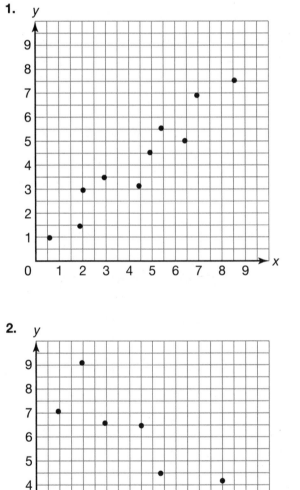

A $r = 0.8$

B $r = -0.8$

C $r = 0.08$

D $r = -0.08$

These data have a positive correlation. Because of this the *r*-value must be positive. Also, the data are fairly close to forming a straight line, so $r = 0.8$ (A) would be the most accurate.

2.

A $r = 0.9$

B $r = -0.6$

C $r = 0.02$

D $r = -0.006$

3.

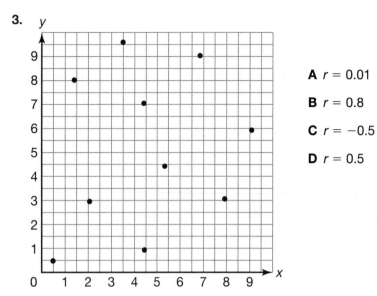

A $r = 0.01$

B $r = 0.8$

C $r = -0.5$

D $r = 0.5$

4.

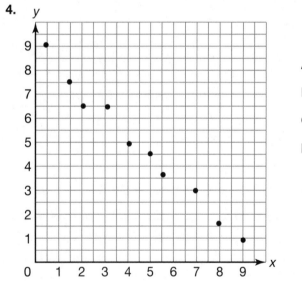

A $r = -0.009$

B $r = 0.8$

C $r = -0.9$

D $r = 0.2$

Name _____ Date _____

5.

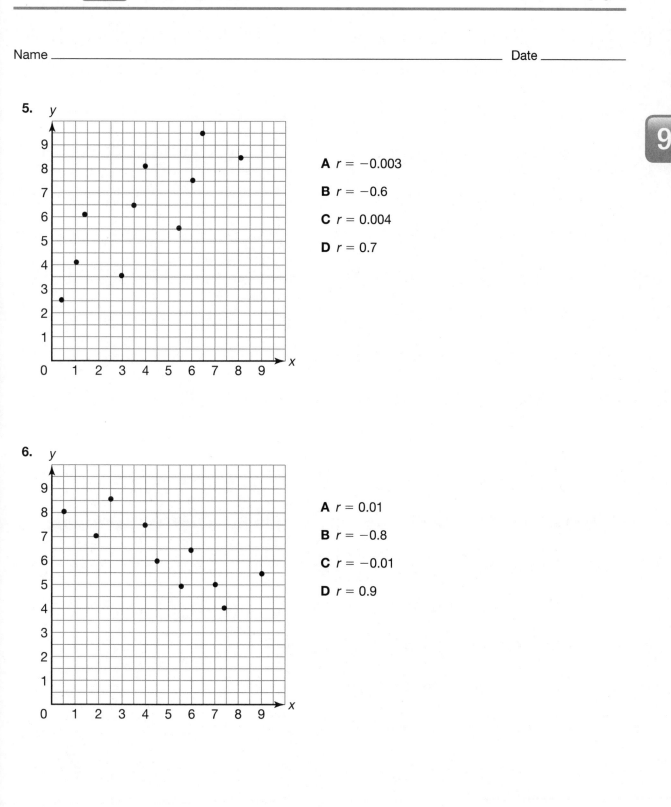

A $r = -0.003$

B $r = -0.6$

C $r = 0.004$

D $r = 0.7$

6.

A $r = 0.01$

B $r = -0.8$

C $r = -0.01$

D $r = 0.9$

Determine the correlation coefficient of each data set. Round your answer to the nearest ten thousandth.

7. (3, 2), (5, 7) and (10, 9)

$$\bar{x} = \frac{3 + 5 + 10}{3}$$

$$= 6$$

$$\bar{y} = \frac{2 + 7 + 9}{3}$$

$$= 6$$

$$\sum_{i=1}^{n}(x_i - \bar{x})^2$$

$$(-3)^2 = 9$$
$$(-1)^2 = 1 \Big\} \, 9 + 1 + 16 = 26$$
$$(4)^2 = 16$$

$(x_i - \bar{x})$

$3 - 6 = -3$

$5 - 6 = -1$

$10 - 6 = 4$

$(y_i - \bar{y})$

$2 - 6 = -4$

$7 - 6 = 1$

$9 - 6 = 3$

$$\sum_{i=1}^{n}(y_i - \bar{y})^2$$

$$(-4)^2 = 16$$
$$(1)^2 = 1 \Big\} \, 16 + 1 + 9 = 26$$
$$(3)^2 = 9$$

$$\sum_{i=1}^{n}(x_i - \bar{x})(y_i - \bar{y})$$

$$-3 \cdot -4 = 12$$
$$-1 \cdot 1 = -1 \Big\} \, 12 + (-1) + (12) = 23$$
$$4 \cdot 3 = 12$$

$$\sqrt{\sum_{i=1}^{n}(x_i - \bar{x})^2} \sqrt{\sum_{i=1}^{n}(y_i - \bar{y})^2} = \sqrt{26} \cdot \sqrt{26}$$

$$= 26$$

$$r = \frac{\sum_{i=1}^{n}(x_i - \bar{x})(y_i - \bar{y})}{\sqrt{\sum_{i=1}^{n}(x_i - \bar{x})^2} \sqrt{\sum_{i=1}^{n}(y_i - \bar{y})^2}}$$

$$= \frac{23}{26}$$

$$\approx 0.8846$$

The correlation coefficient of this data set is 0.8846.

Name _____ Date _____

8. (2, 10), (3, 3) and (10, 5)

9

9. (2, 2), (5, 3) and (7, 6)

Name _____ Date _____

10. (5, 6), (7, 4) and (8, 2)

11. (2, 8), (3, 5) and (6, 6)

9

Name _____ Date _____

12. (4, 8), (6, 11) and (8, 15)

Determine the linear regression equation and correlation coefficient for each data set. State if the linear regression equation is appropriate for the data set. Round your answer to the nearest ten thousandth.

13.

Year	2007	2008	2009	2010	2011	2012
Profit (dollars)	50,000	75,000	150,000	125,000	195,000	225,000

x = years since 2007

$y = 34{,}571.4286x + 50{,}238.0952$

$r = 0.9571$

Because the r-value is close to 1, the linear regression equation is appropriate for the data set.

14.

Year	2007	2008	2009	2010	2011	2012
Profit (dollars)	100,000	85,000	91,000	82,000	79,500	74,000

15.

Time (seconds)	0	1	2	3	4	5
Height (feet)	5	21	34	31	18	3

Name _____ Date _____

16.

Time (seconds)	0	1	2	3	4	5
Height (feet)	63	56	42	36	28	12

17.

Year	2007	2008	2009	2010	2011	2012
Units Sold	1480	14,105	8925	18,750	5250	2650

18.

Year	2007	2008	2009	2010	2011	2012
Units Sold	5245	7840	7075	9130	10,620	12,635

9

Name _____ Date _____

The Residual Effect
Creating Residual Plots

9

Vocabulary

Write a definition for each term.

1. residual

2. residual plot

Problem Set

Complete each table. Round your answers to the nearest tenth. Construct a residual plot.

1. Linear regression equation: $y = 0.5x$

x	y	Predicted Value	Residual Value
5	3	2.5	0.5
10	4	5	−1
15	9	7.5	1.5
20	7	10	−3
25	13	12.5	0.5
30	15	15	0

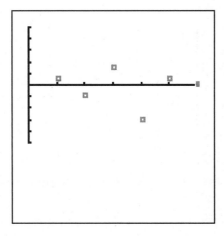

2. Linear regression equation: $y = -0.4x + 16.3$

x	y	Predicted Value	Residual Value
2	5		
4	15		
6	26		
8	23		
10	11		
12	3		

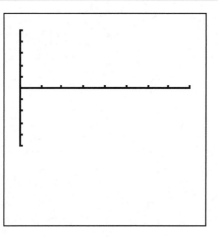

3. Linear regression equation: $y = 3x - 2.1$

x	y	Predicted Value	Residual Value
1	1.5		
3	6.5		
5	12.5		
7	19.5		
9	24.5		
11	31.5		

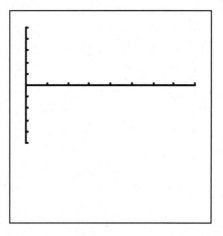

Name _____ Date _____

4. Linear regression equation: $y = -9.6x + 641.7$

x	y	Predicted Value	Residual Value
10	600		
20	450		
30	300		
40	200		
50	150		
60	125		

5. Linear regression equation: $y = 4.9x + 16.4$

x	y	Predicted Value	Residual Value
100	505		
90	460		
80	415		
70	360		
60	305		
50	265		

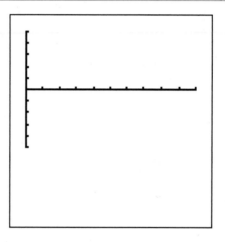

6. Linear regression equation: $y = -x + 19.7$

x	y	Predicted Value	Residual Value
2	17		
4	16		
6	15		
8	12		
10	9		
12	8		

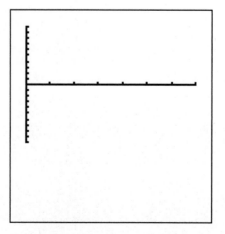

Name _____ Date _____

Consider the scatter plot, its line of best fit, and the corresponding residual plot of each data set. State if a linear model is appropriate for the data.

7. Linear regression equation: $y = 2.96x + 5.30$, $r = 0.9964$

x	2	4	6	8	10	12
y	12	16	22.5	29.5	36	40

Scatter Plot & Line of Best Fit   Residual Plot

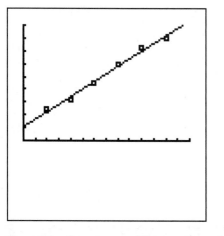
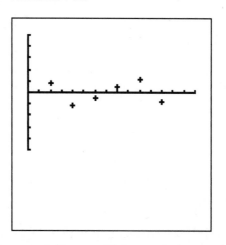

Based on the shape of the scatter plot and the correlation coefficient, a linear model appears to be appropriate for the data. Based on the residual plot, a linear model appears to be appropriate for the data.

8. Linear regression equation: $y = 0.24x + 9.04$, $r = 0.1570$

x	1	3	5	7	9	11
y	4	8	17	18	10	6

Scatter Plot & Line of Best Fit

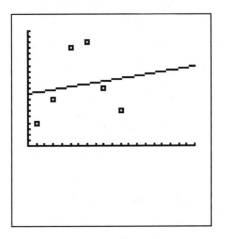

Residual Plot

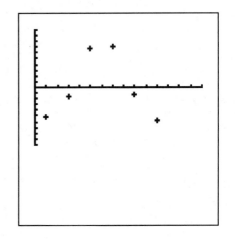

Name _____ Date _____

9. Linear regression equation: $y = 14.08x - 163.13$, $r = 0.9746$

x	10	20	30	40	50	60
y	49	103	207	346	511	762

Scatter Plot & Line of Best Fit

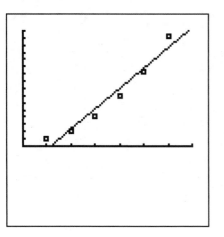

Residual Plot

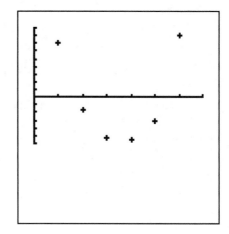

10. Linear regression equation: $y = -1.91x + 59$, $r = -0.9968$

x	5	10	15	20	25	30
y	48	41	32	19	12	1

Scatter Plot & Line of Best Fit

Residual Plot

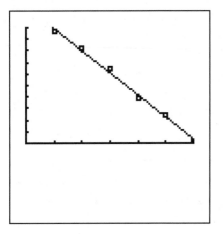

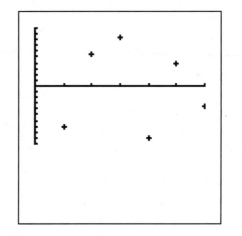

Name _____ Date _____

11. Linear regression equation: $y = 4.01x + 1.43$, $r = 0.9997$

x	1	2	3	4	5	6
y	5.5	9.25	13.5	17.75	21.25	25.5

Scatter Plot & Line of Best Fit

Residual Plot

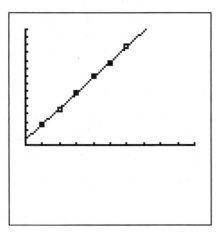

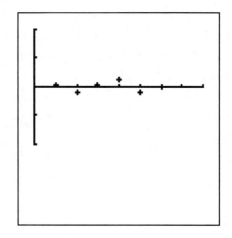

12. Linear regression equation: $y = 3.93x - 11.33$, $r = 0.8241$

x	2	4	6	8	10	12
y	9	2	1	12	25	48

Scatter Plot & Line of Best Fit

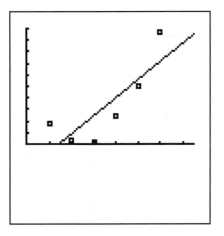

Residual Plot

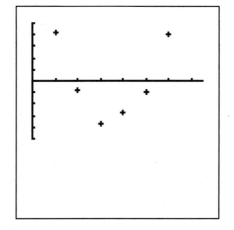

Name _____ Date _____

To Fit or Not To Fit? That Is The Question!
Using Residual Plots

Problem Set

For each data set, determine the linear regression equation. Then, construct a scatter plot and a corresponding residual plot. State if a linear model is appropriate for the data. Round your answers to the nearest hundredth. Round the correlation coefficient to the nearest ten thousandth.

1.

x	10	20	30	40	50	60	70	80
y	351	601	849	1099	1351	1601	1849	2099
Prediction	350.66	600.46	850.26	1100.06	1349.86	1599.66	1849.46	2099.26
Residual	0.34	0.54	−1.26	−1.06	1.14	1.34	−0.46	−0.26

Linear regression equation: $y = 24.98x + 100.86$, $r = 1.0000$

Scatter Plot & Line of Best Fit

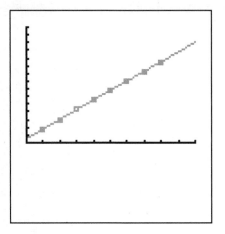

Residual Plot

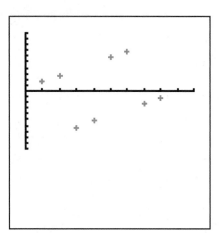

Based on the shape of the scatter plot and the correlation coefficient, a linear model appears to be appropriate for the data. Based on the residual plot, a linear model appears to be appropriate for the data.

9

2.

x	2	4	6	8	10	12	14	16
y	8	14	20	26	32	38	44	50
Prediction								
Residual								

Linear regression equation:

Scatter Plot & Line of Best Fit   Residual Plot

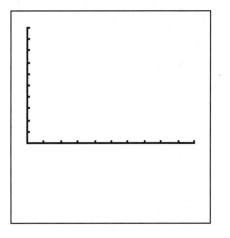   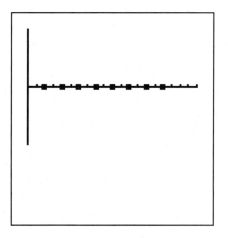

Name _____ Date _____

3.

x	1	3	5	7	9	11	13	15
y	2	10	26	50	82	122	170	226
Prediction								
Residual								

Linear regression equation:

Scatter Plot & Line of Best Fit

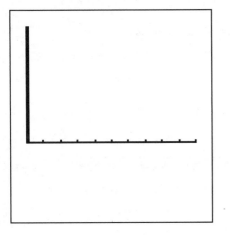

Residual Plot

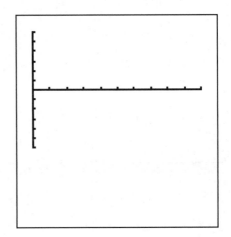

4.

x	2	4	6	8	10	12	14	16
y	2	5	11	25	57	129	291	656
Prediction								
Residual								

Linear regression equation:

Scatter Plot & Line of Best Fit

Residual Plot

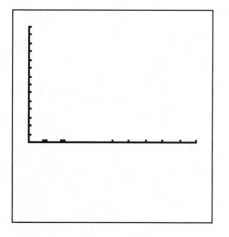
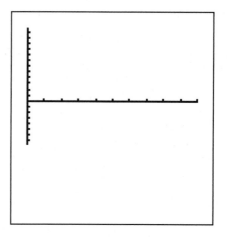

Name _____ Date _____

5.

x	1	2	3	4	5	6	7	8
y	37.5	35.5	32.5	30	27.5	25.5	22.5	20
Prediction								
Residual								

Linear regression equation:

Scatter Plot & Line of Best Fit

Residual Plot

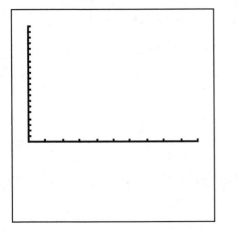
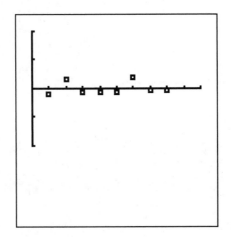

6.

x	2	4	6	8	10	12	14	16
y	50	48	46	44	40	36	30	24
Prediction								
Residual								

Linear regression equation:

Scatter Plot & Line of Best Fit

Residual Plot

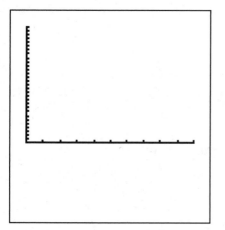
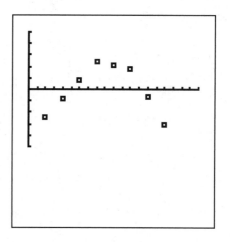

Name _____ Date _____

Who Are You? Who? Who?
Causation vs. Correlation

9

Vocabulary

Choose the word from the box that best completes each sentence.

causation	necessary condition	confounding variable
common response	sufficient condition	

1. A correlation is a _____ for causation, but a correlation is not a _____ for causation.

2. A _____ is when some other reason may cause the same result.

3. _____ is when one event causes a second event.

4. A _____ is when there are other variables that are unknown or unobserved.

Problem Set

Determine whether each correlation implies causation. List reasons why or why not.

1. The amount of ice cream a grocery store sells is negatively correlated to the amount of soup that the grocery store sells.

   The correlation does not imply causation. There may be a correlation between ice cream sales and soup sales. For instance, ice cream sales may increase as soup sales decrease because ice cream sales typically increase in warmer weather and soup sales typically decrease in warmer weather. However, this trend does not mean that an increase in ice cream sales causes the soup sales to decrease.

2. The number of new entry-level jobs in a city is positively correlated to the number of new home sales.

3. There is a positive correlation between the total number of dollars paid toward an education and a person's annual salary.

4. There is a negative correlation between the number of times a person washes their hands during the day and the number of times that person catches a cold.

5. There is a negative correlation between the number of hours a student plays video games per day and the grades a student receives in school.

6. There is a positive correlation between the number of hours a student spends studying and the grades a student receives in school.

Name _____ Date _____

Read each statement. Then answer the questions. Explain your reasoning.

7. A study claims that eating a healthy breakfast improves school performance.

   a. Do you think that eating breakfast every morning is a necessary condition for a student to perform well at school?

   Yes. It is very difficult for a student to perform well in school without a healthy breakfast.

   b. Do you think that eating breakfast every morning is a sufficient condition for a student to perform well at school?

   No. Not every student who eats breakfast every morning performs well at school.

8. A teacher said that students who read a book slowly will understand the story.

   a. Do you think that reading a book slowly is a necessary condition for understanding the story?

   b. Do you think that reading a book slowly is a sufficient condition for a student to understand the story?

9. A reporter claims that when there are a large number of paramedics at a disaster site, there are a large number of fatalities.

   a. Do you think that a large number of paramedics at a disaster site is a necessary condition for a large number of fatalities?

   b. Do you think that a large number of paramedics at a disaster site is a sufficient condition for a large number of fatalities?

9

10. An adult claims that if you play with fire, you are going to have bad dreams.

   a. Do you think that playing with fire is a necessary condition for a person to have bad dreams?

   b. Do you think that playing with fire is a sufficient condition for a person to have bad dreams?

11. A dietician says that if people reduce their caloric intake they will lose weight.

   a. Do you think that reducing caloric intake is a necessary condition for a person to lose weight?

   b. Do you think that reducing caloric intake is a sufficient condition for a person to lose weight?

12. A cosmetic company claims that if you use sunscreen you will not get skin cancer.

   a. Do you think that using sunscreen is a necessary condition for a person to not get skin cancer?

   b. Do you think that using sunscreen is a sufficient condition for a person to not get skin cancer?

Name _____ Date _____

Could You Participate in Our Survey?
Interpreting Frequency Distributions

Vocabulary

Match each definition to its corresponding term.

1. displays the total of the frequencies of the rows or columns of a frequency distribution

   a. categorical data

2. displays the frequencies for categorical data in a two-way table

   b. two-way frequency table

3. non-numerical data that can be grouped into categories

   c. frequency distribution

4. displays categorical data by representing the number of occurrences that fall into each group for two variables

   d. joint frequency

5. any frequency you record within the body of a two-way frequency table

   e. frequency marginal distribution

Problem Set

Organize each data set into a two-way frequency table. Then complete the frequency marginal distribution for the data set.

1.

Class	Favorite Color
A	Red
A	Blue
B	Red
B	Purple
B	Blue
A	Red
B	Green
B	Green
A	Blue
B	Purple

Class	Favorite Color
B	Blue
A	Blue
A	Green
A	Red
B	Blue
B	Blue
A	Purple
B	Green
A	Red
B	Purple

Two-way frequency table:

Favorite Color of Students

		Red	Blue	Purple	Green
Class	Class A	////	///	/	/
	Class B	/	////	///	///

Frequency marginal distribution:

Favorite Color of Students

		Red	Blue	Purple	Green	Total
Class	Class A	4	3	1	1	9
	Class B	1	4	3	3	11
	Total	5	7	4	4	20

Name _____ Date _____

2.

Class	Favorite Sport to Watch on TV
11th Grade	Football
11th Grade	Baseball
12th Grade	Football
12th Grade	Football
11th Grade	Basketball
12th Grade	Football
11th Grade	Baseball
11th Grade	Football
12th Grade	Basketball
11th Grade	Baseball

Class	Favorite Sport to Watch on TV
12th Grade	Football
11th Grade	Basketball
11th Grade	Basketball
12th Grade	Football
12th Grade	Baseball
11th Grade	Football
12th Grade	Basketball
12th Grade	Baseball
11th Grade	Basketball
12th Grade	Football

Two-way frequency table:

Favorite Sport to Watch on TV

Class			

Frequency marginal distribution:

Favorite Sport to Watch on TV

Class				

3.

Class	Favorite Fruit
5th Grade	Apple
6th Grade	Banana
5th Grade	Apple
5th Grade	Apple
5th Grade	Banana
6th Grade	Grapes
6th Grade	Orange
6th Grade	Apple
5th Grade	Orange
5th Grade	Banana

Class	Favorite Fruit
5th Grade	Banana
6th Grade	Apple
6th Grade	Orange
6th Grade	Apple
6th Grade	Banana
5th Grade	Grapes
5th Grade	Banana
5th Grade	Apple
6th Grade	Orange
5th Grade	Grapes

Two-way frequency table:

Favorite Fruit of Students

Class				

Frequency marginal distribution:

Favorite Fruit of Students

Class				

Name _____ Date _____

4.

Class	Favorite Sports Boys Play
A	Soccer
A	Baseball
C	Basketball
B	Soccer
B	Soccer
C	Basketball
B	Football
C	Baseball
A	Baseball
C	Basketball

Class	Favorite Sports Boys Play
C	Soccer
A	Basketball
A	Baseball
B	Soccer
B	Football
B	Football
C	Baseball
A	Football
A	Soccer
C	Basketball

Two-way frequency table:

Favorite Sports Boys Play

Class				

Frequency marginal distribution:

Favorite Sports Boys Play

Class					

5.

Class	Favorite Sports Girls Play
A	Basketball
B	Soccer
B	Swimming
C	Basketball
C	Softball
A	Soccer
B	Soccer
A	Softball
C	Basketball
C	Swimming

Class	Favorite Sports Girls Play
A	Basketball
A	Basketball
B	Soccer
C	Basketball
B	Softball
B	Swimming
A	Swimming
A	Softball
C	Soccer
A	Softball

Two-way frequency table:

Favorite Sports Girls Play

Class				

Frequency marginal distribution:

Favorite Sports Girls Play

Class				

Name _____ Date _____

6.

Class	Favorite Subject
A	Algebra
A	English
B	History
B	History
B	Algebra
A	Algebra
A	English
B	English
A	English
B	History

Class	Favorite Subject
B	History
B	Algebra
A	English
B	Algebra
A	English
A	History
B	Algebra
B	Algebra
A	History
A	English

Two-way frequency table:

Favorite Subject of Students

Class			

Frequency marginal distribution:

Favorite Subject of Students

Class				

Construct a bar graph to represent each data set shown in the frequency marginal distribution table.

7.

Favorite Color of Students

	Red	Blue	Purple	Green	Total
Class A	5	7	3	1	16
Class B	6	5	5	2	18
Total	11	12	8	3	34

Class

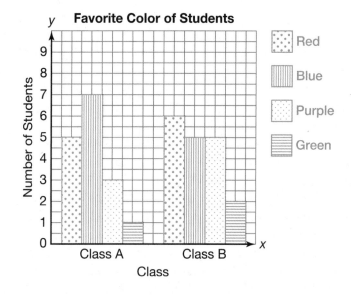

Name _____ Date _____

8.

Favorite Color of Students

	Red	Blue	Purple	Green	Total
Class A	5	7	3	1	16
Class B	6	5	5	2	18
Total	11	12	8	3	34

Class

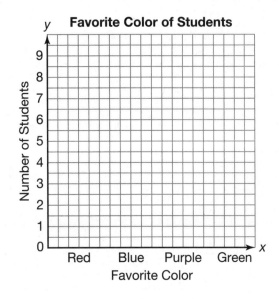

9.

Favorite Sport to Watch on TV

Class	Football	Baseball	Basketball	Total
11th Grade	16	7	12	35
12th Grade	13	5	18	36
Total	29	12	30	71

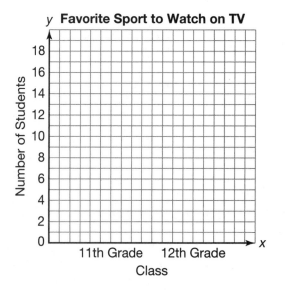

Name _____ Date _____

10.

Favorite Sport to Watch on TV

	Football	Baseball	Basketball	Total
11th Grade	16	7	12	35
12th Grade	13	5	18	36
Total	29	12	30	71

Class

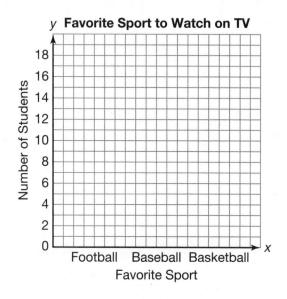

11.

Favorite Fruit of Students

		Apple	Banana	Grapes	Orange	Total
Class	**5th Grade**	17	15	8	6	46
	6th Grade	12	11	3	9	35
	Total	29	26	11	15	81

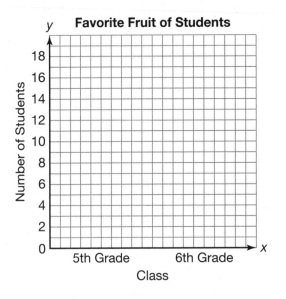

Name _____ Date _____

12.   **Favorite Fruit of Students**

		Apple	Banana	Grapes	Orange	Total
Class	**5th Grade**	17	15	8	6	46
	6th Grade	12	11	3	9	35
	Total	29	26	11	15	81

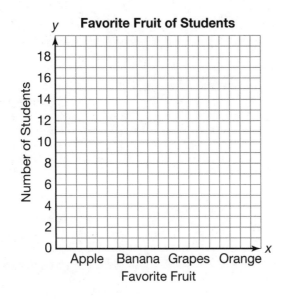

Favorite Fruit of Students

Name _____ Date _____

It's So Hot Outside!
Relative Frequency Distribution

Vocabulary

Write a brief explanation of the difference between a relative frequency distribution and a relative frequency marginal distribution.

Problem Set

Complete the relative frequency distribution and relative frequency marginal distribution for each frequency marginal distribution.

1.

Favorite Music of Students

		Pop	Rap	Country	Rock	Total
Class	Class A	15	10	4	7	36
	Class B	12	17	6	5	40
	Total	27	27	10	12	76

Favorite Music of Students

		Pop	Rap	Country	Rock	Total
Class	Class A	$\frac{15}{76} \approx 0.197$	$\frac{10}{76} \approx 0.132$	$\frac{4}{76} \approx 0.053$	$\frac{7}{76} \approx 0.092$	$\frac{36}{76} \approx 0.474$
	Class B	$\frac{12}{76} \approx 0.158$	$\frac{17}{76} \approx 0.224$	$\frac{6}{76} \approx 0.079$	$\frac{5}{76} \approx 0.066$	$\frac{40}{76} \approx 0.526$
	Total	$\frac{27}{76} \approx 0.355$	$\frac{27}{76} \approx 0.355$	$\frac{10}{76} \approx 0.132$	$\frac{12}{76} \approx 0.158$	$\frac{76}{76} = 1$

2.

Favorite Books of Students

Class	Biography	Mystery	Romance	Historical	Total
Class A	7	12	5	9	33
Class B	11	3	9	12	35
Class C	12	14	6	8	40
Total	30	29	20	29	108

Favorite Books of Students

Class	Biography	Mystery	Romance	Historical	Total
Class A					
Class B					
Class C					
Total					

3.

Favorite Movies of Students

Class	Comedy	Drama	Horror	Total
Class A	20	8	3	31
Class B	18	6	9	33
Total	38	14	12	64

Favorite Books of Students

Class	Comedy	Drama	Horror	Total
Class A				
Class B				
Total				

Name _____ Date _____

4.

Favorite Subject of Students

Class	Biology	History	Geometry	Total
Class A	13	8	9	30
Class B	8	15	5	28
Class C	4	11	14	29
Total	25	34	28	87

Favorite Subject of Students

Class	Biology	History	Geometry	Total
Class A				
Class B				
Class C				
Total				

5.

Favorite Vegetable of Students

Class		Green Beans	Broccoli	Carrots	Corn	Total
	Class A	9	4	12	8	33
	Class B	10	7	6	11	34
	Total	19	11	18	19	67

Favorite Vegetable of Students

Class		Green Beans	Broccoli	Carrots	Corn	Total
	Class A					
	Class B					
	Total					

6.

Favorite Winter Sport of Students

Class		Skiing	Tubing	Sledding	Skating	Total
	Class A	13	7	9	4	33
	Class B	11	5	14	9	39
	Total	24	12	23	13	72

Favorite Winter Sport of Students

Class		Skiing	Tubing	Sledding	Skating	Total
	Class A					
	Class B					
	Total					

Name _____ Date _____

Construct a stacked bar graph of each relative frequency distribution.

7.

Favorite Winter Sport of Students

	Skiing	Tubing	Sledding	Skating	Total
Class 11th Grade	$\frac{20}{163} \approx 0.123$	$\frac{16}{163} \approx 0.098$	$\frac{32}{163} \approx 0.196$	$\frac{11}{163} \approx 0.067$	$\frac{79}{163} \approx 0.485$
12th Grade	$\frac{24}{163} \approx 0.147$	$\frac{18}{163} \approx 0.110$	$\frac{27}{163} \approx 0.166$	$\frac{15}{163} \approx 0.092$	$\frac{84}{163} \approx 0.515$
Total	$\frac{44}{163} \approx 0.270$	$\frac{34}{163} \approx 0.209$	$\frac{59}{163} \approx 0.362$	$\frac{26}{163} \approx 0.160$	$\frac{163}{163} = 1$

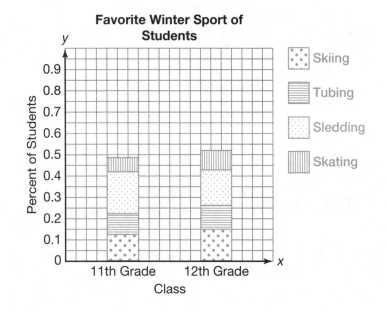

Favorite Winter Sport of Students

Skiing

Tubing

Sledding

Skating

8.

Favorite Winter Sport of Students

		Skiing	Tubing	Sledding	Skating	Total
Class	**11th Grade**	$\frac{20}{163} \approx 0.123$	$\frac{16}{163} \approx 0.098$	$\frac{32}{163} \approx 0.196$	$\frac{11}{163} \approx 0.067$	$\frac{79}{163} \approx 0.485$
	12th Grade	$\frac{24}{163} \approx 0.147$	$\frac{18}{163} \approx 0.110$	$\frac{27}{163} \approx 0.166$	$\frac{15}{163} \approx 0.092$	$\frac{84}{163} \approx 0.515$
	Total	$\frac{44}{163} \approx 0.270$	$\frac{34}{163} \approx 0.209$	$\frac{59}{163} \approx 0.362$	$\frac{26}{163} \approx 0.160$	$\frac{163}{163} = 1$

10

Favorite Winter Sport of Students

Name _____ Date _____

9.

Favorite Movies of Students

Class	Comedy	Drama	Horror	Total
11th Grade	$\frac{42}{164} \approx 0.256$	$\frac{15}{164} \approx 0.091$	$\frac{27}{164} \approx 0.165$	$\frac{84}{164} \approx 0.512$
12th Grade	$\frac{40}{164} \approx 0.244$	$\frac{22}{164} \approx 0.134$	$\frac{18}{164} \approx 0.110$	$\frac{80}{164} \approx 0.488$
Total	$\frac{82}{164} = 0.5$	$\frac{37}{164} \approx 0.226$	$\frac{45}{164} \approx 0.274$	$\frac{164}{164} = 1$

10

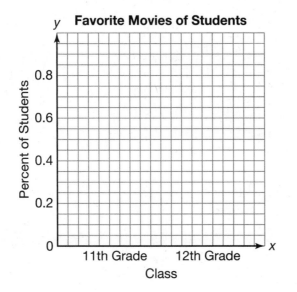

Favorite Movies of Students

10.

Favorite Movies of Students

		Comedy	Drama	Horror	Total
Class	11th Grade	$\frac{42}{164} \approx 0.256$	$\frac{15}{164} \approx 0.091$	$\frac{27}{164} \approx 0.165$	$\frac{84}{164} \approx 0.512$
	12th Grade	$\frac{40}{164} \approx 0.244$	$\frac{22}{164} \approx 0.134$	$\frac{18}{164} \approx 0.110$	$\frac{80}{164} \approx 0.488$
	Total	$\frac{82}{164} = 0.5$	$\frac{37}{164} \approx 0.226$	$\frac{45}{164} \approx 0.274$	$\frac{164}{164} = 1$

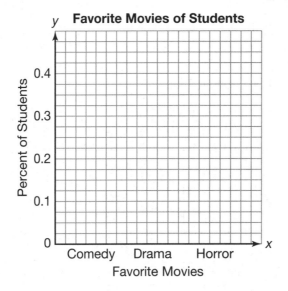

Favorite Movies of Students

Name _____ Date _____

11.   **Favorite Subject of Students**

<table>
<tr><th rowspan="2">Class</th><th></th><th>Chemistry</th><th>English</th><th>Algebra</th><th>Total</th></tr>
<tr><td>Class A</td><td>$\frac{10}{108} \approx 0.093$</td><td>$\frac{17}{108} \approx 0.157$</td><td>$\frac{8}{108} \approx 0.074$</td><td>$\frac{35}{108} \approx 0.324$</td></tr>
<tr><td></td><td>Class B</td><td>$\frac{13}{108} \approx 0.120$</td><td>$\frac{9}{108} \approx 0.083$</td><td>$\frac{15}{108} \approx 0.139$</td><td>$\frac{37}{108} \approx 0.343$</td></tr>
<tr><td></td><td>Class C</td><td>$\frac{8}{108} \approx 0.074$</td><td>$\frac{12}{108} \approx 0.111$</td><td>$\frac{16}{108} \approx 0.148$</td><td>$\frac{36}{108} \approx 0.333$</td></tr>
<tr><td></td><td>Total</td><td>$\frac{31}{108} \approx 0.287$</td><td>$\frac{38}{108} \approx 0.352$</td><td>$\frac{39}{108} \approx 0.361$</td><td>$\frac{108}{108} = 1$</td></tr>
</table>

10

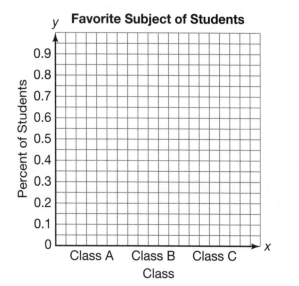

12.

Favorite Subject of Students

Class		Chemistry	English	Algebra	Total
	Class A	$\frac{10}{108} \approx 0.093$	$\frac{17}{108} \approx 0.157$	$\frac{8}{108} \approx 0.074$	$\frac{35}{108} \approx 0.324$
	Class B	$\frac{13}{108} \approx 0.120$	$\frac{9}{108} \approx 0.083$	$\frac{15}{108} \approx 0.139$	$\frac{37}{108} \approx 0.343$
	Class C	$\frac{8}{108} \approx 0.074$	$\frac{12}{108} \approx 0.111$	$\frac{16}{108} \approx 0.148$	$\frac{36}{108} \approx 0.333$
	Total	$\frac{31}{108} \approx 0.287$	$\frac{38}{108} \approx 0.351$	$\frac{39}{108} \approx 0.361$	$\frac{108}{108} = 1$

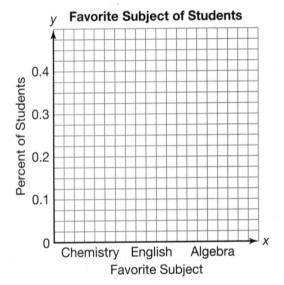

Name _____ Date _____

She Blinded Me with Science!
Relative Frequency Conditional Distribution

Vocabulary

Define the term in your own words.

1. relative frequency conditional distribution

Problem Set

Complete the relative frequency conditional distribution for each two-way table.

1.

Grades of Students

	A	B	C	D	F
Algebra	6	4	8	1	1
Geometry	6	11	9	2	2
Trigonometry	3	7	12	5	3

Class

Grades of Students

	A	B	C	D	F	Total
Algebra	$\frac{6}{20}=30\%$	$\frac{4}{20}=20\%$	$\frac{8}{20}=40\%$	$\frac{1}{20}=5\%$	$\frac{1}{20}=5\%$	$\frac{20}{20}=100\%$
Geometry	$\frac{6}{30}=20\%$	$\frac{11}{30}\approx36.7\%$	$\frac{9}{30}=30\%$	$\frac{2}{30}\approx6.7\%$	$\frac{2}{30}\approx6.7\%$	$\frac{30}{30}=100\%$
Trigonometry	$\frac{3}{30}=10\%$	$\frac{7}{30}\approx23.3\%$	$\frac{12}{30}=40\%$	$\frac{5}{30}\approx16.7\%$	$\frac{3}{30}=10\%$	$\frac{30}{30}=100\%$

Class

2.

Grades of Students

		A	B	C	D	F
Class	Computer Programming	7	13	12	1	2
	Journalism	8	11	4	1	0
	Cinematography	15	9	8	1	0

Grades of Students

		A	B	C	D	F	Total
Class	Computer Programming						
	Journalism						
	Cinematography						

3.

Student's Choice of Shakespeare Play to Study

		Hamlet	Macbeth	King Lear	Othello
Class	Class A	9	10	13	5
	Class B	14	8	7	8

Student's Choice of Shakespeare Play to Study

		Hamlet	Macbeth	King Lear	Othello
Class	Class A				
	Class B				
	Total				

Name _____ Date _____

4.

Student's Choice of Musical to Perform

		Carousel	South Pacific	The King and I	The Sound of Music
Class	Class A	8	5	14	9
	Class B	11	8	12	4

Student's Choice of Musical to Perform

		Carousel	South Pacific	The King and I	The Sound of Music
Class	Class A				
	Class B				
	Total				

5.

Favorite Lunch Item of Students

		Pizza	Salad	Chicken	Burger
Class	Class A	12	3	10	8
	Class B	9	8	13	5
	Class C	7	9	7	12

Favorite Lunch Item of Students

		Pizza	Salad	Chicken	Burger	Total
Class	Class A					
	Class B					
	Class C					

6.

Favorite Gym Activity of Students

	Volleyball	Basketball	Softball	Flag Football
Class A	9	10	4	12
Class B	12	5	7	6
Class C	9	3	14	6

Class

Favorite Gym Activity of Students

	Volleyball	Basketball	Softball	Flag Football	Total
Class A					
Class B					
Class C					

Class

Name _____ Date _____

The relative frequency conditional distribution shows the sports that female and male students choose to participate in. Use the relative frequency conditional distribution to answer each question.

Favorite Sports of Students

		Basketball	Soccer	Track & Field	Swimming	Total
Class	**Female Students**	$\frac{18}{85} \approx 21.2\%$	$\frac{14}{85} \approx 16.5\%$	$\frac{22}{85} \approx 25.9\%$	$\frac{31}{85} \approx 36.5\%$	$\frac{85}{85} = 100\%$
	Male Students	$\frac{24}{97} \approx 24.7\%$	$\frac{19}{97} \approx 19.6\%$	$\frac{20}{97} \approx 20.6\%$	$\frac{34}{97} \approx 35.1\%$	$\frac{97}{97} = 100\%$

10

7. What percent of female students participate in track & field?

Of the female students, 25.9% participate in track & field.

8. What percent of male students participate in basketball?

9. Which sport is the most popular among female students?

10. Which sport is the least popular among male students?

11. Which sport is the least popular among female students?

12. Which sport is the most popular among male students?

10

Name _____ Date _____

Oh! Switch the Station!
Drawing Conclusions from Data

Problem Set

A student committee at South Park High School must decide on a location for this year's senior picnic. They take a survey of three senior classes to help make their decision. The data from the survey is shown in the table. For each question, create a distribution to support your answer.

Class	Location
Class A	Beach
Class A	Beach
Class A	Water Park
Class B	Water Park
Class B	Beach
Class B	Beach
Class B	Amusement Park
Class C	Amusement Park
Class C	Amusement Park
Class A	Beach
Class A	Beach
Class A	Beach
Class C	Amusement Park
Class C	Amusement Park
Class B	Water Park
Class B	Amusement Park
Class A	Amusement Park
Class B	Water Park
Class C	Water Park
Class B	Water Park
Class C	Amusement Park

Class	Location
Class C	Amusement Park
Class B	Water Park
Class B	Water Park
Class C	Amusement Park
Class A	Beach
Class A	Water Park
Class B	Water Park
Class B	Water Park
Class B	Beach
Class C	Beach
Class A	Beach
Class A	Beach
Class C	Beach
Class B	Water Park
Class C	Water Park
Class B	Beach
Class C	Beach
Class B	Water Park
Class C	Water Park
Class A	Amusement Park
Class A	Beach

10

1. Which location is most popular among all three classes?

   Frequency marginal distribution table:

   Favorite Senior Picnic Location of Students

	Beach	Amusement Park	Water Park	Total
Class A	⧸⧸⧸⧸ ⧸⧸⧸⧸ 9	⧸⧸⧸ 2	⧸⧸ 2	13
Class B	⧸⧸⧸⧸ 4	⧸⧸ 2	⧸⧸⧸⧸ ⧸⧸⧸⧸ 10	16
Class C	⧸⧸⧸ 3	⧸⧸⧸⧸ ⧸⧸ 7	⧸⧸⧸ 3	13
Total	16	11	15	42

   The beach is the most popular location among all three classes.

2. Which location is least popular among all three classes?

Name _____ Date _____

3. Which location is most preferred by Class B?

4. Which location is least preferred in Class A?

5. Which class had the highest percentage of students prefer the water park as the location for the senior picnic?

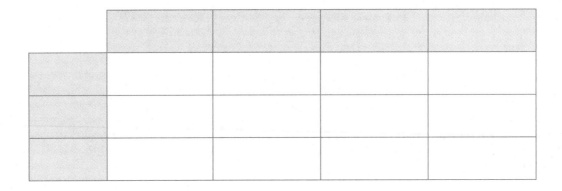

6. Which class least preferred the amusement park as the location for the senior picnic?

Name _____ Date _____

7. Which class had the most students in agreement as to their preferred location within the class?

8. Which class made up the smallest percentage of the students who supported the most popular overall location, the beach?

9. Which class made up the highest percentage of the students who supported the least popular overall location, the amusement park?

10. Which class made up the highest percentage of the students who supported the water park as their favorite senior picnic location?

Name _____ Date _____

Let's Take a Little Trip
Every Graph Tells a Story

Problem Set

For each graph describe the linear piecewise function in words. Be sure to include the domain and range and how the distance changed from hour to hour.

1. John goes for a walk on the beach early in the morning and returns home later that day.

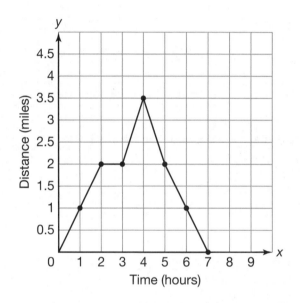

The domain is all times from 0 to 7 hours, which means the trip lasted 7 hours. The range is all distances from 0 to 3.5 miles, which means John went a maximum of 3.5 miles away from home. John traveled 1 mile in each of the first 2 hours. He rested for an hour, and then traveled 1.5 miles in the next hour. At this point he started back toward home. He traveled 1.5 miles in the next hour, and 1 mile in each of the following 2 hours, which brought him back home.

11

2. Peyton takes her dog for a long run on Saturday, stopping at different places along the way.

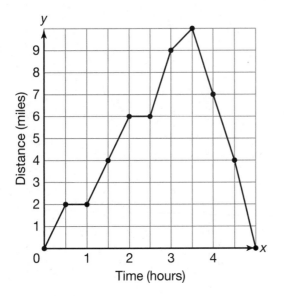

3. Tonya rides her bike to her friend Alexandra's house, stays awhile, and then returns home.

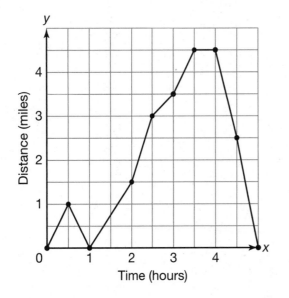

Name _____ Date _____

4. Tim walks to his friend Ryan's house, spends some time there, and comes back home.

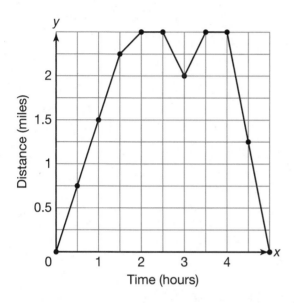

5. Every Tuesday and Thursday, Kurt walks to the community center after school.

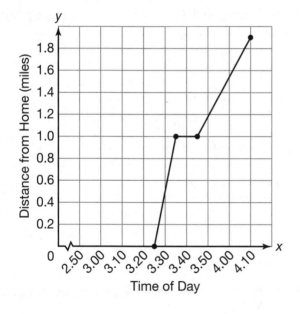

6. Lucy is hiking from her campsite to a waterfall, enjoys the scenery, then returns to the campsite.

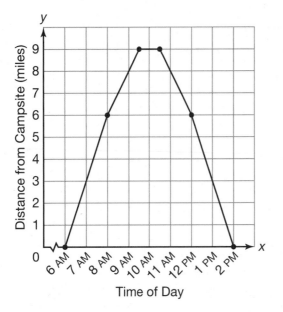

The graph shows the temperature in a restaurant's freezer during Alicia's 10-hour shift. Interpret the graph to answer each question.

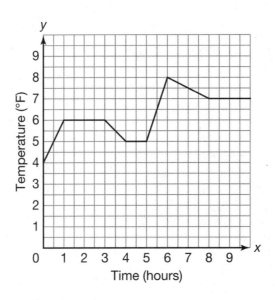

7. State the domain and range as they relate to the problem situation.

The domain, which is from 0 to 10 hours, represents the time of Alicia's shift. The range, which is from 4 to 8°F, represents the temperature in the freezer.

Name _____ Date _____

8. What is the temperature three hours after the start of Alicia's shift?

9. At which time(s) in Alicia's shift is the temperature 5°F?

10. During which time period(s) is the temperature in the freezer remaining constant?

11

11. Identify if the function has any absolute maximum or absolute minimum values and explain what the absolute maximum or absolute minimum means in terms of the problem situation.

12. At which time(s) during Alicia's shift is the temperature changing the fastest? Explain your reasoning.

The graph shows the depth at which a shark swims after a tracking device is attached to its dorsal fin. Interpret the graph to answer each question.

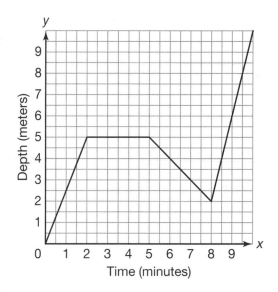

13. Is this relation a function? If so, explain why the relation is a function and identify the function family. If not, explain why the relation is not a function.

The relation is a function because at any time, the shark is exactly one depth. The function is a linear piecewise function.

14. State the domain and range as they relate to the problem situation.

15. What is the shark's depth one minute after the tracking device is installed?

16. How many minutes after the tracking device is installed is the shark's depth 6 meters?

Name _____ Date _____

17. During which time period(s) is the shark swimming toward the surface?

18. What was the shark's speed the first two minutes after the tracking device was attached? Explain your reasoning.

The graph shows Terrence's distance from a car dealership during his 10-minute test drive. Interpret the graph to answer each question.

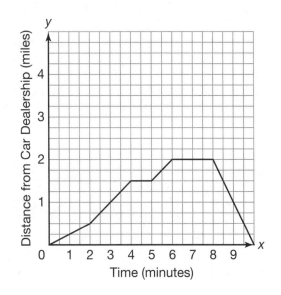

19. How far from the car dealership is Terrence after 7 minutes?

Terrence is 2 miles from the car dealership after 7 minutes.

20. State the domain and range as they relate to the problem situation.

LESSON **11.1** **Skills Practice** *page 8*

21. Identify if the relation has any absolute minimum or maximum values. Explain what the absolute minimum or absolute maximum means in terms of this problem situation.

22. At which time(s) is Terrence 1.5 miles from the car dealership?

23. During which time period(s) is Terrence driving the fastest? What is Terrence's average speed during that interval?

11

24. When is Terrence traveling away from the dealership? When is he traveling toward the dealership? Explain how you know.

Name _____ Date _____

Whodunit? The Function Family Line-Up
Modeling Data with Curves of Best Fit

Problem Set

Create a scatter plot of each data set on the grid. Sketch a function that best models the data. Describe which function family best represents the function you sketched.

1.

x	y
1	33
2	25
3	20
4	11
5	10
6	15
7	15
8	40
9	38

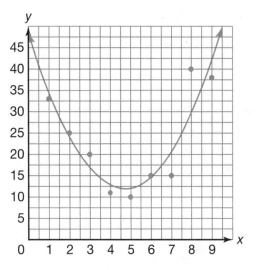

The function belongs to the quadratic function family.

2.

x	y
1	1
2	1
3	1.5
4	1
5	2
6	3
7	4.5
8	6
9	9.5

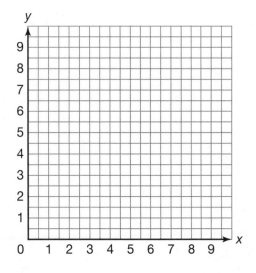

3.

x	y
1	450
2	425
3	350
4	275
5	250
6	250
7	150
8	75
9	25

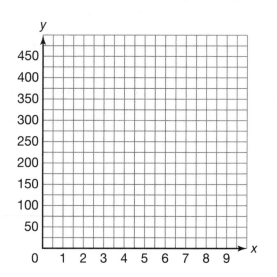

4.

x	y
0	80
1	50
2	40
3	20
4	15
5	12.5
6	7.5
7	10
8	7.5
9	5

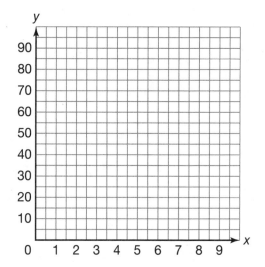

Name _____ Date _____

5.

x	y
1	340
2	400
4	360
5	400
6	490
8	470
10	550
12	570
14	680
15	660
18	740

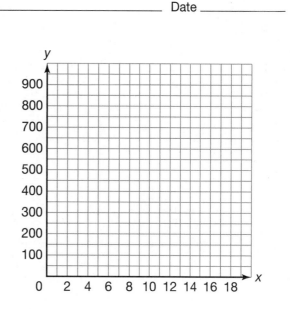

6.

x	y
5	0
10	150
15	325
20	325
25	450
30	450
35	475
40	375
45	400
50	275

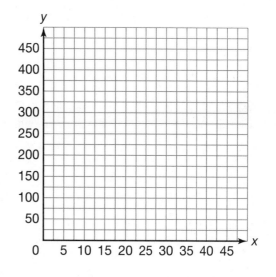

11

The graph shows the amount of snow accumulation at Snowy Ridge Ski Resort over a period of time. The function which best fits the data is also displayed. Analyze the graph of the function to answer each question.

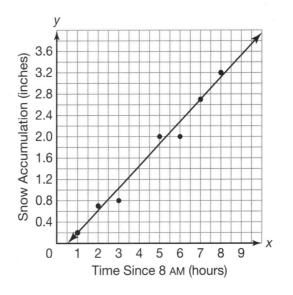

7. State the domain and range of the function.

The domain of the function is all real numbers. The range of the function is all real numbers.

8. Does the function have an absolute minimum or absolute maximum? If so, identify it and describe what it means in terms of the problem situation. If not, explain why not.

9. Does your function represent continuous or discrete data? Explain your reasoning.

10. According to the function, what was the total amount of snow accumulation at 12 PM?

11. Use the function to predict the total amount of snow accumulation at 6 pm.

Name _____ Date _____

12. The Snowy Ridge Ski Resort can expect to see an increase in skiers when there is 3 or more inches of snow accumulation. Around what time should the ski resort expect to see more skiers?

The graph shows the number of ants in an ant farm since the day it was started. The function which best fits the data is also displayed. Analyze the graph of the function to answer each question.

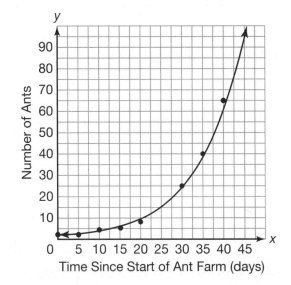

13. Does the function have an absolute minimum, absolute maximum, or neither? If so, describe what it means in terms of this problem situation.

This function has neither an absolute minimum nor an absolute maximum. However, in terms of the problem situation, the number of ants cannot be negative, so the function can never go below the *x*-axis.

14. State the domain and range of the function.

15. Does the function represent continuous or discrete data? Explain your reasoning.

16. According to the function, how many ants were in the ant farm 25 days after it was started?

17. Use the function to predict when the number of ants in the ant farm will reach 100.

18. Use what you know about populations to justify the shape of this graph.

The graph shows the median price of an acre of land in Washington County since 2005. The function which best fits the data is also displayed. Analyze the graph of the function to answer the question.

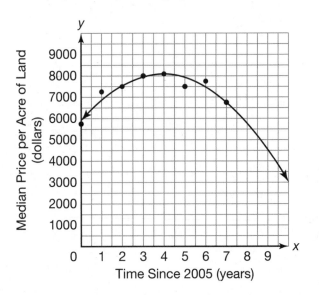

19. Which function family best represents the function shown?

The quadratic function family best represents the function.

20. What do you notice about the median price of an acre of land between 2005 and 2015?

Name _____ Date _____

21. State the domain and range of the function. Determine the domain and range for the problem situation.

22. Over which interval(s) is the function increasing? Over which interval(s) is the function decreasing?

23. Use the function to predict the median price per acre of land in the year 2015.

11

24. A Washington County landowner in the year 2012 is contemplating selling her land, but she also thinks it might be worth it to wait a few years. Make a recommendation to the landowner based on the function.

Name _____ Date _____

People, Tea, and Carbon Dioxide
Modeling Using Exponential Functions

Problem Set

For each given data set determine the exponential regression equation and the value of the correlation coefficient, r. Round all values to the hundredths place.

1.

x	y
10	5
20	6
30	8
40	15
50	32
60	70
70	150

$f(x) = 1.88(1.06)^x$

$r \approx 0.98$

2.

x	y
0	6000
1	2100
2	750
3	275
4	95
5	40
6	15
7	6
8	4

3.

x	5	10	15	20	25	30	35	40
y	12	10	25	21	45	35	80	120

4.

x	100	200	300	400	500	600	700
y	25.4	10.5	4.5	2.1	0.8	0.3	0.4

11

5.

x	0.5	1.0	1.5	2.0	2.5	3.0	3.5	4.0
y	1200	585	272	126	42	40	14	12

6.

x	0	100	200	300	400	500	600
y	10	50	110	160	220	290	350

Evaluate each function for the given value of x. Round your answer to the hundredths place.

7. Evaluate $f(x) = 2.45(1.05)^x$ when $x = 6$.

$f(6) = 2.45(1.05)^6$

≈ 3.28

8. Evaluate $f(x) = 55(0.82)^x$ when $x = 10$.

9. Evaluate $f(x) = 200(1.11)^x$ when $x = 20$.

10. Evaluate $f(x) = 10(2)^x$ when $x = 11$.

11. Evaluate $f(x) = 1200(0.99)^x$ when $x = 100$.

12. Evaluate $f(x) = 0.5(1.094)^x$ when $x = 25$.

13. Evaluate $f(x) = 5000(0.485)^x$ when $x = 7$.

14. Evaluate $f(x) = 180(0.35)^x$ when $x = 5$.

15. Evaluate $f(x) = 2.5(1.5)^x$ when $x = 30$.

16. Evaluate $f(x) = 9000(0.95)^x$ when $x = 90$.

Name _____ Date _____

Use a graphing calculator to determine the exponential regression equation that models each situation. Use the equation to make the associated prediction. Round all values to the hundredths place.

17. Tamara deposited $500 into a savings account in 1970. The table shows the value of Tamara's savings account from 1970 to 2010. Predict the account's value in 2020.

Time Since 1970 (years)	0	5	10	15	20	25	30	35	40
Account Value (dollars)	500	650	900	1150	1600	2100	2750	3850	4800

$f(x) = 497.63(1.06)^x$

$f(50) = 497.63(1.06)^{50}$

≈ 9166.42

The account's value will be approximately $9166.42 in 2020.

18. Tamika deposited $1000 into a savings account in 1980. The table shows the value of Tamika's savings account from 1980 to 2010. Predict when the account's value will be $5000.

Time Since 1980 (years)	0	5	10	15	20	25	30
Account Value (dollars)	1000	1200	1480	1800	2200	2720	3250

19. A marine biologist monitors the population of sunfish in a small lake. He records 800 sunfish in his first year, 600 sunfish in his fourth year, 450 sunfish in his sixth year, and 350 sunfish in his tenth year. Predict the population of sunfish in the lake in his sixteenth year.

20. A marine biologist monitors the population of catfish in a small lake. He records 50 catfish in his first year, 170 catfish in his fourth year, 380 catfish in his sixth year, and 1900 catfish in his tenth year. Predict when the population of catfish in the lake will be 6000.

21. Every hour, a scientist records the number of cells in a colony of bacteria growing in her lab. The sample begins with 15 cells. Predict the number of cells in the colony after 7 hours.

Hour	Number of Cells
0	15
1	40
2	110
3	300
4	850

22. Every hour, a scientist records the number of cells in a colony of bacteria growing in her lab. The sample begins with 50 cells. Predict how long it will take the sample to grow to 2000 cells.

Hour	Number of Cells
0	50
1	90
2	160
3	290
4	530

Name _____ Date _____

BAC Is BAD News
Choosing the Best Function to Model Data

Problem Set

Use a graphing calculator to determine the indicated regression equation for each data set. Round to the nearest tenth. Then explain the meaning of each variable in the regression equation.

1. Determine a quadratic regression equation that shows the relationship between the length of time in months that a new television has been for sale and the price of the television in dollars.

Time (months)	0	6	8	12
Price (dollars)	750	530	450	275

$y = -0.5x^2 - 33.6x + 749.9$

x represents the time in months the television has been for sale

y represents the price in dollars of the television

2. Determine a quadratic regression equation that shows the relationship between the number of years since a collector purchased an antique table and the value of the table in dollars.

Time (years)	0	22	50	100
Price (dollars)	25	9755	15,750	8550

3. Determine an exponential regression equation that shows the relationship between the time in months and the population of a town.

Time (months)	1	2	3	4	5
Population	1000	1050	1175	1340	1450

4. Determine an exponential regression equation that shows the relationship between the time in months and the rabbit population in a park.

Time (months)	1	2	3	4
Rabbit Population	4	5	8	12

5. Determine a quadratic regression equation that shows the relationship between a vehicle's mileage in thousands of miles and the cost for repairs in dollars during the vehicle's last inspection.

Mileage (thousands of miles)	50	100	150	200
Cost for Repairs (dollars)	200	350	675	1425

6. Determine an exponential regression equation that shows the relationship between the time in years and the amount of interest on a mortgage in dollars.

Time (years)	1	5	10	15	20
Interest (dollars)	3500	4750	3200	8525	10,450

Name _____ Date _____

Determine which regression equation is the best fit for each set of data points. Explain your reasoning.

7. The quadratic regression equation is $y = 0.0077056x^2 - 0.161558x + 2.142424$.

The exponential regression equation is $y = (1.0851)(1.045)^x$.

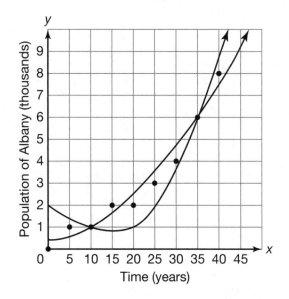

The exponential regression equation fits the data better than the quadratic regression equation. The exponential regression equation is closer to more points in the data set.

8. The quadratic regression equation is $y = -0.220238x^2 + 16.369x - 57.14285.$

The exponential regression equation is $y = (172.2555)(0.9926)^x.$

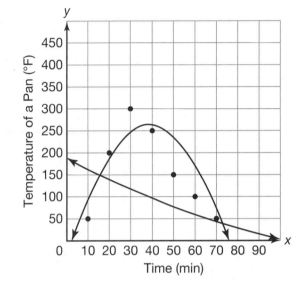

9. The quadratic regression equation is $y = 7.42857x^2 - 44.5714x + 78.4.$

The exponential regression equation is $y = (23.202)(1)^x.$

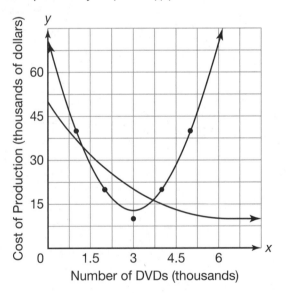

Name _____ Date _____

10. The quadratic regression equation is $y = 0.00205357x^2 + -0.2380357x + 8.05$.

The exponential regression equation is $y = (7.98796)(0.965952)^x$.

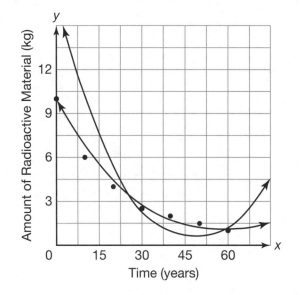

11. The quadratic regression equation is $y = 0.24x^2 - 6.43x + 171$.

The exponential regression equation is $y = (133.56)(1.01)^x$.

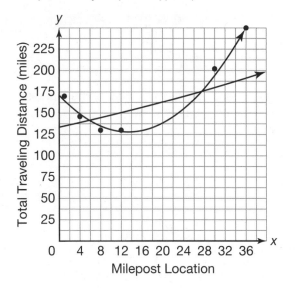

12. The quadratic regression equation is $y = 0.617x^2 - 3.48x + 4.66$.

   The exponential regression equation is $y = 1.12(1.345562)^x$.

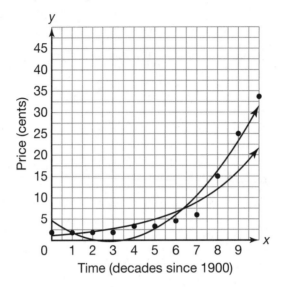

11

Use the given regression equation to answer each question.

13. The height of a ball in feet t seconds after it is projected upward can be modeled by the regression equation $h(t) = -16t^2 + 160t + 5$. What is the height of the ball after 2 seconds?

$h(2) = -16(2)^2 + 160(2) + 5$

$\quad = -16(4) + 320 + 5$

$\quad = -64 + 325$

$\quad = 261$

The height of the ball is 261 feet after 2 seconds.

14. The population of a town after t years can be modeled by the regression equation $p(t) = 15,000(1.07)^t$. What will the population of the town be after 5 years?

Name _____ Date _____

15. A boiling pot of water is removed from a burner. Its temperature in degrees Fahrenheit can be modeled by the regression equation $t(x) = 72 + 140(0.98)^x$, where x represents the number of minutes after the pot is removed from the burner. When does the temperature reach 152 degrees?

16. The balance in a bank account can be modeled by the regression equation $b(t) = 2t^2 - 20t + 400$, where t represents the time in months. When is the balance in the bank account $382?

17. The population of polar bears in a park after t years can be modeled by the regression equation $p(t) = 350(0.98)^t$. What is the population of the polar bears after 20 years?

11

18. The height of a rocket in feet t seconds after it is launched can be modeled by the regression equation $h(t) = -16t^2 + 800t + 15$. What is the height of the rocket 40 seconds after it is launched?

Ralph purchased a new 1970 Chevy Nova in the year it was manufactured for $3000. The scatter plot shows the car's value over a period of time since 1970. The quadratic regression equation that best fits the data is $f(x) = 20.77x^2 - 470.98x + 3685.45$, where $f(x)$ represents the value of the car in dollars and x represents the time since 1970 in years. The function is graphed on the grid. Analyze this information to answer each question.

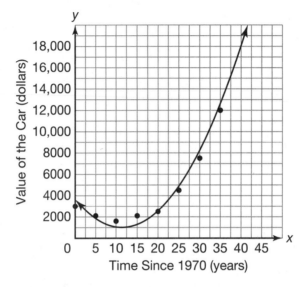

19. Discuss the domain and range of the function as they relate to the problem situation.

The domain is all real numbers greater than or equal to 0, because the car did not have a value prior to the year of its manufacture. The range is all real numbers greater than or equal to approximately $1000, because the function's value starts at approximately $3685, and then drops to approximately $1000 before rising from that point onward.

20. Discuss the intervals of increase and decrease as they relate to the problem situation.

21. Discuss the *x*- and *y*-intercepts of the function as they relate to the problem situation.

22. Discuss any minimums and maximums as they relate to the problem situation.

Name _____ Date _____

23. Predict the value of the car in 2010.

24. Why do you think the value of this car is best represented by a quadratic function? Do you think this is true of all cars?

The scatter plot shows the number of wild Burmese pythons captured in a Florida county over a period of time. The exponential regression equation that best fits the data is $p(x) = 4.96(1.68)^x$, where p represents the number of wild Burmese pythons captured and x represents the number of years since 2005. The function is graphed on the grid. Analyze this information to answer each question.

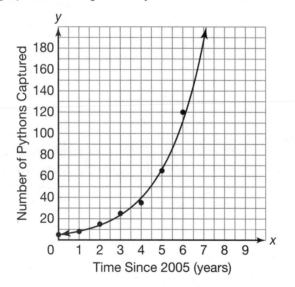

25. Discuss any minimums and maximums as they relate to the problem situation.

The function does not have a maximum value. Even though the given exponential function has no minimum value, the function as it relates to the problem has a minimum value of approximately 5 in the year 2005.

26. Discuss the domain and range of the function as they relate to the problem situation.

27. Discuss the intervals of increase and decrease as they relate to the problem situation.

28. Discuss the *x*- and *y*-intercepts of the function as they relate to the problem situation.

11

29. Predict the number of wild Burmese pythons captured in Florida in 2012.

30. Why might the number of wild Burmese pythons captured increase exponentially?

Name _____ Date _____

Let's Move!
Translating and Constructing Line Segments

Vocabulary

Choose the term from the box that best completes each statement.

Distance Formula	transformation	image
rigid motion	translation	pre-image
congruent line segment	congruent	arc
copying (duplicating) a line segment		

1. A(n) _____ is a transformation of points in space.

2. The new figure created from a translation is called the _____.

3. A(n) _____ is a part of a circle and can be thought of as the curve between two points on a circle.

4. A(n) _____ is the mapping, or movement, of all the points of a figure in a plane according to a common operation.

5. The _____ can be used to calculate the distance between two points on a coordinate place.

6. In a translation, the original figure is called the _____.

7. Line segments that have the same length are called _____.

8. A(n) _____ is a rigid motion that "slides" each point of a figure the same distance and direction.

9. _____ means to have the same size, shape, and measure.

10. A basic geometric construction called _____ can be used to translate a line segment when measurement is not possible.

Problem Set

Calculate the distance between each given pair of points. Round your answer to the nearest tenth, if necessary.

1. (3, 1) and (6, 5)

$x_1 = 3, y_1 = 1, x_2 = 6, y_2 = 5$

$d = \sqrt{(x_2 - x_1)^2 + (y_2 - y_1)^2}$

$d = \sqrt{(6 - 3)^2 + (5 - 1)^2}$

$d = \sqrt{3^2 + 4^2}$

$d = \sqrt{9 + 16}$

$d = \sqrt{25}$

$d = 5$

2. (2, 8) and (4, 3)

3. (−6, 4) and (5, −1)

4. (9, −2) and (2, −9)

5. (0, −6) and (8, 0)

6. (−5, −8) and (−2, −9)

Name _____ Date _____

Calculate the distance between each given pair of points on the coordinate plane. Round your answer to the nearest tenth, if necessary.

7.

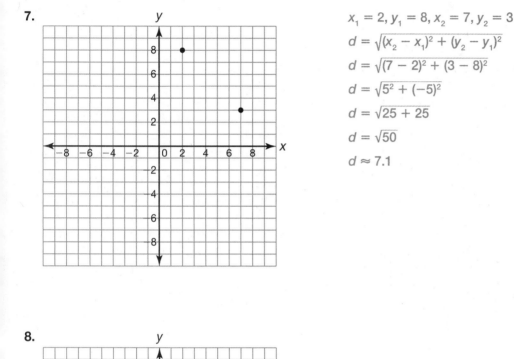

$x_1 = 2, y_1 = 8, x_2 = 7, y_2 = 3$

$d = \sqrt{(x_2 - x_1)^2 + (y_2 - y_1)^2}$

$d = \sqrt{(7 - 2)^2 + (3 - 8)^2}$

$d = \sqrt{5^2 + (-5)^2}$

$d = \sqrt{25 + 25}$

$d = \sqrt{50}$

$d \approx 7.1$

8.

9.

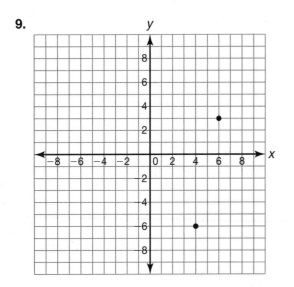

10.

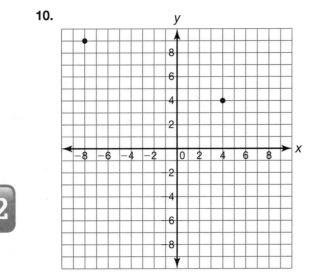

Name _____ Date _____

11.

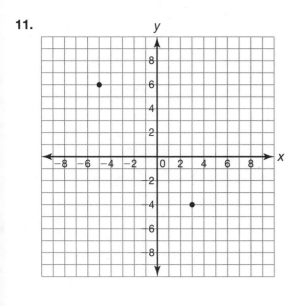

12.

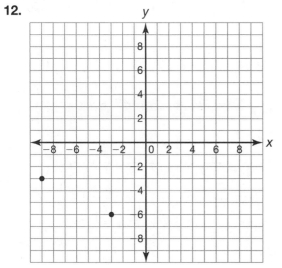

Translate each given line segment on the coordinate plane as described.

13. Translate $\overline{AB}$ 8 units to the left.

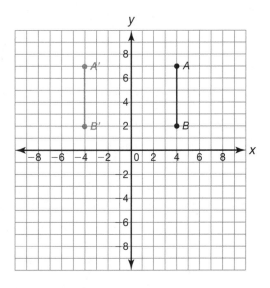

14. Translate $\overline{CD}$ 9 units down.

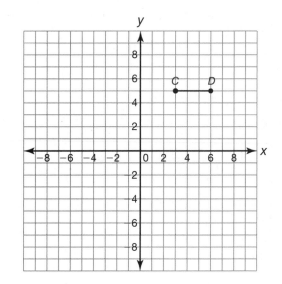

15. Translate $\overline{EF}$ 7 units to the right.

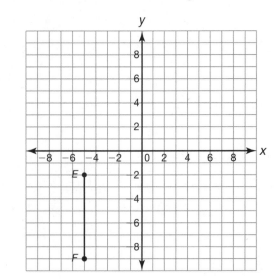

16. Translate $\overline{GH}$ 12 units up.

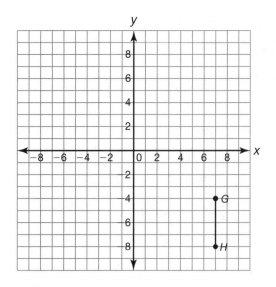

Name _____ Date _____

17. Translate $\overline{JK}$ 12 units down and 7 units to the left.

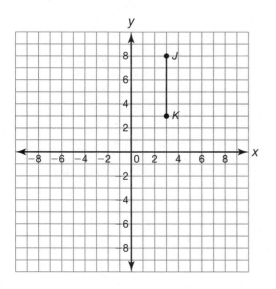

18. Translate $\overline{MN}$ 5 units down and 10 units to the right.

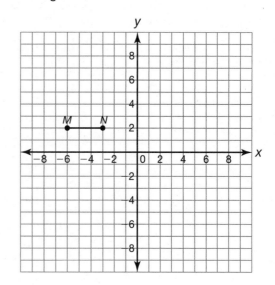

Construct each line segment described.

19. Duplicate $\overline{AB}$.

20. Duplicate $\overline{CD}$.

C●————————●D

21. Duplicate $\overline{EF}$.

E●————————————●F

22. Duplicate $\overline{GH}$.

G●————————————————●H

23. Construct a line segment twice the length of $\overline{JK}$.

J•———————•K

24. Construct a line segment twice the length of $\overline{MN}$.

M•———————•N

12

Name _____ Date _____

Treasure Hunt
Midpoints and Bisectors

Vocabulary

Match each definition to the corresponding term.

1. midpoint

2. Midpoint Formula

3. segment bisector

4. bisecting a line segment

a. a line, line segment, or ray that divides a line segment into two line segments of equal measure

b. a basic geometric construction used to locate the midpoint of a line segment

c. a point exactly halfway between the endpoints of a line segment

d. $\left(\dfrac{x_1 + x_2}{2}, \dfrac{y_1 + y_2}{2}\right)$

Problem Set

Determine the midpoint of a line segment with each set of given endpoints.

1. (8, 0) and (4, 6)

$x_1 = 8, y_1 = 0$
$x_2 = 4, y_2 = 6$
$\left(\dfrac{x_1 + x_2}{2}, \dfrac{y_1 + y_2}{2}\right) = \left(\dfrac{8 + 4}{2}, \dfrac{0 + 6}{2}\right)$
$\qquad\qquad = \left(\dfrac{12}{2}, \dfrac{6}{2}\right)$
$\qquad\qquad = (6, 3)$

2. (3, 8) and (9, 10)

3. (−7, 2) and (3, 6)

4. (6, −3) and (−4, 5)

5. (−10, −1) and (0, 4)

6. (−2, 7) and (−8, −9)

Determine the midpoint of the given line segment on each coordinate plane using the Midpoint Formula.

7.

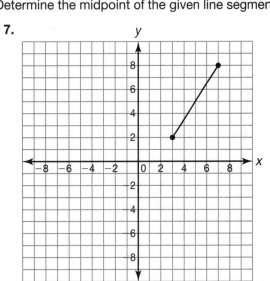

$x_1 = 3, y_1 = 2$

$x_2 = 7, y_2 = 8$

$$\left(\frac{x_1 + x_2}{2}, \frac{y_1 + y_2}{2}\right) = \left(\frac{3 + 7}{2}, \frac{2 + 8}{2}\right)$$

$$= \left(\frac{10}{2}, \frac{10}{2}\right)$$

$$= (5, 5)$$

Name _____ Date _____

8.

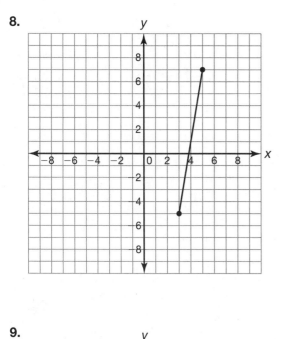

9.

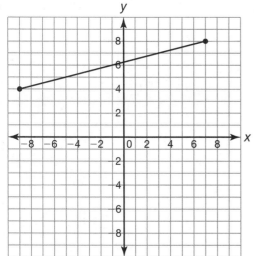

10.

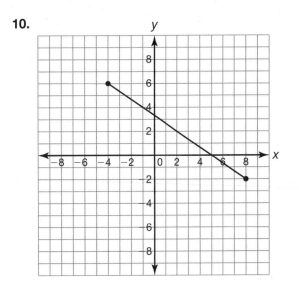

11.

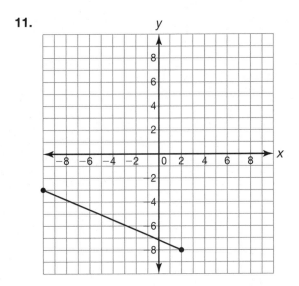

Name _____ Date _____

12.

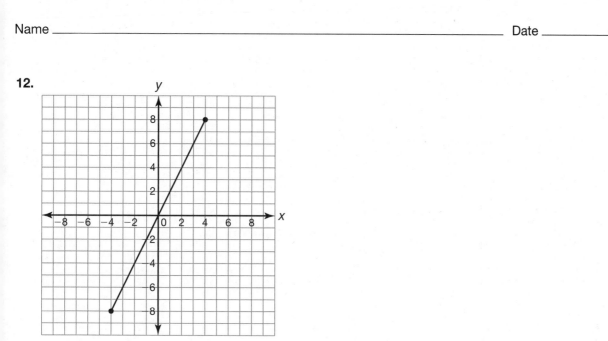

Locate the midpoint of each line segment using construction tools and label it point *M*.

13.

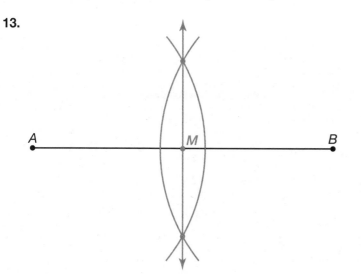

14.

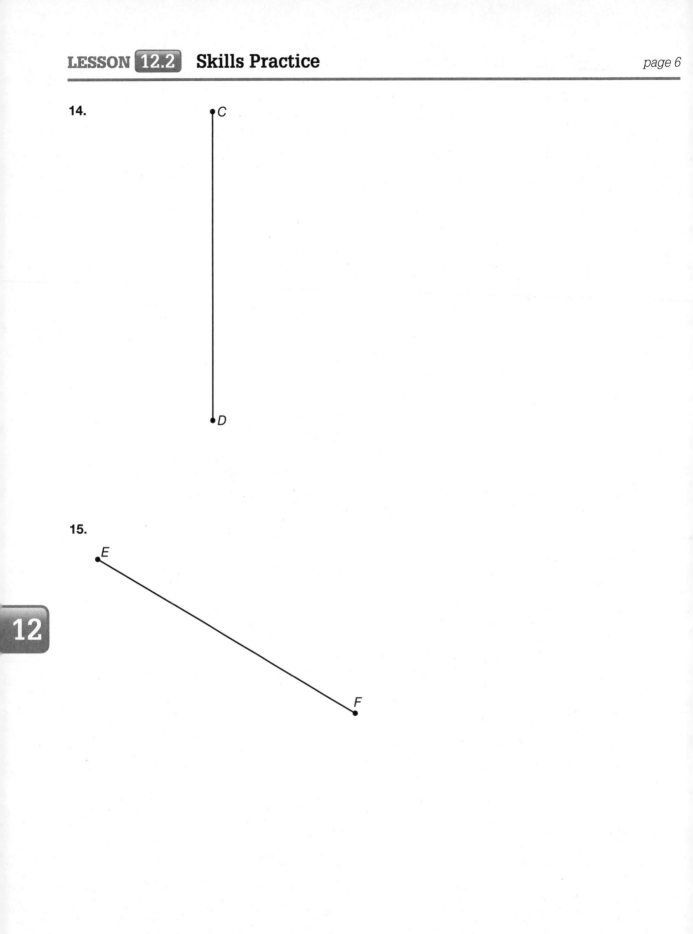

15.

Name _____ Date _____

16.

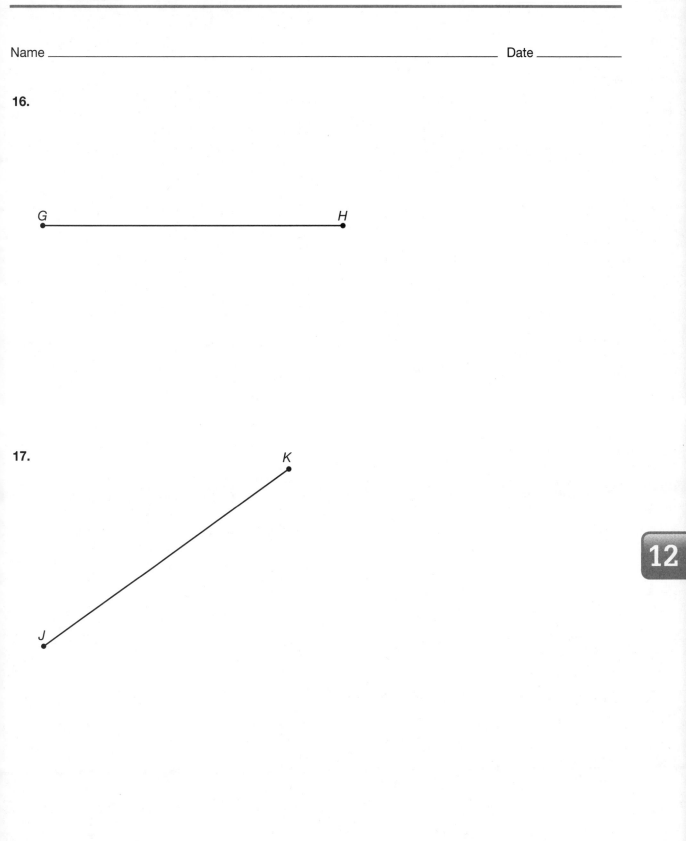

G _____ H

17.

K

J

18.

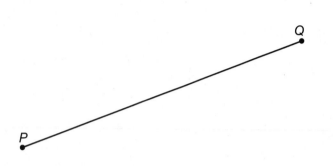

Name _____ Date _____

It's All About Angles
Translating and Constructing Angles and Angle Bisectors

Vocabulary

Define each term in your own words.

1. angle

2. angle bisector

Describe how to perform each construction in your own words.

3. copying or duplicating an angle

4. bisecting an angle

Problem Set

Translate each given angle on the coordinate plane as described.

1. Translate ∠ABC 9 units to the left.

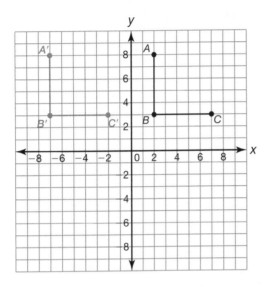

2. Translate ∠DEF 12 units down.

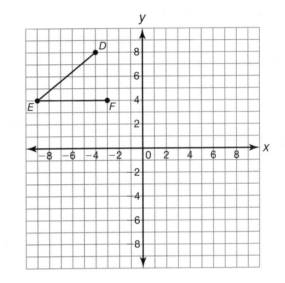

3. Translate ∠GHJ 10 units to the right.

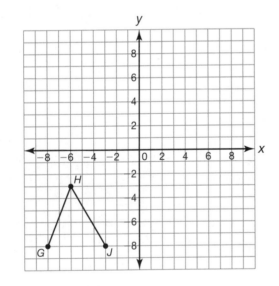

4. Translate ∠KLM 13 units up.

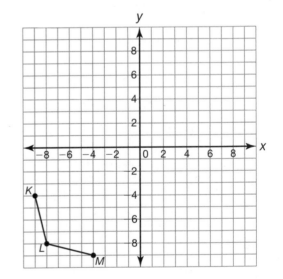

Name _____ Date _____

5. Translate ∠*NPQ* 8 units to the left and 11 units down.

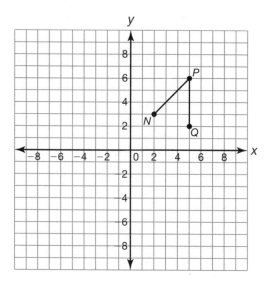

6. Translate ∠*RST* 15 units to the left and 9 units up.

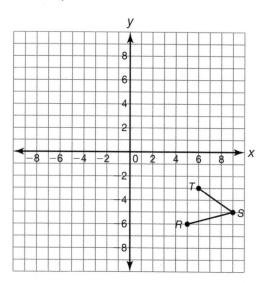

Construct each angle as described using a compass and a straightedge.

7. Copy ∠*B*.

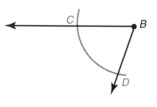

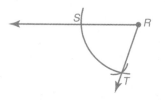

∠*CBD* ≅ ∠*SRT*

8. Copy ∠*D*.

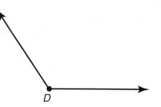

9. Copy ∠*P*.

10. Copy ∠*Z*.

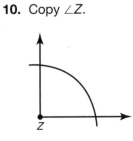

11. Construct an angle that is twice the measure of ∠*K*.

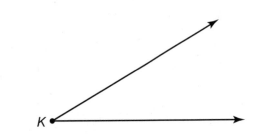

Name _____ Date _____

12. Construct an angle that is twice the measure of ∠M.

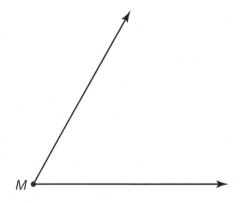

Construct the angle bisector of each given angle.

13.

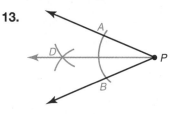

$\overline{PD}$ is the angle bisector of ∠P.

14.

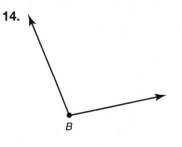

15.

16.

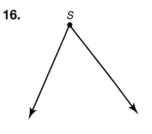

17. Construct an angle that is one-fourth the measure of ∠F.

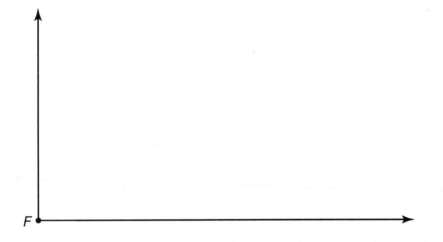

18. Construct an angle that is one-fourth the measure of ∠X.

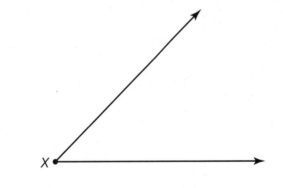

Name _____ Date _____

Did You Find a Parking Space?
Parallel and Perpendicular Lines on the Coordinate Plane

Vocabulary

Complete the sentence.

1. The point-slope form of the equation of the line that passes through (x_1, y_1) and has slope m is _____ .

Problem Set

Determine whether each pair of lines are parallel, perpendicular, or neither. Explain your reasoning.

1. line n: $y = -2x - 4$

line m: $y = -2x + 8$

Parallel. The slope of line n is -2, which is equal to the slope of line m, so the lines are parallel.

2. line p: $y = 3x + 5$

line q: $y = \frac{1}{3}x + 5$

3. line r: $y = -5x + 12$

line s: $y = \frac{1}{5}x - 6$

4. line n: $y = 6x + 2$

line m: $y = -6x - 2$

5. line p: $y - x = 4$

line q: $2x + y = 8$

6. line r: $2y + x = 6$

line s: $3x + 6y = 12$

Determine whether the lines shown on each coordinate plane are parallel, perpendicular, or neither. Explain your reasoning.

7.

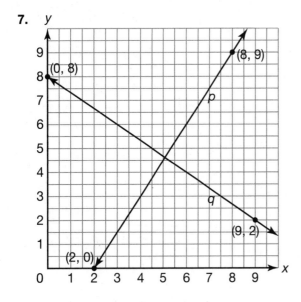

The lines are perpendicular. The slope of line p is $\frac{3}{2}$ and the slope of line q is $-\frac{2}{3}$.
Because $\frac{3}{2}\left(-\frac{2}{3}\right) = -1$, the lines are perpendicular.

Name _____ Date _____

8.

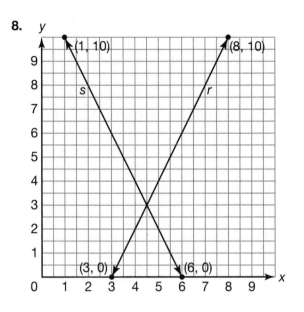

9.

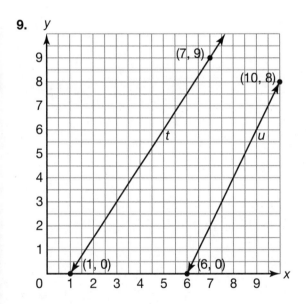

10.

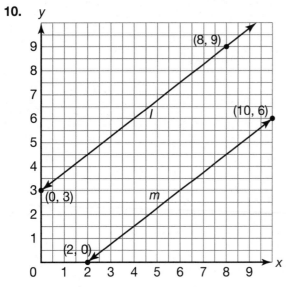

11.

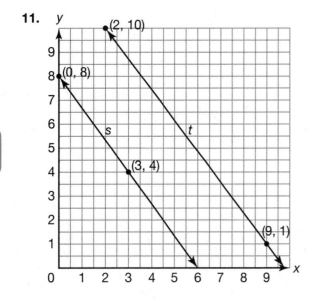

Name _____ Date _____

12.

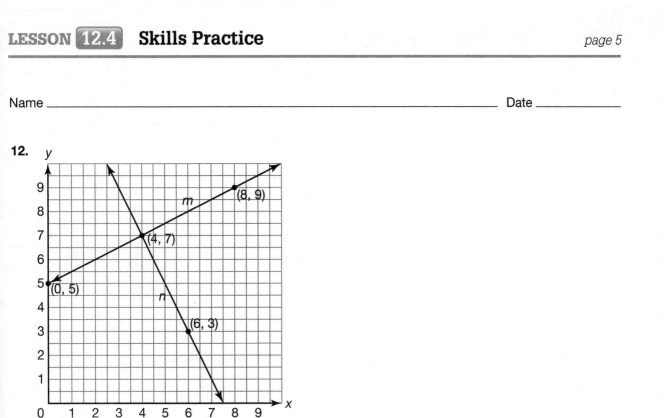

Determine an equation for each parallel line described. Write your answer in both point-slope form and slope-intercept form.

13. What is the equation of a line parallel to $y = \frac{4}{5}x + 2$ that passes through (1, 2)?

Point-slope form: $(y - 2) = \frac{4}{5}(x - 1)$

Slope-intercept form:

$y - 2 = \frac{4}{5}x - \frac{4}{5}$

$y = \frac{4}{5}x - \frac{4}{5} + 2$

$y = \frac{4}{5}x + \frac{6}{5}$

14. What is the equation of a line parallel to $y = -5x + 3$ that passes through (3, 1)?

15. What is the equation of a line parallel to $y = 7x - 8$ that passes through $(5, -2)$?

16. What is the equation of a line parallel to $y = -\frac{1}{2}x + 6$ that passes through $(-4, 1)$?

12

17. What is the equation of a line parallel to $y = \frac{1}{3}x - 4$ that passes through $(9, 8)$?

Name _____ Date _____

18. What is the equation of a line parallel to $y = -4x - 7$ that passes through $(2, -9)$?

Determine an equation for each perpendicular line described. Write your answer in both point-slope form and slope-intercept form.

19. What is the equation of a line perpendicular to $y = 2x - 6$ that passes through $(5, 4)$?

The slope of the new line must be $-\frac{1}{2}$.

Point-slope form: $(y - 4) = -\frac{1}{2}(x - 5)$

Slope-intercept form:
$$y - 4 = -\frac{1}{2}x + \frac{5}{2}$$
$$y = -\frac{1}{2}x + \frac{5}{2} + 4$$
$$y = -\frac{1}{2}x + \frac{13}{2}$$

20. What is the equation of a line perpendicular to $y = -3x + 4$ that passes through $(-1, 6)$?

21. What is the equation of a line perpendicular to $y = -\frac{2}{5}x - 1$ that passes through $(2, -8)$?

22. What is the equation of a line perpendicular to $y = \frac{3}{4}x + 12$ that passes through $(12, 3)$?

23. What is the equation of a line perpendicular to $y = 6x - 5$ that passes through $(6, -3)$?

24. What is the equation of a line perpendicular to $y = \frac{5}{2}x - 1$ that passes through $(-1, -4)$?

Name _____ Date _____

Determine the equation of a vertical line that passes through each given point.

25. (−2, 1)

$x = -2$

26. (3, 15)

27. (9, −7)

28. (−11, −8)

29. (−5, −10)

30. (0, −4)

Determine the equation of a horizontal line that passes through each given point.

31. (4, 7)

$y = 7$

32. (−6, 5)

33. (−8, −3)

34. (2, −9)

35. (−7, 8)

36. (6, −2)

12

Calculate the distance from each given point to the given line.

37. Point: (0, 4); Line: $f(x) = 2x - 3$

Write the equation for the line perpendicular to the given line that goes through the given point.

Since the slope of f is 2, the slope of the perpendicular segment is $-\frac{1}{2}$.

$y = mx + b$

$4 = -\frac{1}{2}(0) + b$

$4 = b$

The equation of the line containing the perpendicular segment is $y = -\frac{1}{2}x + 4$.

Calculate the point of intersection of the segment and the line $f(x) = 2x - 3$.

$-\frac{1}{2}x + 4 = 2x - 3$

$-x + 8 = 4x - 6$

$-5x = -14$

$x = \frac{-14}{-5} = 2.8$

$y = -\frac{1}{2}(2.8) + 4 = 2.6$

The point of intersection is (2.8, 2.6).

Calculate the distance.

$d = \sqrt{(0 - 2.8)^2 + (4 - 2.6)^2}$

$d = \sqrt{(-2.8)^2 + (1.4)^2}$

$d = \sqrt{7.84 + 1.96}$

$d = \sqrt{9.8} \approx 3.13$

The distance from the point (0, 4) to the line $f(x) = 2x - 3$ is approximately 3.13 units.

12

Name _____ Date _____

38. Point: $(-1, 3)$; Line: $f(x) = -\dfrac{1}{2}x - 4$

Write the equation for the line perpendicular to the given line that goes through the given point.

39. Point: $(-2, 5)$; Line: $f(x) = \dfrac{2}{3}x - \dfrac{1}{6}$

Write the equation for the line perpendicular to the given line that goes through the given point.

12

Name _____ Date _____

40. Point: $(-1, -2)$; Line: $f(x) = -4x + 11$

Write the equation for the line perpendicular to the given line that goes through the given point.

41. Point: $(3, -1)$; Line: $f(x) = \frac{1}{3}x - 6$

Write the equation for the line perpendicular to the given line that goes through the given point.

12

Name _____ Date _____

42. Point: $(-4, -2)$; Line: $f(x) = -\frac{1}{2}x + 4$

Write the equation for the line perpendicular to the given line that goes through the given point.

Name _____ Date _____

Making Copies—Just as Perfect as the Original!
Constructing Perpendicular Lines, Parallel Lines, and Polygons

Problem Set

Construct a line perpendicular to each given line and through the given point.

1. Construct a line that is perpendicular to $\overleftrightarrow{CD}$ and passes through point T.

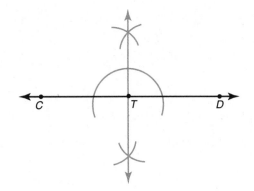

2. Construct a line that is perpendicular to $\overleftrightarrow{AB}$ and passes through point X.

12

3. Construct a line that is perpendicular to $\overleftrightarrow{RS}$ and passes through point *W*.

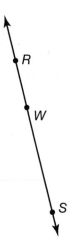

4. Construct a line that is perpendicular to $\overleftrightarrow{YZ}$ and passes through point *G*.

Name _____ Date _____

5. Construct a line that is perpendicular to $\overleftrightarrow{MN}$ and passes through point J.

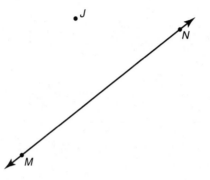

6. Construct a line that is perpendicular to $\overleftrightarrow{PQ}$ and passes through point R.

Construct a line parallel to each given line and through the given point.

7. Construct a line that is parallel to $\overleftrightarrow{AB}$ and passes through point C.

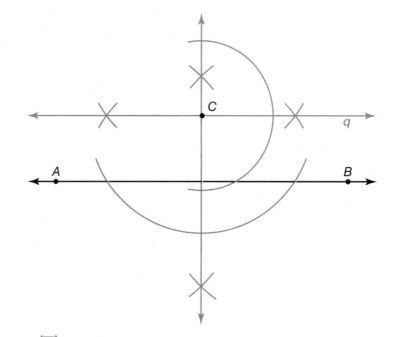

Line q is parallel to $\overleftrightarrow{AB}$.

8. Construct a line that is parallel to $\overleftrightarrow{DE}$ and passes through point F.

$_\bullet F$

Name _____ Date _____

9. Construct a line that is parallel to $\overleftrightarrow{GH}$ and passes through point J.

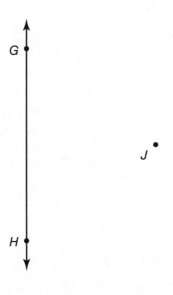

10. Construct a line that is parallel to $\overleftrightarrow{KL}$ and passes through point M.

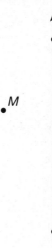

11. Construct a line that is parallel to $\overleftrightarrow{NP}$ and passes through point Q.

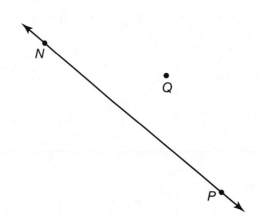

12. Construct a line that is parallel to $\overleftrightarrow{RT}$ and passes through point W.

Name _____ Date _____

Construct each geometric figure.

13. Construct an equilateral triangle. The length of one side is given.

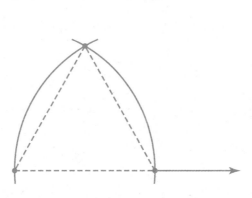

14. Construct an equilateral triangle. The length of one side is given.

15. Construct an isosceles triangle that is not an equilateral triangle such that each leg is longer than the base. The length of the base is given.

•————————————————•

16. Construct an isosceles triangle that is not an equilateral triangle such that each leg is shorter than the base. The length of the base is given.

•————————————•

Name _____ Date _____

17. Construct a square. The perimeter of the square is given.

•———————————•

18. Construct a square. The perimeter of the square is given.

•———————————•

19. Construct a rectangle that is not a square. The perimeter of the rectangle is given.

——————————————————————

20. Construct a rectangle that is not a square. The perimeter of the rectangle is given.

——————————————————————

12

Name _____ Date _____

Slide, Flip, Turn: The Latest Dance Craze?
Translating, Rotating, and Reflecting Geometric Figures

Vocabulary

Match each definition to its corresponding term.

1. rotation

    a. a line over which a figure is reflected so that corresponding points are the same distance from the line

2. point of rotation

    b. the angle measure by which a geometric figure is rotated about the point of rotation

3. angle of rotation

    c. a rigid motion that turns a figure about a fixed point for a given angle and given direction

4. reflection

    d. a rigid motion that "flips" a figure over a given line of reflection

5. line of reflection

    e. the fixed point about which a geometric figure is rotated during a rotation

13

Problem Set

Transform each given geometric figure on the coordinate plane as described.

1. Translate trapezoid *ABCD* 11 units to the right.

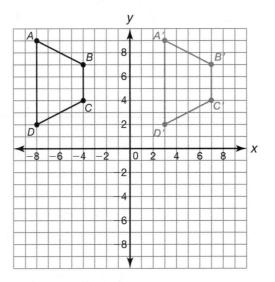

2. Translate triangle *EFG* 8 units up.

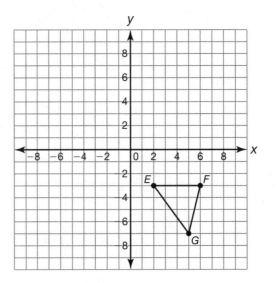

Name _____ Date _____

3. Rotate rectangle *HJKL* about the origin 90° counterclockwise.

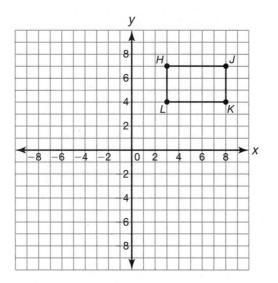

4. Rotate triangle *MNP* about the origin 180° counterclockwise.

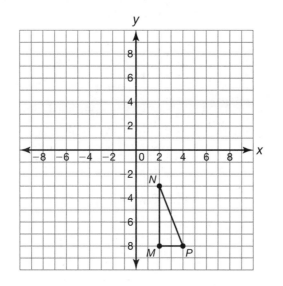

5. Rotate trapezoid *QRST* about the origin 90° counterclockwise.

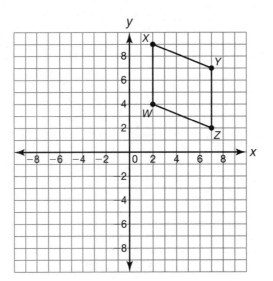

6. Rotate parallelogram *WXYZ* about the origin 180° counterclockwise.

Name _____ Date _____

7. Reflect triangle *ABC* over the *y*-axis.

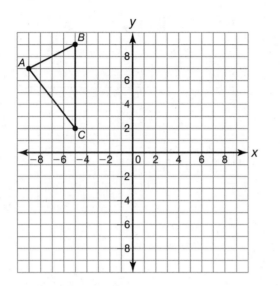

8. Reflect parallelogram *DEFG* over the *x*-axis.

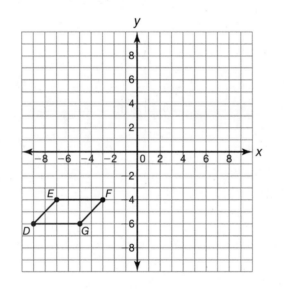

9. Reflect trapezoid *HJKL* over the *x*-axis.

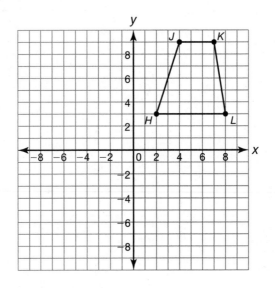

10. Reflect quadrilateral *MNPQ* over the *y*-axis.

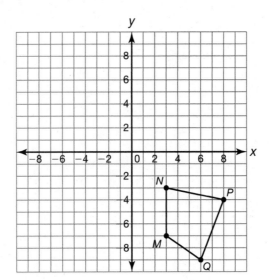

Name _____ Date _____

Determine the coordinates of each translated image without graphing.

11. The vertices of triangle *ABC* are *A* (5, 3), *B* (2, 8), and *C* (−4, 5). Translate the triangle 6 units to the left to form triangle *A′ B′ C′*.

The vertices of triangle *A′ B′ C′* are *A′* (−1, 3), *B′* (−4, 8), and *C′* (−10, 5).

12. The vertices of rectangle *DEFG* are *D* (−7, 1), *E* (−7, 8), *F* (1, 8), and *G* (1, 1). Translate the rectangle 10 units down to form rectangle *D′ E′ F′ G′*.

13. The vertices of parallelogram *HJKL* are *H* (2, −6), *J* (3, −1), *K* (7, −1), and *L* (6, −6). Translate the parallelogram 7 units up to form parallelogram *H′ J′ K′ L′*.

14. The vertices of trapezoid *MNPQ* are *M* (−6, −5), *N* (0, −5), *P* (−1, 2), and *Q* (−4, 2). Translate the trapezoid 4 units to the right to form trapezoid *M′ N′ P′ Q′*.

15. The vertices of triangle *RST* are *R* (0, 3), *S* (2, 7), and *T* (3, −1). Translate the triangle 5 units to the left and 3 units up to form triangle *R′ S′ T′*.

16. The vertices of quadrilateral *WXYZ* are *W* (−10, 8), *X* (−2, −1), *Y* (0, 0), and *Z* (3, 7). Translate the quadrilateral 5 units to the right and 8 units down to form quadrilateral *W′ X′ Y′ Z′*.

Determine the coordinates of each rotated image without graphing.

17. The vertices of triangle *ABC* are *A* (5, 3), *B* (2, 8), and *C* (−4, 5). Rotate the triangle about the origin 90° counterclockwise to form triangle *A′ B′ C′*.

The vertices of triangle *A′ B′ C′* are *A′* (−3, 5), *B′* (−8, 2), and *C′* (−5, −4).

18. The vertices of rectangle *DEFG* are *D* (−7, 1), *E* (−7, 8), *F* (1, 8), and *G* (1, 1). Rotate the rectangle about the origin 180° counterclockwise to form rectangle *D′ E′ F′ G′*.

13

19. The vertices of parallelogram *HJKL* are *H* (2, −6), *J* (3, −1), *K* (7, −1), and *L* (6, −6). Rotate the parallelogram about the origin 90° counterclockwise to form parallelogram *H′ J′ K′ L′*.

20. The vertices of trapezoid *MNPQ* are *M* (−6, −5), *N* (0, −5), *P* (−1, 2), and *Q* (−4, 2). Rotate the trapezoid about the origin 180° counterclockwise to form trapezoid *M′ N′ P′ Q′*.

21. The vertices of triangle *RST* are *R* (0, 3), *S* (2, 7), and *T* (3, −1). Rotate the triangle about the origin 90° counterclockwise to form triangle *R′ S′ T′*.

22. The vertices of quadrilateral *WXYZ* are *W* (−10, 8), *X* (−2, −1), *Y* (0, 0), and *Z* (3, 7). Rotate the quadrilateral about the origin 180° counterclockwise to form quadrilateral *W′ X′ Y′ Z′*.

Determine the coordinates of each reflected image without graphing.

23. The vertices of triangle *ABC* are *A* (5, 3), *B* (2, 8), and *C* (−4, 5). Reflect the triangle over the *x*-axis to form triangle *A′ B′ C′*.

The vertices of triangle *A′ B′ C′* are *A′* (5, −3), *B′* (2, −8), and *C′* (−4, −5).

24. The vertices of rectangle *DEFG* are *D* (−7, 1), *E* (−7, 8), *F* (1, 8), and *G* (1, 1). Reflect the rectangle over the *y*-axis to form rectangle *D′ E′ F′ G′*.

25. The vertices of parallelogram *HJKL* are *H* (2, −6), *J* (3, −1), *K* (7, −1), and *L* (6, −6). Reflect the parallelogram over the *x*-axis to form parallelogram *H′ J′ K′ L′*.

26. The vertices of trapezoid *MNPQ* are *M* (−6, −5), *N* (0, −5), *P* (−1, 2), and *Q* (−4, 2). Reflect the trapezoid over the *y*-axis to form trapezoid *M′ N′ P′ Q′*.

27. The vertices of triangle *RST* are *R* (0, 3), *S* (2, 7), and *T* (3, −1). Reflect the triangle over the *x*-axis to form triangle *R′ S′ T′*.

28. The vertices of quadrilateral *WXYZ* are *W* (−10, 8), *X* (−2, −1), *Y* (0, 0), and *Z* (3, 7). Reflect the quadrilateral over the *y*-axis to form quadrilateral *W′ X′ Y′ Z′*.

Name _____ Date _____

All the Same to You
Congruent Triangles

Vocabulary

Complete each problem related to the key terms of the lesson.

1. Draw and label a pair of congruent triangles. Write a congruence statement for the triangles.

   a. Identify each pair of congruent line segments in the drawing.

   b. Identify each pair of congruent angles in the drawing.

   c. Identify each pair of corresponding sides in the drawing.

   d. Identify each pair of corresponding angles in the drawing.

13

Problem Set

Identify the transformation used to create △*XYZ* on each coordinate plane. Identify the congruent angles and the congruent sides. Then write a triangle congruence statement.

1.

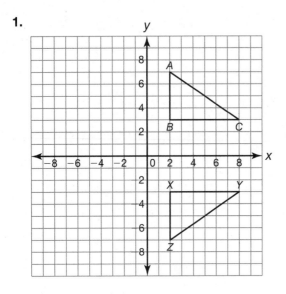

Triangle *BCA* was reflected over the *x*-axis to create triangle *XYZ*.

$BC \cong \overline{XY}$, $\overline{CA} \cong \overline{YZ}$, and $\overline{BA} \cong \overline{XZ}$; $\angle B \cong \angle X$, $\angle C \cong \angle Y$, and $\angle A \cong \angle Z$.

$\triangle BCA \cong \triangle XYZ$

2.

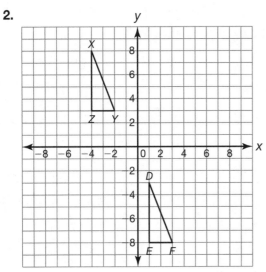

Name _____ Date _____

3.

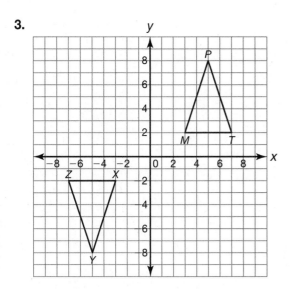

4.

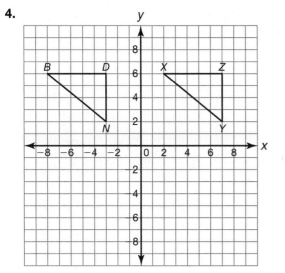

5.

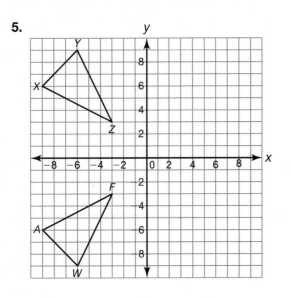

6.

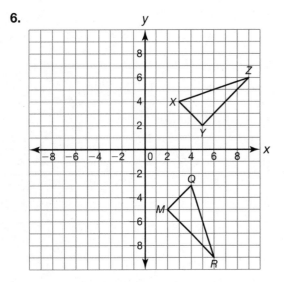

Name _____ Date _____

7.

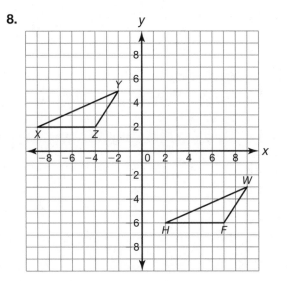

8.

9.

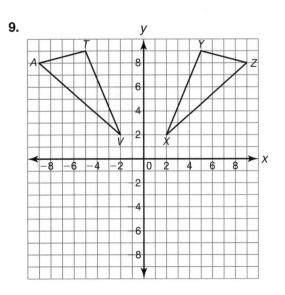

10.

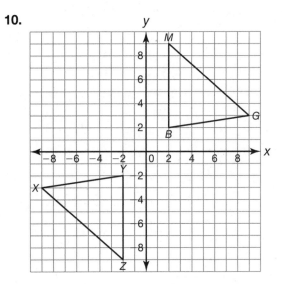

Name _____ Date _____

List the corresponding sides and angles using congruence symbols for each pair of triangles represented by the given congruence statement.

11. $\triangle JPM \cong \triangle TRW$

$\overline{JP} \cong \overline{TR}, \overline{PM} \cong \overline{RW}$, and $\overline{JM} \cong \overline{TW}$; $\angle J \cong \angle T$, $\angle P \cong \angle R$, and $\angle M \cong \angle W$.

12. $\triangle AEU \cong \triangle BCD$

13. $\triangle LUV \cong \triangle MTH$

14. $\triangle RWB \cong \triangle VCQ$

15. $\triangle TOM \cong \triangle BEN$

16. $\triangle JKL \cong \triangle RST$

17. $\triangle CAT \cong \triangle SUP$

18. $\triangle TOP \cong \triangle GUN$

13

Name _____ Date _____

Side-Side-Side
SSS Congruence Theorem

Vocabulary

Define each term in your own words.

1. theorem

2. postulate

3. Side-Side-Side (SSS) Congruence Theorem

13

Problem Set

Determine whether each pair of given triangles are congruent by SSS. Use the Distance Formula when necessary.

1.

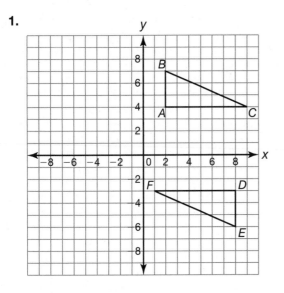

$AB = DE = 3$

$AC = DF = 7$

$d = \sqrt{(x_2 - x_1)^2 + (y_2 - y_1)^2}$

$BC = \sqrt{(9 - 2)^2 + (4 - 7)^2}$

$BC = \sqrt{7^2 + (-3)^2}$

$BC = \sqrt{49 + 9}$

$BC = \sqrt{58} \approx 7.62$

$d = \sqrt{(x_2 - x_1)^2 + (y_2 - y_1)^2}$

$EF = \sqrt{(1 - 8)^2 + (-3 - (-6))^2}$

$EF = \sqrt{(-7)^2 + 3^2}$

$EF = \sqrt{49 + 9}$

$EF = \sqrt{58} \approx 7.62$

$BC = EF$

The triangles are congruent by the SSS Congruence Theorem.

Name _____ Date _____

2.

3.

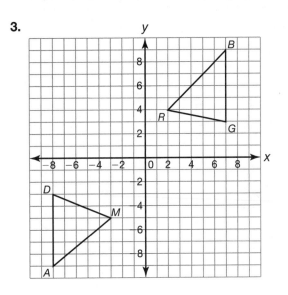

Name _____ Date _____

4.

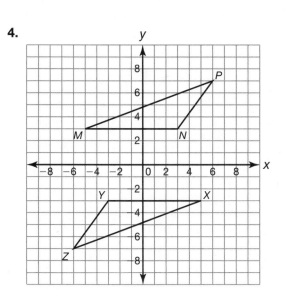

5.

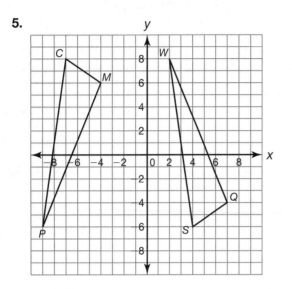

Name _____ Date _____

6.

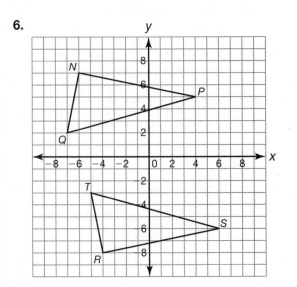

Perform the transformation described on each given triangle. Then verify that the triangles are congruent by SSS. Use the Distance Formula when necessary.

7. Reflect $\triangle ABC$ over the y-axis to form $\triangle XYZ$. Verify that $\triangle ABC \cong \triangle ABC$ by SSS.

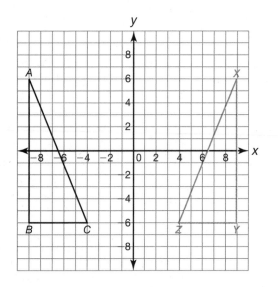

$AB = XY = 12$

$BC = YZ = 5$

$d = \sqrt{(x_2 - x_1)^2 + (y_2 - y_1)^2}$

$AC = \sqrt{(-4 - (-9))^2 + (-6 - 6)^2}$

$AC = \sqrt{5^2 + (-12)^2}$

$AC = \sqrt{25 + 144}$

$AC = \sqrt{169} = 13$

$d = \sqrt{(x_2 - x_1)^2 + (y_2 - y_1)^2}$

$XZ = \sqrt{(4 - 9)^2 + (-6 - 6)^2}$

$XZ = \sqrt{(-5)^2 + (-12)^2}$

$XZ = \sqrt{25 + 144}$

$XZ = \sqrt{169} = 13$

$AC = XZ$

The triangles are congruent by the SSS Congruence Theorem.

Name _____ Date _____

8. Rotate △*DEF* 180° clockwise to form △*QRS*. Verify that △*DEF* ≅ △*QRS* by SSS.

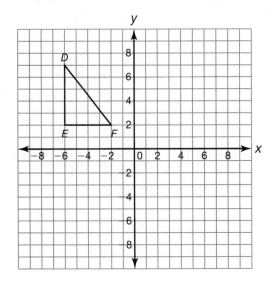

9. Reflect △*JKL* over the *x*-axis to form △*MNP*. Verify that △*JKL* ≅ △*MNP* by SSS.

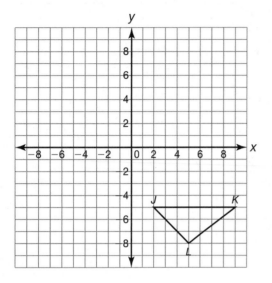

Name _____ Date _____

10. Translate △*HMZ* 10 units to the left and 1 unit down to form △*BNY*. Verify that △*HMZ* ≅ △*BNY* by SSS.

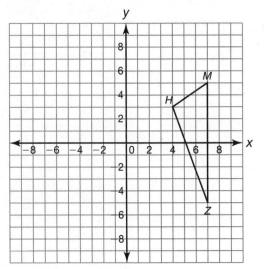

11. Rotate △AFP 90° counterclockwise to form △DHW. Verify that △AFP ≅ △DHW by SSS.

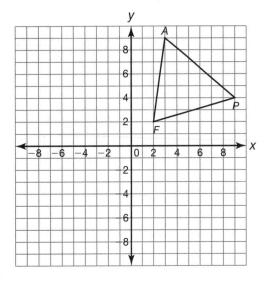

Name _____ Date _____

12. Translate △ACE 3 units to the right and 9 units up to form △JKQ. Verify that △ACE ≅ △JKQ by SSS.

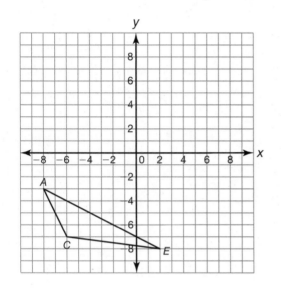

13

Side-Angle-Side
SAS Congruence Theorem

Vocabulary

Describe how to prove the given triangles are congruent. Use the key terms *included angle* and *Side-Angle-Side Congruence Theorem* in your answer.

1.

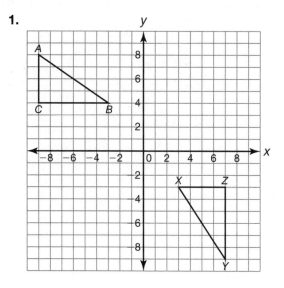

13

Problem Set

Determine whether each pair of given triangles are congruent by SAS. Use the Distance Formula when necessary.

1. Determine whether △ABC is congruent to △DEF by SAS.

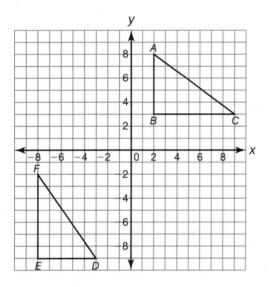

$AB = DE = 5$
$BC = EF = 7$
$m\angle B = m\angle E = 90°$
The triangles are congruent by the SAS Congruence Theorem.

2. Determine whether △CKY is congruent to △DLZ by SAS.

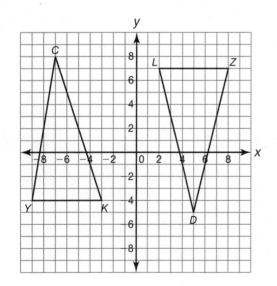

Name _____ Date _____

3. Determine whether △FMR is congruent to △JQW by SAS.

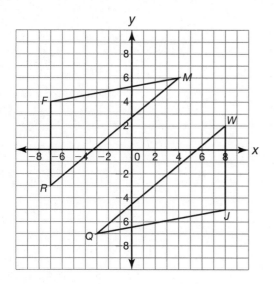

4. Determine whether △QRS is congruent to △XYZ by SAS.

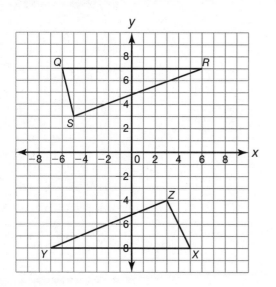

5. Determine whether △*JKL* is congruent to △*MNP* by SAS.

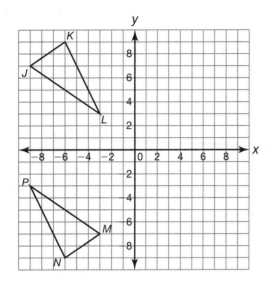

Name _____ Date _____

6. Determine whether △*ATV* is congruent to △*DNP* by SAS.

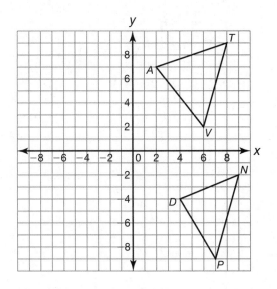

Perform the transformation described on each given triangle. Then verify that the triangles are congruent by SAS. Use the Distance Formula when necessary.

7. Reflect △ABC over the y-axis to form △XYZ. Verify that △ABC ≅ △XYZ by SAS.

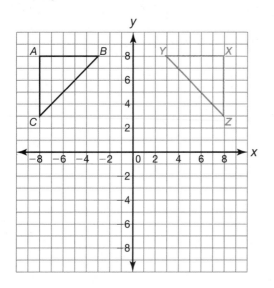

$AB = XY = 5$
$AC = XZ = 5$
$m\angle A = m\angle X = 90°$
The triangles are congruent by the SAS Congruence Theorem.

8. Translate △DEF 11 units to the left and 10 units down to form △QRS. Verify that △DEF ≅ △QRS by SAS.

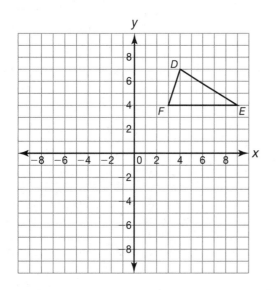

Name _____ Date _____

9. Rotate △*JKL* 180° counterclockwise to form △*MNP*. Verify that △*JKL* ≅ △*MNP* by SAS.

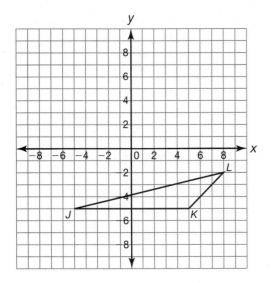

10. Reflect △*AFP* over the *y*-axis to form △*DHW*. Verify that △*AFP* ≅ △*DHW* by SAS.

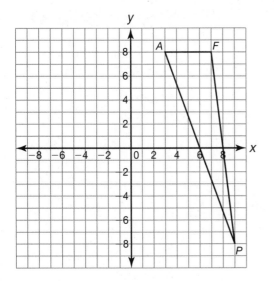

11. Translate △*ACE* 4 units to the right and 4 units down to form △*JKQ*. Verify that △*ACE* ≅ △*JKQ* by SAS.

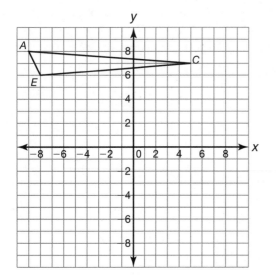

Name _____ Date _____

12. Rotate △*BMZ* 90° counterclockwise to form △*DRT*. Verify that △*BMZ* ≅ △*DRT* by SAS.

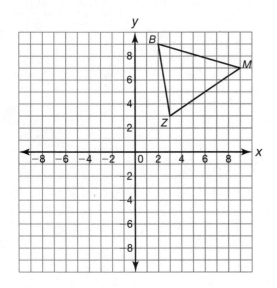

Determine the angle measure or side measure that is needed in order to prove that each set of triangles are congruent by SAS.

13. In △ART, AR = 12, RT = 8, and m∠R = 70°. In △BSW, BS = 12 and m∠S = 70°.

  SW = 8

14. In △CDE, CD = 7, DE = 11, In △FGH, FG = 7, GH = 11 and m∠G = 45°.

15. In △JKL, JK = 2, KL = 3, and m∠K = 60°. In △MNP, NP = 3 and m∠N = 60°.

16. In △QRS, QS = 6, RS = 4, and m∠S = 20°. In △TUV, TV = 6 and UV = 4.

17.

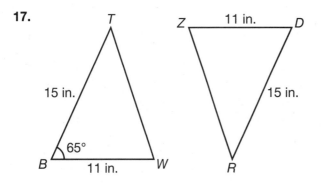

18.

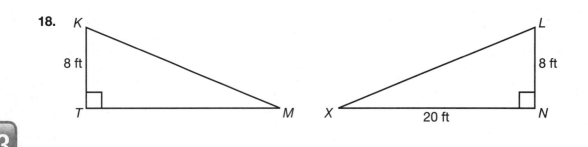

Name _____ Date _____

19.

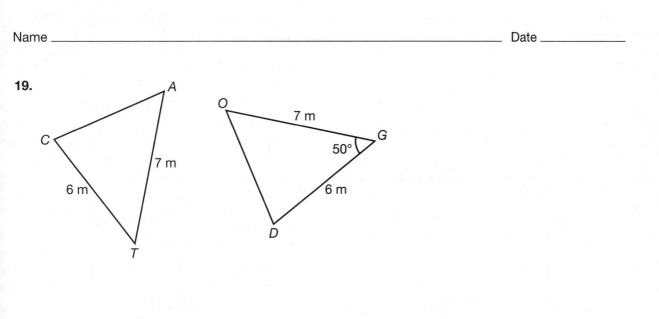

20.

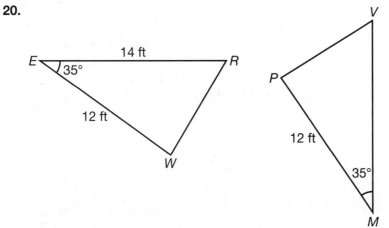

13

Determine whether there is enough information to prove that each pair of triangles are congruent by SSS or SAS. Write the congruence statements to justify your reasoning.

21. $\triangle MNP \overset{?}{\cong} \triangle PQM$

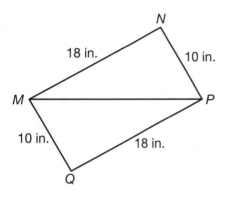

The triangles are congruent by SSS.

$\overline{MN} \cong \overline{PQ}$

$\overline{NP} \cong \overline{QM}$

$\overline{MP} \cong \overline{PM}$

22. $\triangle WXY \overset{?}{\cong} \triangle ZYX$

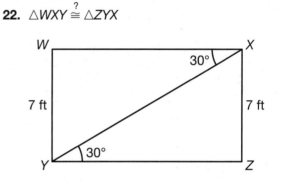

23. $\triangle BCE \overset{?}{\cong} \triangle DAF$

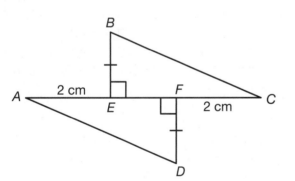

24. $\triangle HJM \overset{?}{\cong} \triangle MKH$

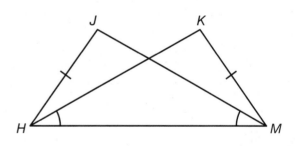

Name _____ Date _____

25. $\triangle PQR \overset{?}{\cong} \triangle STW$

26. $\triangle MAT \overset{?}{\cong} \triangle MHT$

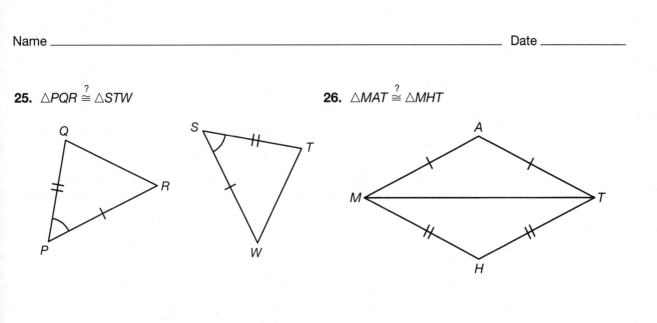

27. $\triangle BDW \overset{?}{\cong} \triangle BRN$

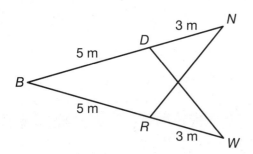

28. $\triangle ABC \overset{?}{\cong} \triangle EDC$

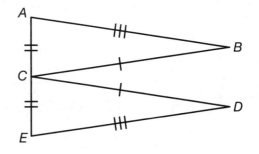

13

Name _____ Date _____

You Shouldn't Make Assumptions
Angle-Side-Angle Congruence Theorem

Vocabulary

Describe how to prove the given triangles are congruent. Use the key terms *included side* and *Angle-Side-Angle Congruence Theorem* in your answer.

1.

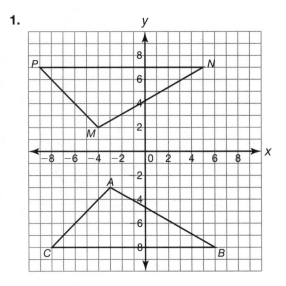

Problem Set

Determine whether each pair of given triangles are congruent by ASA.

1. Determine whether △ABC is congruent to △DEF by ASA.

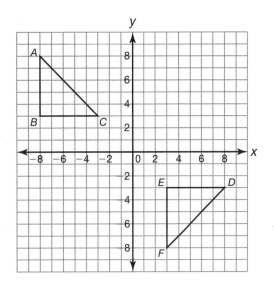

$m\angle B = m\angle E = 90°$

$m\angle C = m\angle F = 45°$

$BC = EF = 5$

The triangles are congruent by the ASA Congruence Theorem.

2. Determine whether △NPQ is congruent to △RST by ASA.

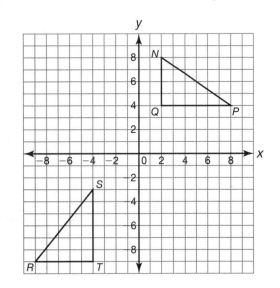

Name _____ Date _____

3. Determine whether △*AGP* is congruent to △*BHQ* by ASA.

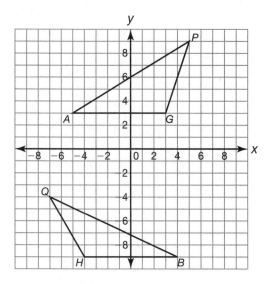

4. Determine whether △*CKY* is congruent to △*DLZ* by ASA.

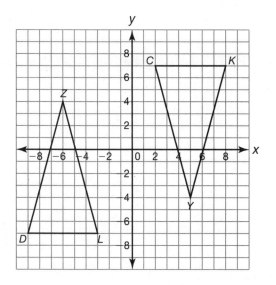

5. Determine whether △*FMR* is congruent to △*JQW* by ASA.

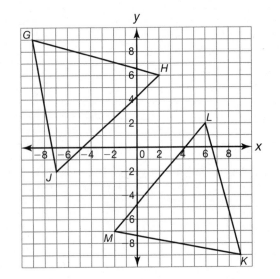

6. Determine whether △*GHJ* is congruent to △*KLM* by ASA.

Name _____ Date _____

Perform the transformation described on each given triangle. Then verify that the triangles are congruent by ASA.

7. Reflect △ABC over the y-axis to form △XYZ. Verify that △ABC ≅ △XYZ by SAS.

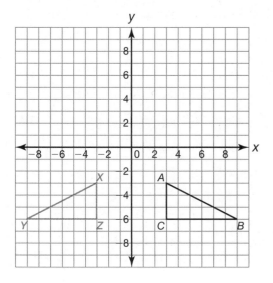

$m\angle C = m\angle Z = 90°$

$m\angle A = m\angle X = 63°$

$AC = XZ = 3$

The triangles are congruent by the ASA Congruence Theorem.

8. Rotate △DEF 90° counterclockwise to form △QRS. Verify that △DEF ≅ △QRS by SAS.

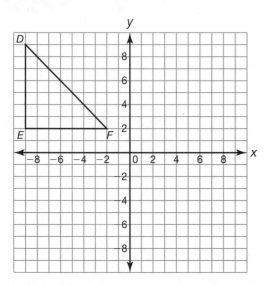

13

9. Translate △*HMZ* 6 units to the right and 10 units up to form △*BNY*. Verify that △*HMZ* ≅ △*BNY* by ASA.

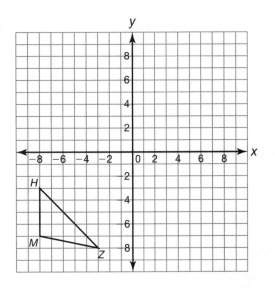

10. Reflect △*AFP* over the *y*-axis to form △*DHW*. Verify that △*AFP* ≅ △*DHW* by ASA.

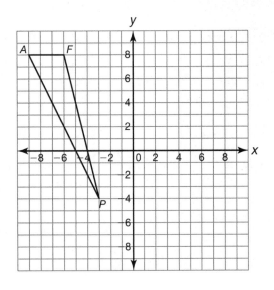

Name _____ Date _____

11. Rotate △*ACE* 180° counterclockwise to form △*JKQ*. Verify that △*ACE* ≅ △*JKQ* by SAS.

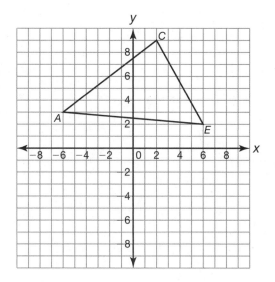

12. Reflect △*JKL* over the *x*-axis to form △*MNP*. Verify that △*JKL* ≅ △*MNP* by ASA.

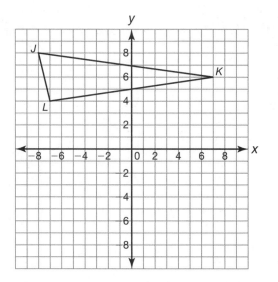

Determine the angle measure or side measure that is needed in order to prove that each set of triangles are congruent by ASA.

13. In $\triangle ADZ$, $m\angle A = 20°$, $AD = 9$, and $m\angle D = 70°$. In $\triangle BEN$, $BE = 9$ and $m\angle E = 70°$.

$m\angle B = 20°$

14. In $\triangle CUP$, $m\angle U = 45°$, and $m\angle P = 55°$, In $\triangle HAT$, $AT = 14$, $m\angle A = 45°$. and $m\angle T = 55°$.

15. In $\triangle HOW$, $m\angle H = 10°$, $HW = 3$, and $m\angle W = 60°$. In $\triangle FAR$, $FR = 3$ and $m\angle F = 10°$.

16. In $\triangle DRY$, $m\angle D = 100°$, $DR = 25$, and $m\angle R = 30°$, In $\triangle WET$, $m\angle W = 100°$ and $m\angle E = 30°$.

17.

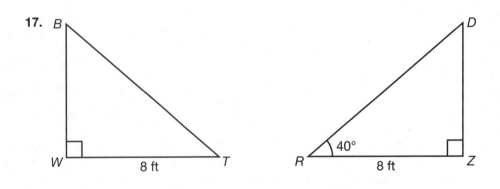

18.

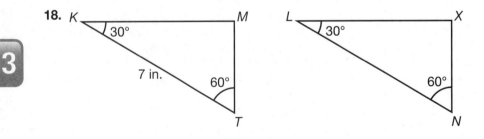

Name _____ Date _____

19.

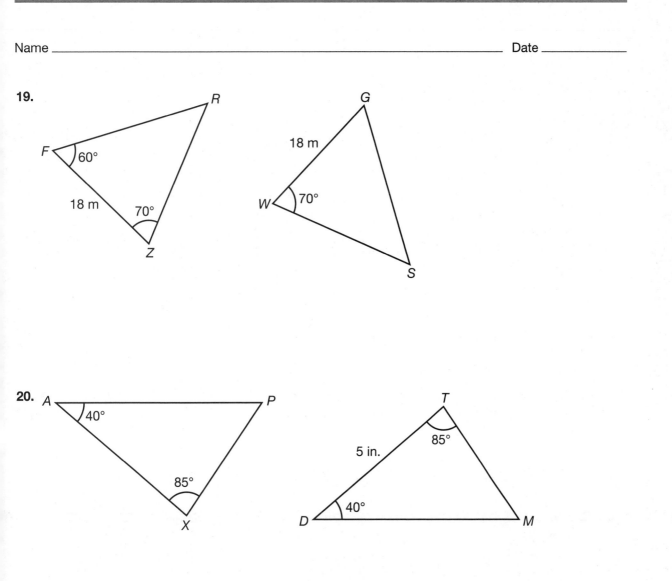

20.

Name _____ Date _____

Ahhhhh ... We're Sorry We Didn't Include You!
Angle-Angle-Side Congruence Theorem

Vocabulary

Describe how to prove the given triangles are congruent. Use the key terms *non-included side* and *Angle-Angle-Side Congruence Theorem* in your answer.

1.

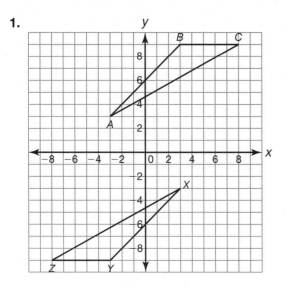

13

Problem Set

Determine whether each set of given triangles are congruent by AAS.

1. Determine whether △ABC is congruent to △DEF by AAS.

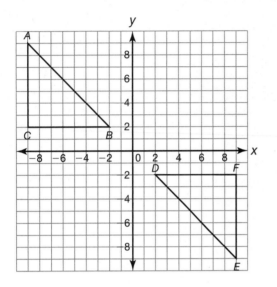

Methods may vary.

$m\angle A = m\angle D = 45°$

$m\angle B = m\angle E = 45°$

$BC = EF = 7$

The triangles are congruent by the AAS Congruence Theorem.

2. Determine whether △GHJ is congruent to △KLM by AAS.

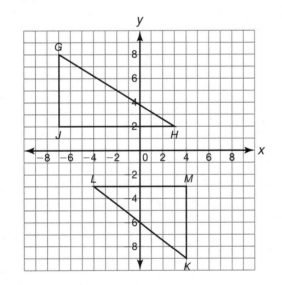

Name _____ Date _____

3. Determine whether △*AGP* is congruent to △*BHQ* by AAS.

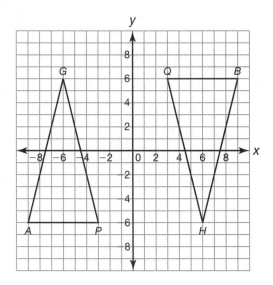

4. Determine whether △*CKY* is congruent to △*DLZ* by AAS.

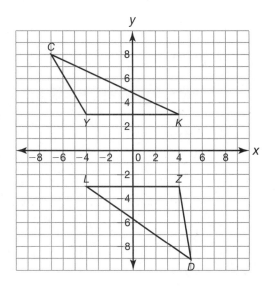

5. Determine whether △*FMR* is congruent to △*JQW* by AAS.

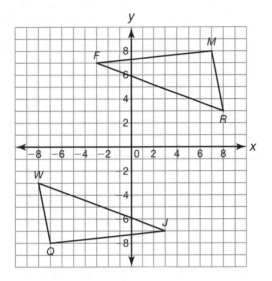

6. Determine whether △*NPQ* is congruent to △*RST* by AAS.

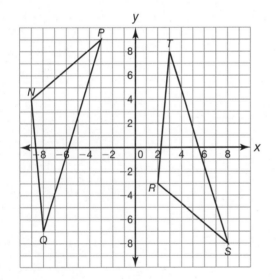

Name _____ Date _____

Perform the transformation described on each given triangle. Then verify that the triangles are congruent by AAS.

7. Reflect △ABC over the y-axis to form △XYZ. Verify that △ABC ≅ △XYZ by AAS.

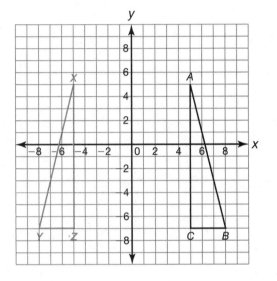

Methods may vary.

$m\angle B = m\angle Y = 76°$

$m\angle C = m\angle Z = 90°$

$AC = XZ = 12$

The triangles are congruent by the AAS Congruence Theorem.

8. Translate △DEF 11 units to the left and 11 units down to form △QRS. Verify that △DEF ≅ △QRS by AAS.

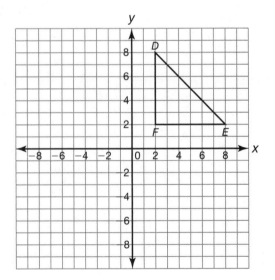

9. Rotate △*JKL* 180° counterclockwise to form △*MNP*. Verify that △*JKL* ≅ △*MNP* by AAS.

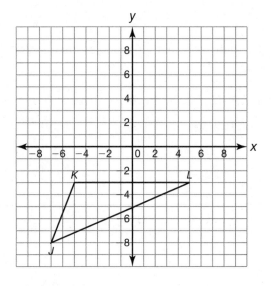

10. Translate △*CUP* 9 units to the left and 4 units up to form △*JAR*. Verify that △*CUP* ≅ △*JAR* by AAS.

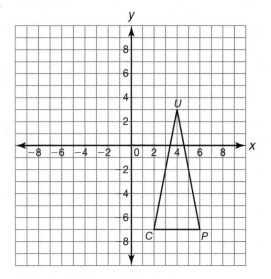

Name _____ Date _____

11. Reflect △*AFP* over the *x*-axis to form △*DHW*. Verify that △*AFP* ≅ △*DHW* by AAS.

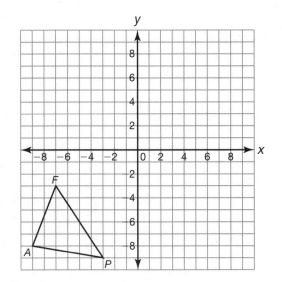

12. Rotate △ACE 270° counterclockwise to form △JKQ. Verify that △ACE ≅ △JKQ by AAS.

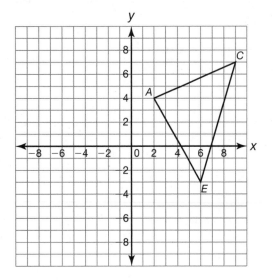

Determine the angle measure or side measure that is needed in order to prove that each set of triangles are congruent by AAS.

13. In △ANT, m∠A = 30°, m∠N = 60°, and NT = 5. In △BUG, m∠U = 60° and UG = 5.

   m∠B = 30°

14. In △BCD, m∠B = 25°, and m∠D = 105°. In △RST, RS = 12, m∠R = 25°, and m∠T = 105°.

15. In △EMZ, m∠E = 40°, EZ = 7, and m∠M = 70°. In △DGP, DP = 7 and m∠D = 40°.

16. In △BMX, m∠M = 90°, BM = 16, and m∠X = 15°. In △CNY, m∠N = 90° and m∠Y = 15°.

Name _____ Date _____

17.

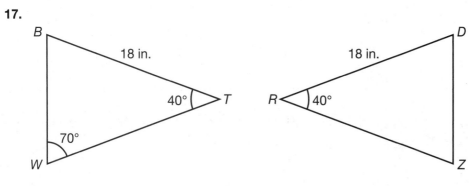

18.

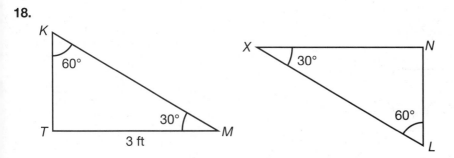

19.

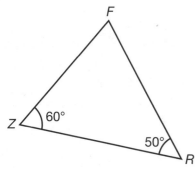

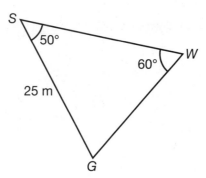

20.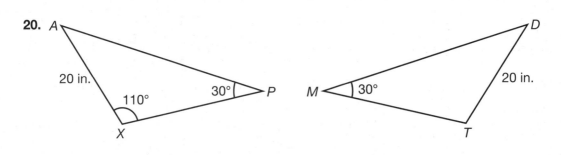

Determine whether there is enough information to prove that each pair of triangles are congruent by ASA or AAS. Write the congruence statements to justify your reasoning.

21. △ABD ≟ △CBD

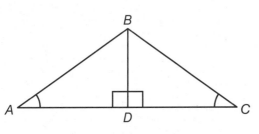

The triangles are congruent by AAS.

∠BAD ≅ ∠BCD

∠ADB ≅ ∠CDB

$\overline{BD} \cong \overline{BD}$

22. △EFG ≟ △HJK

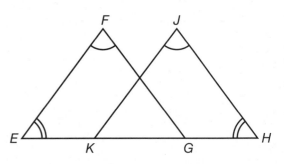

23. △MNQ ≟ △PQN

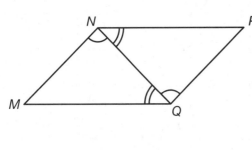

24. △RST ≟ △WZT

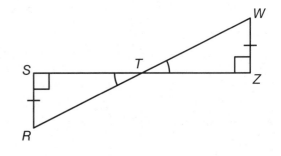

Name _____ Date _____

25. $\triangle BDM \overset{?}{\cong} \triangle MDH$

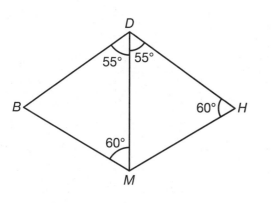

26. $\triangle FGH \overset{?}{\cong} \triangle JHG$

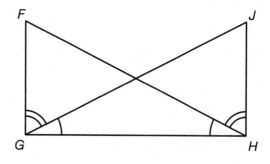

27. $\triangle DFG \overset{?}{\cong} \triangle JMT$

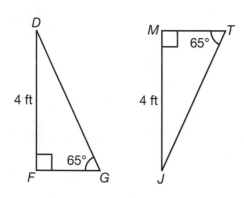

28. $\triangle RST \overset{?}{\cong} \triangle WXY$

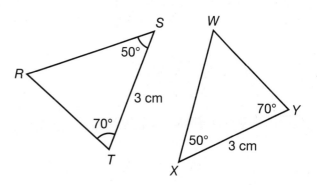

Name _____ Date _____

Transforming to a New Level!
Using Transformations to Determine Perimeter and Area

Problem Set

Translate each given rectangle or square such that one vertex of the image is located at the origin and label the vertices of the image. Calculate the perimeter and area of the image.

1. Rectangle *ABCD*

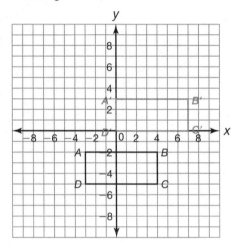

$A'B' = 7, B'C' = 3, C'D' = 7, A'D' = 3$

Perimeter of $A'B'C'D' = A'B' + B'C' + C'D' + A'D'$
$$= 7 + 3 + 7 + 3$$
$$= 20$$
The perimeter of $A'B'C'D'$ is 20 units.

Area of $A'B'C'D' = bh$
$$= 7(3)$$
$$= 21$$
The area of $A'B'C'D'$ is 21 square units.

2. Square *EFGH*

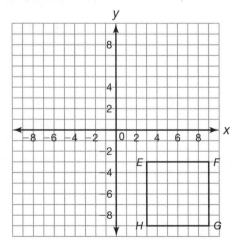

3. Rectangle *JKLM*

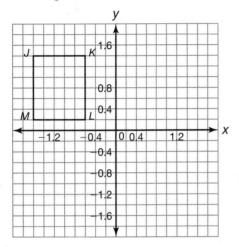

4. Square *PQRS*

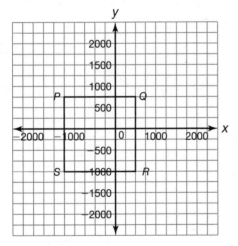

Name _____ Date _____

5. Rectangle *WXYZ*

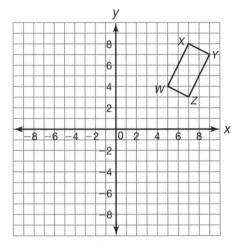

6. Square *AFTZ*

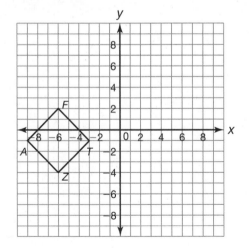

14

7. Rectangle *BHQY*

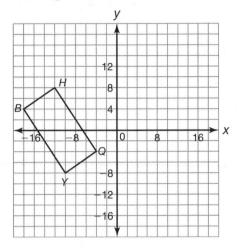

8. Square *DMTW*

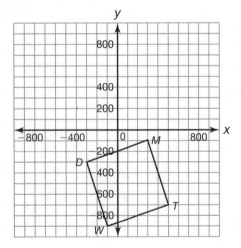

Name _____ Date _____

Looking at Something Familiar in a New Way
Area and Perimeter of Triangles on the Coordinate Plane

Problem Set

Determine the perimeter of each given triangle on the coordinate plane. Round your answer to the nearest hundredth, if necessary.

1. Triangle *ABC*

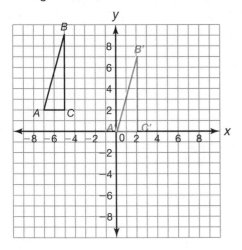

$A'C' = 2, B'C' = 7$

$A'B' = \sqrt{(x_2 - x_1)^2 + (y_2 - y_1)^2}$

$\qquad = \sqrt{(2 - 0)^2 + (7 - 0)^2}$

$\qquad = \sqrt{(2)^2 + (7)^2}$

$\qquad = \sqrt{4 + 49}$

$\qquad = \sqrt{53}$

Perimeter $= A'B' + B'C' + A'C'$

$\qquad\quad = \sqrt{53} + 7 + 2$

$\qquad\quad \approx 16.28$

The perimeter is approximately 16.28 units.

2. Triangle *DEF*

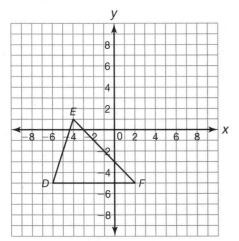

3. Triangle *GHJ*

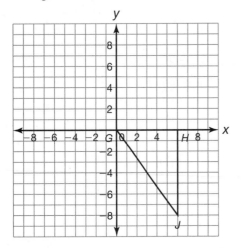

4. Triangle *RST*

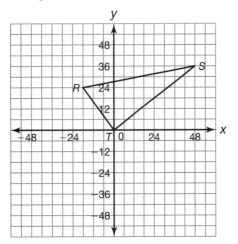

14

Name _____ Date _____

5. Triangle *JKL*

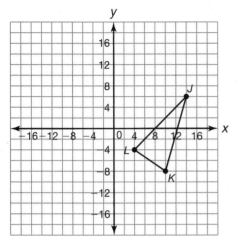

6. Triangle *TUV*

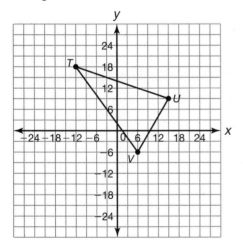

14

Determine the area of each given triangle on the coordinate plane. Round your answer to the nearest hundredth, if necessary.

7. Triangle *WXY*

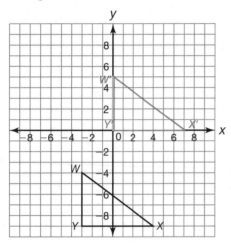

$W'Y' = 5, X'Y' = 7$

$Area = \frac{1}{2} bh$

$= \frac{1}{2} (7)(5)$

$= 17.5$

The area is 17.5 square units.

8. Triangle *ACE*

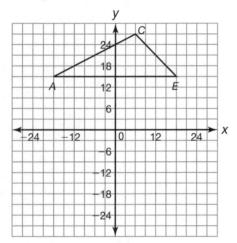

Name _____ Date _____

9. Triangle *DEF*

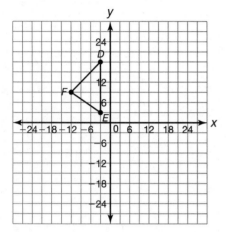

10. Triangle *JKL*

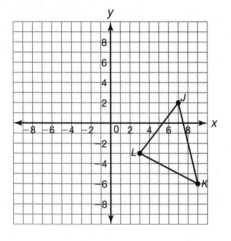

14

11. Triangle *KMN*

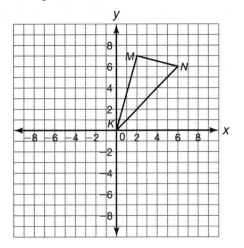

Name _____ Date _____

12. Triangle *ATV*

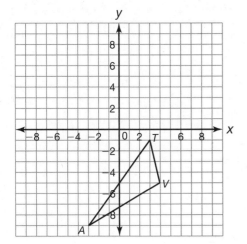

14

Double the area of each triangle as directed. Label the image then calculate the area of the pre-image and the area of the image to verify your solution.

13. Double the area of triangle *DMP* by manipulating the height. Label the image *DM'P*.

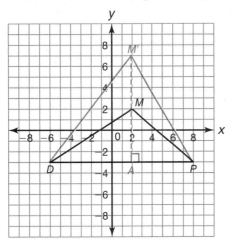

$AM = 5, DP = 14$

Area of triangle *DMP*:

$Area = \dfrac{1}{2} bh$

$= \dfrac{1}{2}(14)(5)$

$= 35$

The area of triangle *DMP* is 35 square units.

$AM' = 10$

Area of triangle *DM'P*:

$Area = \dfrac{1}{2} bh$

$= \dfrac{1}{2}(14)(10)$

$= 70$

The area of triangle *DM'P* is 70 square units.

The area of triangle *DM'P* is double the area of triangle *DMP*.

14. Double the area of triangle *HNW* by manipulating the height. Label the image *HN'W*.

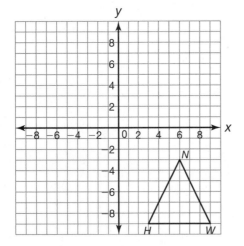

14

Name _____ Date _____

15. Double the area of triangle *MLP* manipulating the height. Label the image *MLP'*.

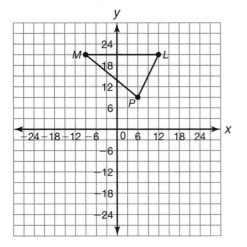

16. Double the area of triangle *MFD* by manipulating the base. Label the image *M'FD*.

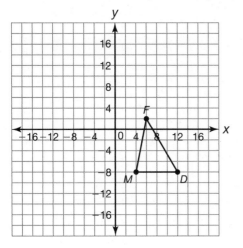

17. Double the area of triangle *ART* by manipulating the base. Label the image *AR'T*.

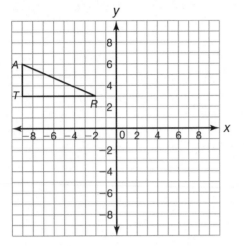

18. Double the area of triangle *QTZ* by manipulating the base. Label the image *Q'TZ*.

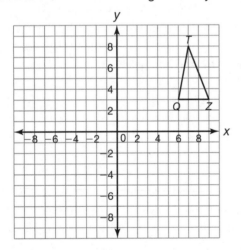

Name _____ Date _____

One Figure, Many Names
Area and Perimeter of Parallelograms on the Coordinate Plane

Problem Set

Determine the perimeter of each given parallelogram on the coordinate plane. Round your answer to the nearest hundredth, if necessary.

1. Parallelogram *ABCD*

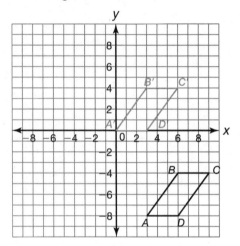

$A'D' = B'C' = 3$

$A'B' = \sqrt{(x_2 - x_1)^2 + (y_2 - y_1)^2}$

$\quad\;\; = \sqrt{(3 - 0)^2 + (4 - 0)^2}$

$\quad\;\; = \sqrt{(3)^2 + (4)^2}$

$\quad\;\; = \sqrt{9 + 16}$

$\quad\;\; = \sqrt{25}$

$\quad\;\; = 5$

$C'D' = A'B' = 5$

Perimeter $= A'B' + B'C' + C'D' + A'D'$

$\quad\quad\quad\;\;\; = 5 + 3 + 5 + 3$

$\quad\quad\quad\;\;\; = 16$

The perimeter is 16 units.

2. Parallelogram *EFGH*

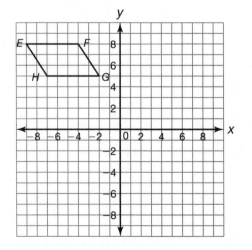

3. Parallelogram *RSTU*

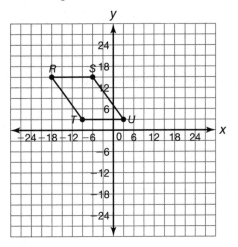

4. Parallelogram *WXYZ*

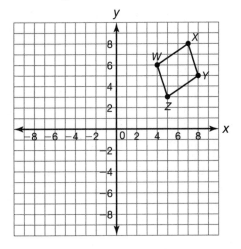

Name _____ Date _____

5. Parallelogram *JKLM*

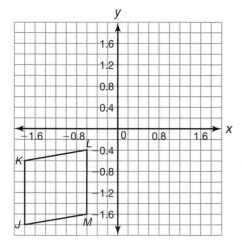

6. Parallelogram *NPQR*

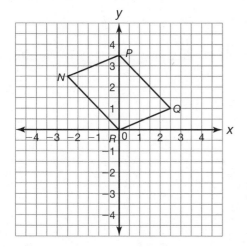

14

Determine the area of each given parallelogram on the coordinate plane. Round your answer to the nearest hundredth, if necessary.

7. Parallelogram *STVZ*

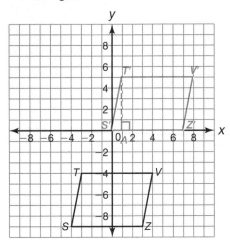

$AT' = 5, S'Z' = 7$

$Area = bh$

$\quad = (7)(5)$

$\quad = 35$

The area is 35 square units.

8. Parallelogram *AFMT*.

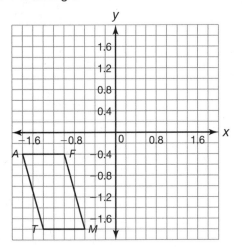

Name _____ Date _____

9. Parallelogram *NEST*

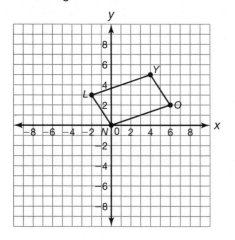

10. Parallelogram *LYON*

14

11. Parallelogram *BGNP*

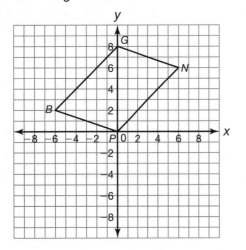

Name _____ Date _____

12. Parallelogram *DJQW*

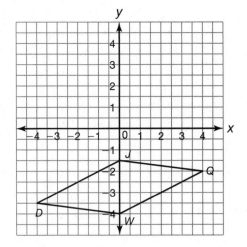

14

Double the area of each parallelogram as directed. Label the image, and then calculate the area of the pre-image and the image to verify your solution.

13. Double the area of parallelogram *GNRT* by manipulating the base. Label the image *GN'R'T*.

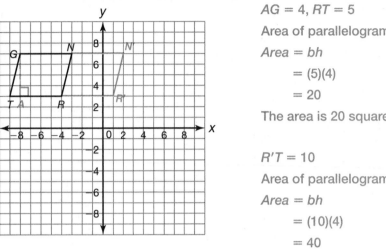

$AG = 4$, $RT = 5$

Area of parallelogram *GNRT*:

$Area = bh$

$= (5)(4)$

$= 20$

The area is 20 square units.

$R'T = 10$

Area of parallelogram *GN'R'T*:

$Area = bh$

$= (10)(4)$

$= 40$

The area is 40 square units.

The area of parallelogram *GN'R'T* is double the area of parallelogram *GNRT*.

14. Double the area of parallelogram *AHSW* by manipulating the base. Label the image *A'H'SW*.

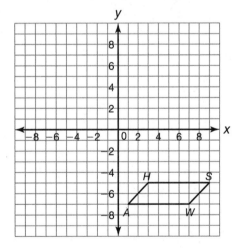

14

Name _____ Date _____

15. Double the area of parallelogram *BASK* by manipulating the base. Label the image *BA'S'K*.

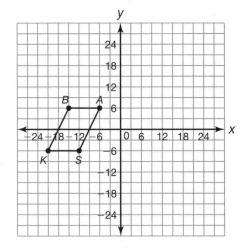

16. Double the area of parallelogram *DOGZ* by manipulating the height. Label the image *DOG'Z'*.

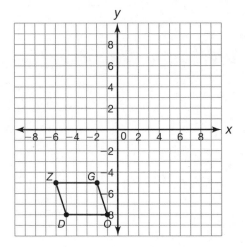

14

17. Double the area of parallelogram *CFTV* by manipulating the height. Label the image *C'FTV'*.

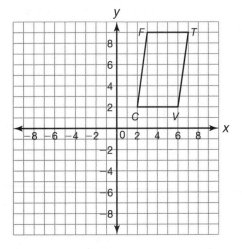

18. Double the area of parallelogram *JMTW* by manipulating the height. Label the image *JMT'W'*.

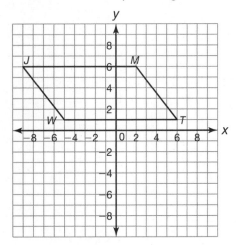

Name _____ Date _____

Let's Go Halfsies!
Determining the Perimeter and Area of Trapezoids and Composite Figures

Vocabulary

Define each term in your own words.

1. bases of a trapezoid

2. legs of a trapezoid

3. regular polygon

4. composite figures

Problem Set

Determine the perimeter of each given figure on the coordinate plane. Round your answer to the nearest hundredth, if necessary.

1. Trapezoid *ABCD*

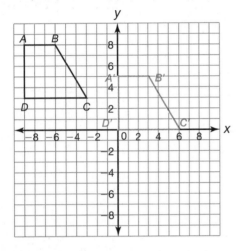

$A'B' = 3, A'D' = 5, C'D' = 6$

$B'C' = \sqrt{(x_2 - x_1)^2 + (y_2 - y_1)^2}$

$\quad = \sqrt{(6 - 3)^2 + (0 - 5)^2}$

$\quad = \sqrt{(3)^2 + (-5)^2}$

$\quad = \sqrt{9 + 25}$

$\quad = \sqrt{34}$

Perimeter $= A'B' + B'C' + C'D' + A'D'$

$\quad = 3 + \sqrt{34} + 6 + 5$

$\quad \approx 19.83$

The perimeter is approximately 19.83 units.

2. Trapezoid *EFGH*

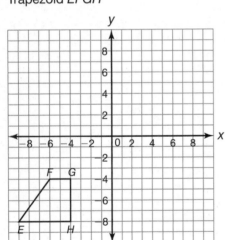

14

Name _____ Date _____

3. Figure *PQRST*

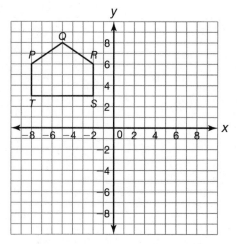

4. Figure *ABCDEF*

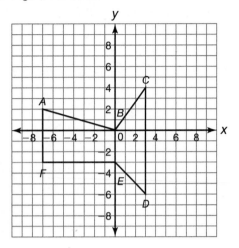

Name _____ Date _____

5. Regular hexagon *ABCDEF* with coordinates $A(-5\sqrt{3}, 15)$, $B(0, 20)$, $C(5\sqrt{3}, 15)$, $D(5\sqrt{3}, 5)$, $E(0, 0)$, and $F(-5\sqrt{3}, 5)$

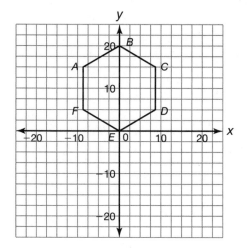

6. Regular octagon *JKLMNPQR* with coordinates $J(-6 - 6\sqrt{2}, 6)$, $K(-6, 6 + 6\sqrt{2})$, $L(6, 6 + 6\sqrt{2})$, $M(6 + 6\sqrt{2}, 6)$, $N(6 + 6\sqrt{2}, -6)$, $P(6, -6 - 6\sqrt{2})$, $Q(-6, -6 - 6\sqrt{2})$, and $R(-6 - 6\sqrt{2}, -6)$

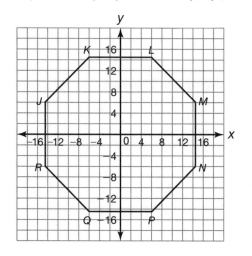

14

Determine the area of each given figure in the coordinate plane. Round your answer to the nearest hundredth, if necessary.

7. Trapezoid *WXYZ*

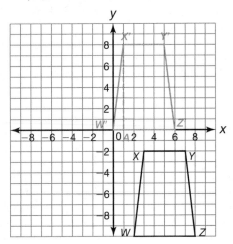

$AX' = 8$, $W'Z' = 6$, $X'Y' = 4$

$Area = \dfrac{1}{2}(b_1 + b_2)h$

$\quad = \dfrac{1}{2}(6 + 4)(8)$

$\quad = \dfrac{1}{2}(10)(8)$

$\quad = 40$

The area is 40 square units.

8. Trapezoid *ACES*

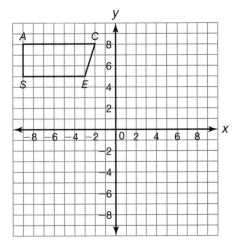

Name _____ Date _____

9. Trapezoid *BEST*

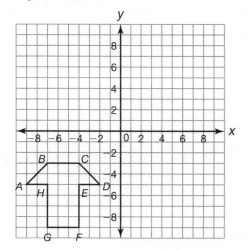

10. Figure *ABCDEFGH*

11. Figure *JKLMNOPQ*

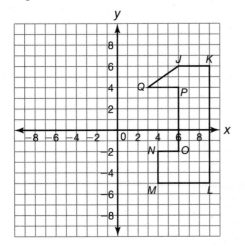

Name _____ Date _____

12. Figure *MNPQRST*

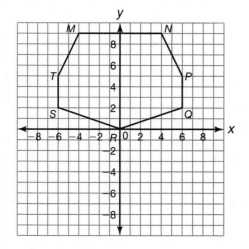

14

Name _____ Date _____

Name That Triangle!
Classifying Triangles on the Coordinate Plane

Problem Set

Determine the location of point C such that triangle ABC has each given characteristic. The graph shows line segment AB.

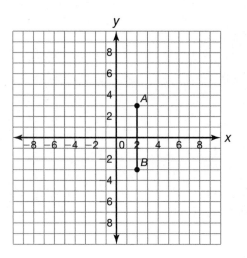

1. Triangle ABC is a right triangle.

Point C can have an infinite number of locations as long as the location satisfies one of the following conditions:
- Point C could be located anywhere on line $y = 3$ except where $x = 2$.
- Point C could be located anywhere on line $y = -3$ except where $x = 2$.

2. Triangle ABC is an acute triangle.

3. Triangle *ABC* is an obtuse triangle.

4. Triangle *ABC* is an equilateral triangle.

5. Triangle *ABC* is an isosceles triangle.

6. Triangle *ABC* is a scalene triangle.

Name _____ Date _____

Graph triangle *ABC* using each set of given points. Determine if triangle *ABC* is scalene, isosceles, or equilateral.

7. $A(-3, 1)$, $B(-3, -3)$, $C(1, 0)$

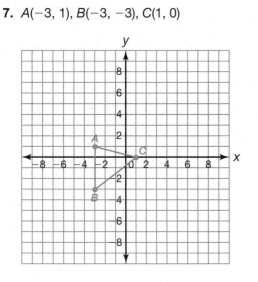

$$AB = 1 - (-3)$$
$$= 4$$

$$BC = \sqrt{(x_2 - x_1)^2 + (y_2 - y_1)^2}$$
$$= \sqrt{(1 - (-3))^2 + (0 - (-3))^2}$$
$$= \sqrt{(4)^2 + (3)^2}$$
$$= \sqrt{16 + 9}$$
$$= \sqrt{25}$$
$$= 5$$

$$AC = \sqrt{(x_2 - x_1)^2 + (y_2 - y_1)^2}$$
$$= \sqrt{(-3 - 1)^2 + (1 - 0)^2}$$
$$= \sqrt{(-4)^2 + (1)^2}$$
$$= \sqrt{16 + 1}$$
$$= \sqrt{17}$$

Because each of the side lengths are different, triangle *ABC* is scalene.

8. $A(8, 5)$, $B(8, 1)$, $C(4, 3)$

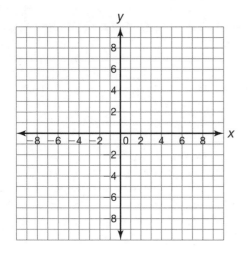

9. A(5, 8), B(5, 2), C(−3, 5)

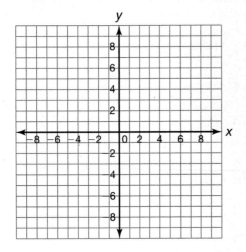

10. A(−2, −6), B(6, −6), C(2, −3)

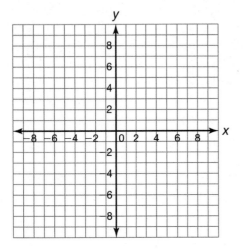

Name _____ Date _____

11. $A(0, 0)$, $B(4, 0)$, $C(3, 7)$

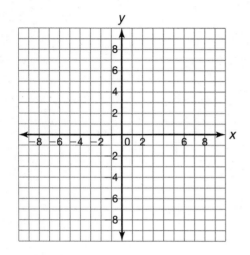

12. $A(-6, 4)$, $B(0, 4)$, $C(-2, -2)$

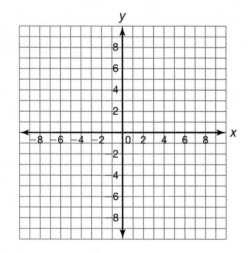

Graph triangle *ABC* using each set of given points. Determine if triangle *ABC* is a right triangle, an acute triangle, or an obtuse triangle.

13. *A*(0, 4), *B*(4, 5), *C*(1, 0)

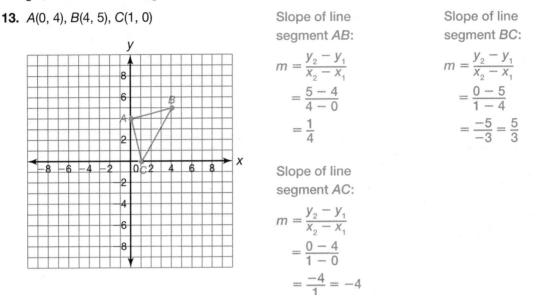

Slope of line segment *AB*:

$$m = \frac{y_2 - y_1}{x_2 - x_1}$$

$$= \frac{5 - 4}{4 - 0}$$

$$= \frac{1}{4}$$

Slope of line segment *BC*:

$$m = \frac{y_2 - y_1}{x_2 - x_1}$$

$$= \frac{0 - 5}{1 - 4}$$

$$= \frac{-5}{-3} = \frac{5}{3}$$

Slope of line segment *AC*:

$$m = \frac{y_2 - y_1}{x_2 - x_1}$$

$$= \frac{0 - 4}{1 - 0}$$

$$= \frac{-4}{1} = -4$$

The slope of line segments *AB* and *AC* are negative reciprocals and therefore form a right angle. Triangle *ABC* is a right triangle.

14. *A*(−6, 1), *B*(−6, −4), *C*(4, 0)

Name _____ Date _____

15. $A(-5, 7), B(7, 7), C(1, 4)$

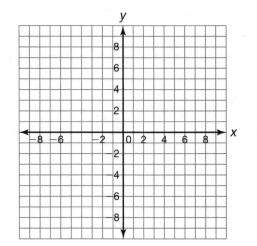

16. $A(-4, -1), B(1, 3), C(3, -4)$

17. A(2, 6), B(8, −3), C(2, −7)

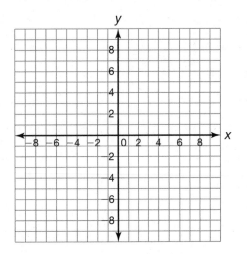

18. A(−2, 6), B(6, −3), C(0, 0)

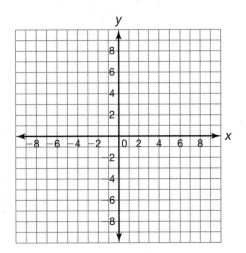

Name _____ Date _____

Name That Quadrilateral!
Classifying Quadrilaterals on the Coordinate Plane

Problem Set

For each set of given points, determine the location of a fourth point such that the described figure is created.

1. The graph shows vertices $A(1, 6)$, $B(-1, 0)$ and $C(5, -2)$. Determine the location of vertex D such that quadrilateral $ABCD$ is a square.

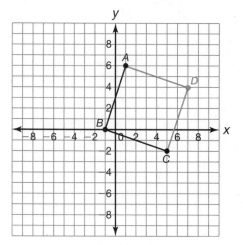

Slope of AB and CD:

$$m = \frac{y_2 - y_1}{x_2 - x_1}$$

$$= \frac{0 - 6}{-1 - 1}$$

$$= \frac{-6}{-2} = 3$$

Slope of BC and AD:

$$m = \frac{y_2 - y_1}{x_2 - x_1}$$

$$m = \frac{-2 - 0}{5 - (-1)}$$

$$= \frac{-2}{6} = -\frac{1}{3}$$

Equation of line that passes through point C:

$$y - y_1 = m(x - x_1)$$
$$y - (-2) = 3(x - 5)$$
$$y + 2 = 3x - 15$$
$$y = 3x - 17$$

Equation of line that passes through point A:

$$y - y_1 = m(x - x_1)$$
$$y - 6 = -\frac{1}{3}(x - 1)$$
$$y - 6 = -\frac{1}{3}x + \frac{1}{3}$$
$$y = -\frac{1}{3}x + \frac{19}{3}$$

Solution to the system of equations:

$$3x - 17 = -\frac{1}{3}x + \frac{19}{3}$$
$$9x - 51 = -x + 19$$
$$10x = 70$$
$$x = 7$$

$$y = 3x - 17$$
$$y = 3(7) - 17$$
$$y = 21 - 17$$
$$y = 4$$

The coordinates of point D are $(7, 4)$.

2. The graph shows vertices $A(2, 4)$, $B(8, 0)$ and $C(4, -6)$. Determine the location of vertex D such that quadrilateral $ABCD$ is a square.

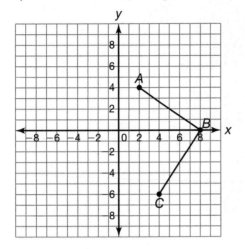

Name _____ Date _____

3. The graph shows vertices $A(-3, 5)$, $B(-5, 1)$ and $C(-1, -1)$. Determine the location of vertex D such that quadrilateral $ABCD$ is a trapezoid.

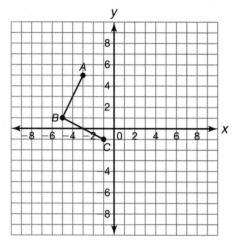

4. The graph shows vertices $A(6, 2)$, $B(2, -4)$ and $C(-4, 0)$. Determine the location of vertex D such that quadrilateral $ABCD$ is a trapezoid.

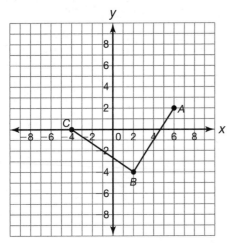

Name _____ Date _____

5. The graph shows vertices $A(-2, -2)$, $B(0, 6)$ and $C(8, 4)$. Determine the location of vertex D such that quadrilateral $ABCD$ is a square.

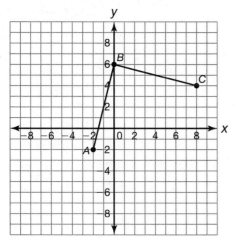

6. The graph shows vertices $A(-3, 2)$, $B(-2, 7)$, and $C(3, 6)$. Determine the location of vertex D such that quadrilateral $ABCD$ is a trapezoid.

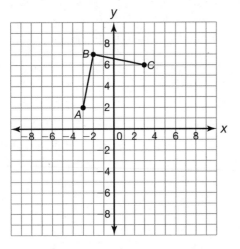

Name _____ Date _____

Graph quadrilateral *ABCD* using each set of given points. Determine if quadrilateral *ABCD* can be best described as a trapezoid, a square, a rectangle, or a rhombus.

7. $A(-4, -2)$, $B(2, 4)$, $C(8, -2)$, $D(2, -8)$

The slopes of the line segments have a negative reciprocal relationship. This means the line segments are perpendicular, which means the angles must be right angles. Also, the opposite sides have the same slope, so the opposite sides are parallel. Finally, all four sides are congruent. Quadrilateral *ABCD* can best be described as a square.

$$AB = \sqrt{(x_2 - x_1)^2 + (y_2 - y_1)^2}$$
$$= \sqrt{(-4 - 2)^2 + (-2 - 4)^2}$$
$$= \sqrt{(-6)^2 + (-6)^2}$$
$$= \sqrt{36 + 36}$$
$$= \sqrt{72}$$

$$BC = \sqrt{(x_2 - x_1)^2 + (y_2 - y_1)^2}$$
$$= \sqrt{(2 - 8)^2 + (4 - (-2))^2}$$
$$= \sqrt{(-6)^2 + (6)^2}$$
$$= \sqrt{36 + 36}$$
$$= \sqrt{72}$$

$$CD = \sqrt{(x_2 - x_1)^2 + (y_2 - y_1)^2}$$
$$= \sqrt{(8 - 2)^2 + (-2 - (-8))^2}$$
$$= \sqrt{(6)^2 + (6)^2}$$
$$= \sqrt{36 + 36}$$
$$= \sqrt{72}$$

$$AD = \sqrt{(x_2 - x_1)^2 + (y_2 - y_1)^2}$$
$$= \sqrt{(-4 - 2)^2 + (-2 - (-8))^2}$$
$$= \sqrt{(-6)^2 + (6)^2}$$
$$= \sqrt{36 + 36}$$
$$= \sqrt{72}$$

Slope of line segment *AB*: $m = \dfrac{y_2 - y_1}{x_2 - x_1}$
$$= \dfrac{-2 - 4}{-4 - 2}$$
$$= \dfrac{-6}{-6} = 1$$

Slope of line segment *BC*: $m = \dfrac{y_2 - y_1}{x_2 - x_1}$
$$= \dfrac{4 - (-2)}{2 - 8}$$
$$= \dfrac{6}{-6} = -1$$

Slope of line segment *CD*: $m = \dfrac{y_2 - y_1}{x_2 - x_1}$
$$= \dfrac{-2 - (-8)}{8 - 2}$$
$$= \dfrac{6}{6} = 1$$

Slope of line segment *AD*: $m = \dfrac{y_2 - y_1}{x_2 - x_1}$
$$= \dfrac{-2 - (-8)}{-4 - 2}$$
$$= \dfrac{6}{-6} = -1$$

8. $A(0, 6)$, $B(3, 4)$, $C(-1, -2)$, $D(-4, 0)$

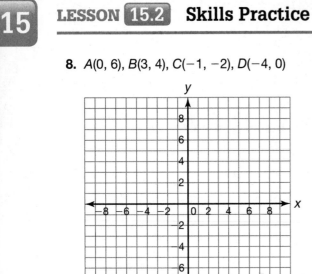

Name _____ Date _____

9. $A(1, 0)$, $B(2, 4)$, $C(10, 2)$, $D(5, -1)$

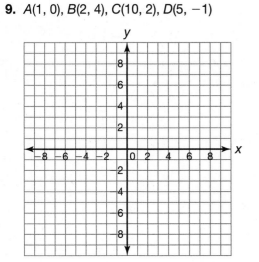

10. *A*(−5, 3), *B*(0, 6), *C*(5, 3), *D*(0, 0)

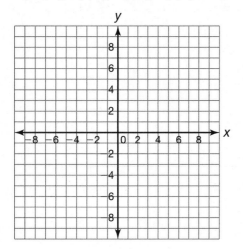

Name _____ Date _____

Is That Point on the Circle?
Determining Points on a Circle

Problem Set

For each question assume circle A has a center at the origin and the given radius or diameter. Determine if each point B lies on the circle.

1. radius: 13; $B(5, 12)$

$$AB = \sqrt{(x_2 - x_1)^2 + (y_2 - y_1)^2}$$
$$= \sqrt{(5 - 0)^2 + (12 - 0)^2}$$
$$= \sqrt{(5)^2 + (12)^2}$$
$$= \sqrt{25 + 144}$$
$$= \sqrt{169}$$
$$= 13$$

The length of segment AB is the same length as the radius of circle A. Therefore point B must lie on circle A.

2. diameter: 12; $B(4, 5)$

3. radius: 10; $B(6, 8)$

4. diameter: 10; $B(-3, 4)$

5. radius: 2.5; $B(-1.5, -2.5)$

6. radius: 7.5; $B(-4.5, -6)$

For each question assume circle A has the given center and radius or a point, C, that lies on the circle. Determine if each point B lies on circle A.

7. center: $(6, 5)$; radius: 5; $B(3, 9)$

$$AB = \sqrt{(x_2 - x_1)^2 + (y_2 - y_1)^2}$$
$$= \sqrt{(6 - 3)^2 + (5 - 9)^2}$$
$$= \sqrt{(3)^2 + (-4)^2}$$
$$= \sqrt{9 + 16}$$
$$= \sqrt{25}$$
$$= 5$$

The length of segment AB is the same length as the radius of circle A. Therefore point B must lie on circle A.

8. center: $(-8, -7)$; radius: 15; $B(1, 4)$

Name _____ Date _____

9. center: $(-2, 4)$; $C(4, 1.5)$; $B(4, 5.5)$

10. center: $(2, -6)$; $C(7, 6)$; $B(-3, 6)$

11. center: $(8, 2)$; radius: 2; $B(7, -1)$

12. center: $(-5, 0)$; $C(-1, -7.5)$; $B(2.5, 4)$

Transform each circle as described then determine if point *B* lies on the image.

13. Circle *A* has a center at $(-5, -4)$ and a radius of 3.25. Circle *A* is reflected over the *x*-axis to form the image circle *A'*. Graph circle *A* and circle *A'*. Determine if $B(-2, 5.25)$ lies on circle *A'*.

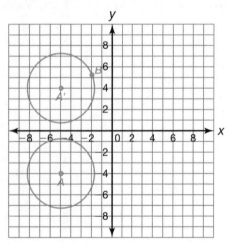

The radius of circle *A'* equals the radius of circle *A*.

The center of circle *A'* is at $(-5, 4)$.

$$A'B = \sqrt{(x_2 - x_1)^2 + (y_2 - y_1)^2}$$
$$= \sqrt{(-5 - (-2))^2 + (4 - 5.25)^2}$$
$$= \sqrt{(-3)^2 + (-1.25)^2}$$
$$= \sqrt{9 + 1.5625}$$
$$= \sqrt{10.5625}$$
$$= 3.25$$

The length of segment *A'B* is the same length as the radius of circle *A'*. Therefore point *B* must lie on circle *A'*.

Name _____ Date _____

14. Circle *A* has a center at (3, 5) and includes point *C*(7, 2). Circle *A* is reflected over the *x*-axis to form the image circle *A'*. Graph circle *A* and circle *A'*. Determine if *B*(−1, −2) lies on circle *A'*.

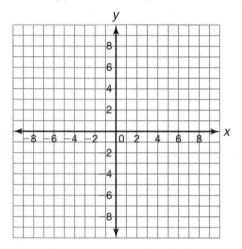

15. Circle *A* has a center at (8, 4) and a radius of 10. Circle *A* is reflected over the *y*-axis to form the image circle *A'*. Graph circle *A* and circle *A'*. Determine if *B*(−6, 14) lies on circle *A'*.

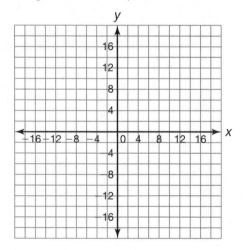

16. Circle *A* has a center at (7, −3) and includes *C*(5, −1). Circle *A* is reflected over the *y*-axis to form the image circle *A'*. Graph circle *A* and circle *A'*. Determine if *B*(−4, −3) lies on circle *A'*.

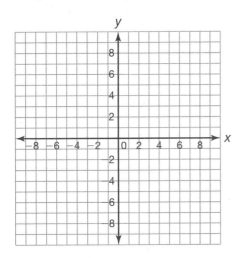

17. Circle *A* has a center at (−5, −6) and a radius of √13. Circle *A* is reflected over the *x*-axis to form the image circle *A'*. Graph circle *A* and circle *A'*. Determine if *B*(−2, 8) lies on circle *A'*.

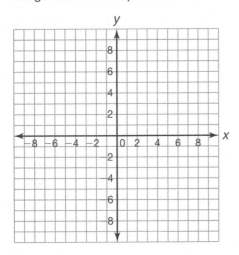

Name _____ Date _____

18. Circle A has a center at (2, 5) and includes C(5, 2). Circle A is reflected over the x-axis to form the image circle A'. Graph circle A and circle A'. Determine if B(4, −1) lies on circle A'.

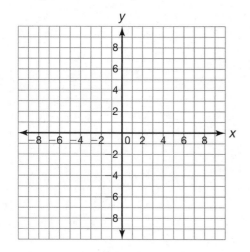

Name _____ Date _____

Name That Point on the Circle
Circles and Points on the Coordinate Plane

Problem Set

For each question assume circle A is centered at the origin and has the given radius. Complete each table by determining the coordinates of five points described.

1.

Radius of circle A	x-intercepts	y-intercepts	Point in Quadrant I
13	(13, 0)	(0, 13)	(12, 5)
	(−13, 0)	(0, −13)	

Answers will vary.

$a^2 + b^2 = c^2$

$12^2 + b^2 = 13^2$

$144 + b^2 = 169$

$b^2 = 25$

$b = \pm 5$

2.

Radius of circle A	x-intercepts	y-intercepts	Point in Quadrant II
15			

3.

Radius of circle *A*	*x*-intercepts	*y*-intercepts	Point in Quadrant III
2.5			

4.

Radius of circle *A*	*x*-intercepts	*y*-intercepts	Point in Quadrant IV
7.5			

5.

Radius of circle *A*	*x*-intercepts	*y*-intercepts	Point in Quadrant I
6.5			

Name _____ Date _____

6.

Radius of circle A	x-intercepts	y-intercepts	Point in Quadrant II
17			

Complete each table by determining the coordinates of the points described.

7. Circle *A* is centered at (3, 2) and has a radius of 5. Determine the coordinates of four points on the circle such that the points lie directly above, below, right and left of the center point. Determine the *y*-coordinate of point *B* on circle *A* if the *x*-coordinate of point *B* is 6. Determine the coordinates of point *C* which is the result of reflecting point *B* horizontally about the center point of circle *A*.

Center	Radius	Points Above & Below Center	Points Right & Left of Center	Point B	Point C
(3, 2)	5	(3, 7)	(8, 2)	(6, 6)	(0, 6)
		(3, −3)	(−2, 2)		

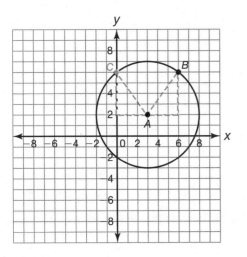

Vertical distance to Point *B*:

$a^2 + b^2 = c^2$

$3^2 + b^2 = 5^2$

$9 + b^2 = 25$

$b^2 = 16$

$b = \pm 4$

$2 + 4 = 6$

The coordinates of Point *B* are (6, 6).

Reflection of Point *B*:

$3 - 3 = 0$

$2 + 4 = 6$

The coordinates of Point *C* are (0, 6).

8. Circle *A* is centered at (−5, 4) and has a radius of 2.5. Determine the coordinates of four points on the circle such that the points lie directly above, below, right, and left of the center point. Determine the *y*-coordinate of point *B* on circle *A* if the *x*-coordinate of point *B* is −3. Determine the coordinates of point *C* which is the result of reflecting point *B* horizontally about the center point of circle *A*.

Center	Radius	Points Above & Below Center	Points Right & Left of Center	Point *B*	Point *C*

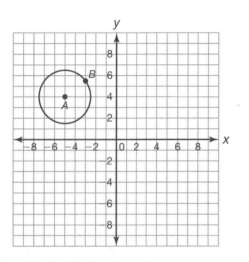

Name _____ Date _____

9. Circle *A* is centered at (3, 4) and has a radius of $3\sqrt{2}$. Determine the coordinates of four points on the circle such that the points lie directly above, below, right, and left of the center point. Determine the *y*-coordinate of point *B* on circle *A* if the *x*-coordinate of point *B* is 6. Determine the coordinates of point *C* which is the result of reflecting point *B* vertically about the center point of circle *A*.

Center	Radius	Points Above & Below Center	Points Right & Left of Center	Point *B*	Point *C*

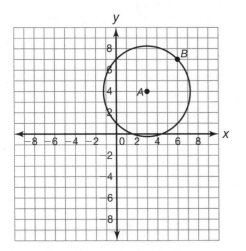

10. Circle *A* is centered at (−1, 1) and has a radius of 7.5. Determine the coordinates of four points on the circle such that the points lie directly above, below, right, and left of the center point. Determine the *y*-coordinate of point *B* on circle *A* if the *x*-coordinate of point *B* is −7. Determine the coordinates of point *C* which is the result of reflecting point *B* vertically about the center point of circle *A*.

Center	Radius	Points Above & Below Center	Points Right & Left of Center	Point *B*	Point *C*

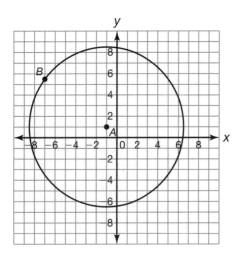

Name _____ Date _____

11. Circle *A* is centered at (8, −6) and has a radius of 10. Determine the coordinates of four points on the circle such that the points lie directly above, below, right, and left of the center point. Determine the *y*-coordinate of point *B* on circle *A* if the *x*-coordinate of point *B* is 16. Determine the coordinates of point *C* which is the result of reflecting point *B* horizontally about the center point of circle *A*.

Center	Radius	Points Above & Below Center	Points Right & Left of Center	Point *B*	Point *C*

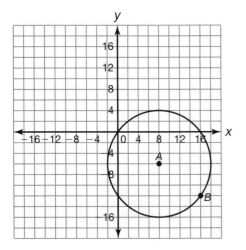

12. Circle *A* is centered at (4, 8) and has a radius of 6. Determine the coordinates of four points on the circle such that the points lie directly above, below, right, and left of the center point. Determine the *y*-coordinate of point *B* on circle *A* if the *x*-coordinate of point *B* is 6. Determine the coordinates of point *C* which is the result of reflecting point *B* horizontally about the center point of circle *A*.

Center	Radius	Points Above & Below Center	Points Right & Left of Center	Point *B*	Point *C*

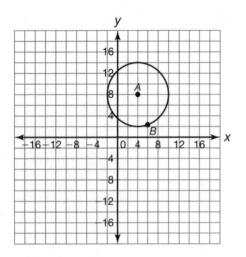

Name _____ Date _____

A Little Dash of Logic
Two Methods of Logical Reasoning

Vocabulary

Define each term in your own words.

1. inductive reasoning

2. deductive reasoning

Problem Set

Identify the specific information, the general information, and the conclusion for each problem situation.

1. You read an article in the paper that says a high-fat diet increases a person's risk of heart disease. You know your father has a lot of fat in his diet, so you worry that he is at higher risk of heart disease.

Specific information: Your father has a lot of fat in his diet.

General information: High-fat diets increase the risk of heart disease.

Conclusion: Your father is at higher risk of heart disease.

2. You hear from your teacher that spending too much time in the sun without sunblock increases the risk of skin cancer. Your friend Susan spends as much time as she can outside working on her tan without sunscreen, so you tell her that she is increasing her risk of skin cancer when she is older.

16

3. Janice tells you that she has been to the mall three times in the past week, and every time there were a lot of people there. "It's always crowded at the mall," she says.

4. John returns from a trip out West and reports that it was over 100 degrees every day. "It's always hot out West," he says.

5. Mario watched 3 parades this summer. Each parade had a fire truck lead the parade. He concluded "A fire truck always leads a parade."

6. Ava read an article that said eating too much sugar can lead to tooth decay and cavities. Ava noticed that her little brother Phillip eats a lot of sugar. She concludes that Phillip's teeth will decay and develop cavities.

Determine whether inductive reasoning or deductive reasoning is used in each situation. Then determine whether the conclusion is correct and explain your reasoning.

7. Jason sees a line of 10 school buses and notices that each is yellow. He concludes that all school buses must be yellow.

It is inductive reasoning because he has observed specific examples of a phenomenon—the color of school buses—and come up with a general rule based on those specific examples.

The conclusion is not necessarily true. It may be the case, for example, that all or most of the school buses in this school district are yellow, while another school district may have orange school buses.

Name _____ Date _____

8. Caitlyn has been told that every taxi in New York City is yellow. When she sees a red car in New York City, she concludes that it cannot be a taxi.

9. Miriam has been told that lightning never strikes twice in the same place. During a lightning storm, she sees a tree struck by lightning and goes to stand next to it, convinced that it is the safest place to be.

10. Jose is shown the first six numbers of a series of numbers: 7, 11, 15, 19, 23, 27. He concludes that the general rule for the series of numbers is $a_n = 4n + 3$.

11. Isabella sees 5 red fire trucks. She concludes that all fire trucks are red.

12. Carlos is told that all garter snakes are not venomous. He sees a garter snake in his backyard and concludes that it is not venomous.

In each situation, identify whether each person is using inductive or deductive reasoning. Then compare and contrast the two types of reasoning.

13. When Madison babysat for the Johnsons for the first time, she was there 2 hours and was paid $30. The next time she was there for 5 hours and was paid $75. She decided that the Johnsons were paying her $15 per hour. The third time she went, she stayed for 4 hours. She tells her friend Jennifer that she makes $15 per hour babysitting. So, Jennifer predicted that Madison made $60 for her 4-hour babysitting job.

Madison used inductive reasoning to conclude that the Johnsons were paying her at a rate of $15 per hour. From that general rule, Jennifer used deductive reasoning to conclude that 4 hours of babysitting should result in a payment of $60. The inductive reasoning looks at evidence and creates a general rule from the evidence. By contrast, the deductive reasoning starts with a general rule and makes a prediction or deduction about what will happen in a particular instance.

14. When Holly was young, the only birds she ever saw were black crows. So, she told her little brother Walter that all birds are black. When Walter saw a bluebird for the first time, he was sure it had to be something other than a bird.

15. Tamika is flipping a coin and recording the results. She records the following results: heads, tails, heads, tails, heads, tails, heads. She tells her friend Javon that the coin alternates between heads and tails for each toss. Javon tells her that the next time the coin is flipped, it will definitely be tails.

Name _____ Date _____

16
16. John likes to watch the long coal trains moving past his house. Over the weeks of watching he notices that every train going east is filled with coal, but the trains heading west are all empty. He tells his friend Richard that all trains heading east have coal and all trains heading west are empty. When Richard hears a train coming from the west, he concludes that it will certainly be filled with coal.

17. Vance earned $60 mowing 5 lawns last weekend for the Greenvalley Homeowners Association. Vance concluded that he earned $12 for each lawn. Vance told Sherwin that he planned to mow 7 lawns for Greenvalley next weekend. Sherwin concluded that Vance would earn $84 mowing the 7 lawns.

18. As a child, the only frogs Emily ever saw were green. Emily told Juan that all frogs are green. When Juan visited a zoo and saw a blue poison dart frog he concluded that it must be something other than a frog.

16

Name _____ Date _____

What's Your Conclusion?
Understanding Conditional Statements, Arguments, and Truth Tables

16

Vocabulary

Choose the term or terms from the box that best completes each statement.

conditional statement	propositional form	hypothesis
propositional variables	conclusion	truth value
truth table		

1. The _____ of a conditional statement is the variable q.

2. A _____ is a statement that can be written in the form "If p, then q." This form is also known as the _____.

3. A _____ is a table that summarizes all possible truth values for a conditional statement $p \rightarrow q$.

4. The _____ of a condition statement is the variable p.

5. In a conditional statement, the variables p and q are _____.

6. The _____ of a conditional statement is whether the statement is true or false.

Problem Set

Read each conditional statement and conclusion. Then write the additional statement required to reach the conclusion.

16

1. Conditional Statement: If my age is 15 now, then I will be 16 on my next birthday.

   Statement: I am not 15 now.

   Conclusion: Therefore, I will not be 16 on my next birthday.

2. Conditional Statement: If it rains today, then I will need to take my umbrella.

   Statement:

   Conclusion: Therefore, I need to take my umbrella.

3. Conditional Statement: If you had read the notice, then you would have known there was no class today.

   Statement:

   Conclusion: Therefore, I knew there was no class today.

4. Conditional Statement: If I had studied more, then I could have gotten an A on my logic test.

   Statement:

   Conclusion: Therefore, I did not get an A on my logic test.

5. Conditional Statement: If the sun is shining today, then I will wear my sunglasses.

   Statement:

   Conclusion: Therefore, I am not wearing my sunglasses.

6. Conditional Statement: If it snows today, then I will go skiing.

   Statement:

   Conclusion: Therefore, I am going skiing.

Name _____ Date _____

For each conditional statement, draw a solid line beneath the hypothesis. Then draw a dotted line beneath the conclusion.

7. If it is sunny tomorrow, we will go to the beach.

8. If the groundhog sees its shadow, there will be six more weeks of winter.

9. If a and b are real numbers, then $a^2 + b^2$ is greater than or equal to 0.

10. If I am smiling, then I am happy.

11. If I get a raise, then I will buy a new car.

12. If I pass my final exam, then I will pass my finance course.

Complete the truth table for each conditional statement. Then explain what each row means in the truth table.

13. "If I can play the violin, then I can join the orchestra."

p	q	$p \rightarrow q$
T	T	T
T	F	F
F	T	T
F	F	T

Row 1: If p is true, then I can play the violin. If q is true, then I can join the orchestra. It is true that if I can play the violin, I can join the orchestra, so the truth value of the conditional statement is true.

Row 2: If p is true, then I can play the violin. If q is false, then I cannot join the orchestra. It is false that if I can play the violin, I cannot join the orchestra, so the truth value of the conditional statement is false.

Row 3: If p is false, then I cannot play the violin. If q is true, then I can join the orchestra. It could be true that if I cannot play the violin, I can join the orchestra, so the truth value of the conditional statement in this case is true. (For instance, if I play another instrument.)

Row 4: If p is false, then I cannot play the violin. If q is false, then I cannot join the orchestra. It could be true that if I cannot play the violin, I cannot join the orchestra, so the truth value of the conditional statement in this case is true.

14. "If $n = 2$, then $n^2 = 4$."

p	q	$p \rightarrow q$
T	T	
T	F	
F	T	
F	F	

15. "If a plant is an oak, then the plant is a tree."

p	q	$p \rightarrow q$
T	T	
T	F	
F	T	
F	F	

Name _____ Date _____

16. "If your mode of transportation is a motorcycle, then your mode of transportation has two wheels."

p	*q*	*p → q*
T	T	
T	F	
F	T	
F	F	

17. If the traffic light is red, then the car is stopped.

p	q	$p \rightarrow q$
T	T	
T	F	
F	T	
F	F	

18. If the electricity is on, then the light is lit.

p	q	$p \rightarrow q$
T	T	
T	F	
F	T	
F	F	

Name _____ Date _____

Write the converse of each conditional statement.

19. If today is Tuesday, then Janis has a piano lesson after school.

If Janis has a piano lesson after school, then today is Tuesday.

20. If that animal is a dog, then it has four legs.

21. If he believed that the sky is green, then he would be crazy.

22. If one book costs $10, then five books cost $50.

23. If the flower if red, then it is a rose.

24. If Jamal is sleeping, then it is nighttime.

Write the inverse of each conditional statement.

25. If you go to the grocery store on Saturday, then there will be very long lines.

If you do not go to the grocery store on Saturday, then there will not be very long lines.

26. If Krista gets an A on her history test, then she is allowed to spend the weekend with her friend.

27. If the bus does not arrive on time, then Milo will be late for work.

28. If there is a chance of rain this weekend, then Liza will cancel her camping trip.

29. If the figure has 3 sides, then the figure is a triangle.

30. If a number is less than 0, then it is negative.

Write the contrapositive of each conditional statement.

31. If a triangle is an equilateral triangle, then all of its sides are equal.

If the sides of a triangle are not all equal, then the triangle is not an equilateral triangle.

32. If it is dark outside, then it is nighttime.

33. If there are more than 30 students in this classroom, then it is too crowded.

34. If the next animal you see is a kangaroo, then you are in Australia.

35. If a figure has 10 sides, then the figure is a decagon.

36. If a number is greater than zero, then the number is positive.

For each conditional statement, write the converse of that statement. If possible, write a true biconditional statement. If not possible, explain why.

37. If N is divisible by 10, then the last digit in N is 0.

If the last digit in N is 0, then N is divisible by 10. True.

Biconditional statement: N is divisible by 10 if and only if the last digit in N is 0.

38. If two triangles are congruent, then the triangles have equal angles.

Name _____ Date _____

39. If the last digit in *N* is 5, then *N* is divisible by 5.

40. If *x* is greater than 0, then x^3 is greater than 0.

41. If a triangle has no equal sides, then the triangle is scalene.

42. If a triangle has an angle more than 90°, then the triangle is obtuse.

16

Name _____ Date _____

Proofs Aren't Just for Geometry
Introduction to Direct and Indirect Proof with the Properties of Numbers

16

Vocabulary

Define the term in your own words.

1. proof by contradiction

Problem Set

Identify whether the commutative property, associative property, identity property, inverse property of addition, or inverse property of multiplication explains why each statement is true.

1. $(5 + 3) + 4 = 5 + (3 + 4)$

Associative property of addition

2. $172.3 + (-172.3) = 0$

3. $107 \cdot \dfrac{1}{107} = 1$

4. $12 \cdot 23 = 23 \cdot 12$

5. $13{,}416.7 \cdot 1 = 13{,}416.7$

6. $37 + 92 = 92 + 37$

7. $13(24 \cdot 117) = (13 \cdot 24)117$

8. $16\dfrac{3}{5} + 0 = 16\dfrac{3}{5}$

Use the distributive property to calculate each value.

9. $12(6 + 10)$

$12(6 + 10) = 12(6) + 12(10) = 72 + 120 = 192$

10. $(13 + 22) \cdot 4$

11. $4(x + y)$

12. $13(a - b)$

13. $mn - mp$

14. $4d + 4e$

Prove or disprove each statement.

15. If $a(b + c) = b(a + c) + ac$, then either $b = 0$ or $c = 0$ (or both).

$$a(b + c) = b(a + c) + ac$$

$ab + ac = ba + bc + ac$	Distributive property
$ab + ac = ab + bc + ac$	Commutative property of multiplication
$ab + ac - ac = ab + bc + ac - ac$	Subtraction law of equality
$ab = ab + bc$	Inverse property of addition
$ab - ab = ab + bc - ab$	Subtraction property of equality
$0 = bc + ab - ab$	Commutative property
$0 = bc$	Additive inverse
$b = 0$ or $c = 0$ (or both)	If a product is equal to zero, at least 1 factor in the product is equal to zero.

Name _____ Date _____

16. If $ab + bc + ac = a(b + c)$, then either $b = 0$ or $c = 0$ (or both).

17. If $(x + a)(x + b) = x^2 + ab$ for all x, then either $a = 0$ or $b = 0$.

18. If $(a + b)c = c(a - b)$, then either $b = 0$ or $c = 0$.

16

19. If a and b are real numbers, then $a(b + 2) = ab + 2$.

20. If a, b, and c are real numbers, then $\dfrac{a}{b + c} = \dfrac{a}{b} + \dfrac{a}{c}$.

Name _____ Date _____

Your Oldest Likes Spinach?
Using Logic to Solve Problems, Part 1

16

Problem Set

Solve each problem.

1. When Tia asked her neighbor Shelia her birth date, she answered her with this riddle: The sum of the month, day, and the last two digits of the year is 87. The day is four times the month and is the last two digits of the year divided by 6. What is the date of Shelia's birthday?

   Day = 4 × *month*, so *day* must be a multiple of 4.

   Days of the month that are multiples of 4 are: 4, 8, 12, 16, 20, 24, and 28.

   $Day = \dfrac{year}{6}$, or *year* = *day* × 6

   Multiply each possible day by 6: 4 × 6 = 24, 8 × 6 = 48, 12 × 6 = 72, and 16 × 6 = 96
   (Stop there because further calculations produce a three-digit number.)

   So, the day is 4, 8, 12, or 16, and the year is 1924, 1948, 1972, or 1996.

   Because the sum of *day*, *month*, and *the last 2 digits of the year* is 87, you can eliminate 1996 as the year (and thus 16 as the day). Going back to *day* = 4 × *month*, the month is 1, 2, or 3.

   Try the combinations: 4 + 1 + 24 ≠ 87, 8 + 2 + 48 ≠ 87, and 12 + 3 + 72 = 87

   So, Shelia's birthday is March 12, 1972.

2. Suzanne is 3 years younger than Chloe. Theodore is older than Chloe. The sum of Theodore and Suzanne's ages is 11. Theodore and Chloe are both in elementary school. Chloe is closer in age to Theodore than to Suzanne. How old is Chloe?

16

3. Franklin has 50¢ in his pocket. There are less than 10 coins in his pocket. There are three different types of coins in his pocket. The number of the smallest-sized coins is the same as the number of the largest-sized coins. There is more than one of the least-value coin. What coins are in Franklin's pocket?

4. Eva, Mei, and Grace each did something different on Saturday (movies, party, or bowling). Assume only one of the following statements is true. Determine who did what activity.

   A. Grace went to the movies.

   B. Grace did not go to a party.

   C. Mei did not go to a party.

   D. Mei did not go bowling.

5. James was helping his grandmother hang three framed photos on the wall. She gave him the following directions. Hang the black frame to the left of the silver frame. Hang the flower photo to the right of the bird photo. Hang the tree photo to the left of the brown frame. Hang the brown frame to the left of the silver frame. Which photo is in which frame and in what order are they from left to right?

Name _____ Date _____

6. Rita lives on Miller Street. There are five houses on her side of the street. The house numbers on her side of the street are consecutive odd numbers. Angelo's house number is the highest number on Rita's side. The sum of the house numbers is 545. What is Angelo's address?

Complete the logic puzzle grid to solve each problem.

7. Marcus signed up for Math Club, Yearbook, and Jazz Band this year. He asked his counselor where each after-school activity meets. His counselor gave him the following instructions:

Mr. Juarez meets his group in room 10. Yearbook meets in room 6. Mr. Dalton advises either Yearbook or Jazz band. Jazz is not advised by Mrs. Aiello, but it meets in room 9.

Complete the grid and then list each of Marcus's after-school activities, their advisors, and their room numbers.

		Advisor			Activity		
		Mr. Juarez	Mr. Dalton	Mrs. Aiello	Math Club	Yearbook	Jazz Band
Room	Room 6	X	X	O	X	O	X
	Room 9	X	O	X	X	X	O
	Room 10	O	X	X	O	X	X
Activity	Math Club	O	X	X			
	Yearbook	X	X	O			
	Jazz Band	X	O	X			

Math Club is advised by Mr. Juarez and meets in Room 10.

Yearbook is advised by Mrs. Aiello and meets in Room 6.

Jazz Band is advised by Mr. Dalton and meets in Room 9.

8. The Student Council is organizing information about the Fall Carnival Fundraiser. Three booths are planned: a basketball shoot, a dunking booth, and a balloon pop. Each booth has two, three, or four volunteers and key rings, homework passes, or glow sticks for prizes. The basketball shoot has glow sticks for prizes. The dunking booth has more than two volunteers and does not have key rings for prizes. The booth with three volunteers has homework passes for prizes. The balloon pop has fewer volunteers than the basketball shoot.

Complete the grid and then list each booth with the correct number of volunteers and prize offered.

		Prizes			Booths		
		Key rings	Homework passes	Glow sticks	Basketball shoot	Dunking booth	Balloon pop
Volunteers	Two						
	Three						
	Four						
Booths	Basketball shoot						
	Dunking booth						
	Balloon pop						

Name _____ Date _____

9. Hector, Ella, and Mitsu placed first, second, and third in the Science Fair. Ella's project won first place. Hector's project was neither in Physics nor in third place. The person who placed third did a Chemistry experiment.

Complete the grid and then list each student with the type of science and the place their project won.

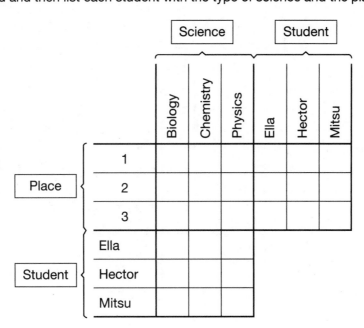

16

10. All of the trophies in the school's trophy case were removed for cleaning. The secretary must use the following instructions to put them back on the proper shelves. The case has three shelves each holding trophies from a different sport: football, basketball, and field hockey. Trophies from each sport are different types: statues, plaques, and cups. The bottom shelf does not display field hockey trophies. The middle shelf displays plaques. Basketball trophies are statues. The top shelf does not display football trophies or cups.

Complete the grid and then list each shelf with the correct sport and type of trophy.

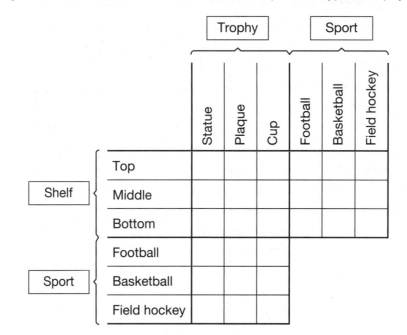

Name _____ Date _____

11. John, Yasmine, and Zach each have a different type of bag: backpack, messenger bag, or duffle bag. Each bag is made of a different type of material: leather, canvas, or nylon. The backpack is leather. John's bag is not canvas or leather. Yasmine's bag is not a duffle bag or leather.

Label and complete the grid and then list each student with the type and material of his or her bag.

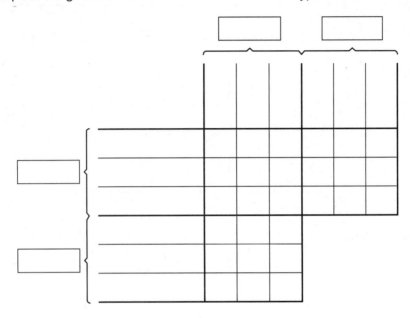

16

12. There are three middle schools in Clayton County: Carver, Wiley, and Taft. Each school has a different school mascot (eagle, bulldog, or hawk) and school colors (orange/red, red/black, or black/gold). The hawk's colors do not include black and Wiley's colors do not include red. Taft does not have a bird as its mascot.

Label and complete the grid and then list each school, its mascot, and its colors.

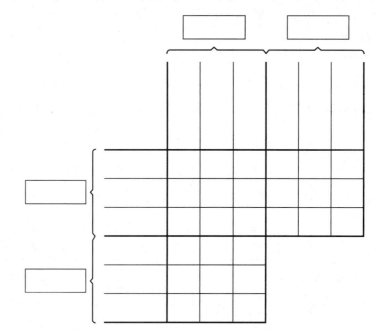

Name _____ Date _____

Shoes and Math Scores?
Using Logic to Solve Problems, Part 2

Problem Set

Complete the grid to solve each problem.

1. Farmer Gray, Farmer White, Farmer Brown, and Farmer Green each grow a different crop (wheat, cotton, soy, or corn) and each has a different number of acres (250, 400, 500, and 750). Complete the grid and then list each farmer, his crop, and the number of acres on his farm.

   - Farmer Brown grows corn.

   - The farmer who grows soy has the largest farm.

   - Farmer Green and Farmer White do not grow crops that start with a "c."

   - Farmer Green is allergic to soy and does not have the smallest farm.

   - There are 500 acres of cotton.

	Wheat	Cotton	Soy	Corn	250 acres	400 acres	500 acres	750 acres
Farmer Gray	X	O	X	X	X	X	O	X
Farmer White	X	X	O	X	X	X	X	O
Farmer Brown	X	X	X	O	O	X	X	X
Farmer Green	O	X	X	X	X	O	X	X
250 acres	X	X	X	O				
400 acres	O	X	X	X				
500 acres	X	O	X	X				
750 acres	X	X	O	X				

Farmer Gray grows cotton on 500 acres.

Farmer White grows soy on 750 acres.

Farmer Brown grows corn on 250 acres.

Farmer Green grows wheat on 400 acres.

16

2. Noah, J.J., Demari, and Victor each go to and from school in different ways. The possible ways are: walking, riding the bus, riding in a car, or biking. Complete the grid and then list each student, his method for getting to school, and his method for getting home from school.

- The boy who bikes to school also bikes home.

- Victor walks to school but is too tired in the afternoon to walk home.

- Noah and Demari both ride the bus.

- J.J. does not ride in a car.

- Noah's dad drops him off at school on his way to work.

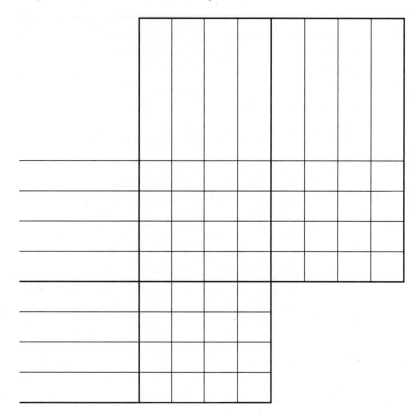

Name _____ Date _____

3. There are four types of recycling bins at the school. Each is for a different material: aluminum, paper, glass, or plastic. Each is a different color: yellow, blue, green, or gray. Each bin is also a different shape: round, octagonal, rectangular, or square. Complete the grid and then list the color and shape of each bin and the type of material it holds.

- The bin for plastic is not round or octagonal.
- The green bin is for glass.
- Either paper or glass is collected in the square bin.
- The rectangular bin is yellow.
- Kyle threw a soda can in the round, blue bin.
- The square bin is not green.

16

4. Angelo, Rashan, Vance, Chen, and Adam ran the 800-meter run. They finished first, second, third, fourth, and fifth. Each participant received a different colored ribbon (red, gold, blue, purple, and white) for his achievement. Complete the grid and then list each runner, the place he finished, and the color of his ribbon.

- The blue and white ribbons are for first and last place (not necessarily in that order).

- Adam was not first or last.

- Angelo finished fourth.

- Chen got the purple ribbon and finished just before Angelo.

- Rashan broke the school record.

- The red, purple, and white ribbons were given to the top three runners (not necessarily in that order).

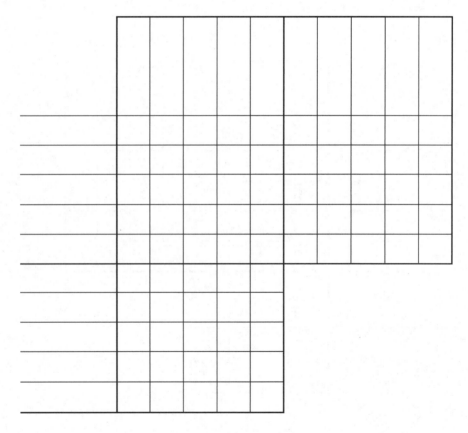

Name _____ Date _____

5. The Bryants, the Levines, the Smiths, the Fogartys, and the Singhs all live on the same street in houses 425, 427, 429, 431, and 433. Each of their houses is a different style: brick, Tudor, modern, Victorian, or farmhouse. Complete the grid and then list each family, their house style, and their house number.

- The Fogartys live in the Victorian at the end of the block.

- The Singhs do not live in the brick house or the farmhouse.

- The house at 431 is a modern house.

- The Levines live in the brick house between the Singhs and the Bryants.

- The modern house is between the Victorian and the Tudor.

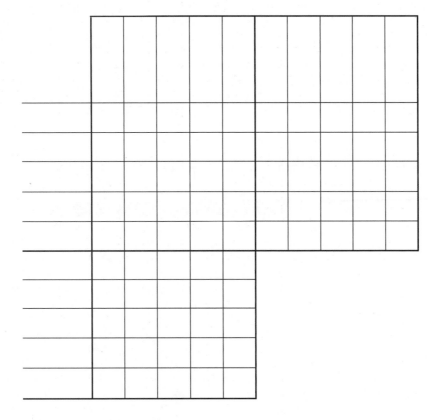

16

6. There are five dogs at the shelter: Jack, Lady, Sadie, Butch, and Max. Each dog is a different size: extra large, large, medium, small, or toy. Each dog is a different color: black, brown, yellow, gray, or white. Complete the grid and then list each dog, its size, and its fur color.

- The largest dog is not yellow, gray, or black.

- Jack is a small dog.

- Neither Butch nor Lady is the toy dog.

- Sadie is a big, white dog.

- A boy wanted the large, yellow dog, but wanted a girl dog, so he adopted the smaller, brown dog.

- Max is not black.

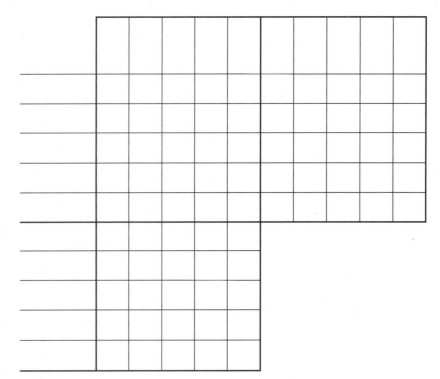

Name _____ Date _____

7. Parker polled her friends Ty, Maddie, Eva, Ben, and Zoe. She found that their favorite school subjects are math, art, science, drama, and history. Their favorite lunches are pizza, salad, tacos, turkey sub, and spaghetti. Their favorite activities are reading, riding a bike, walking the dog, playing on the computer, and listening to music. Complete the grid and then list each friend and their favorite subject, lunch, and activity.

- Eva loves spaghetti.

- Ben does not have a dog.

- Maddie brings her sketchbook with her on her bike rides in the park.

- Zoe is a vegetarian and an animal lover.

- Ben likes math and science.

- The person who likes science spends a lot of time on the computer.

- Eva does not like acting, but she likes to read plays.

- Ty likes pizza, but Maddie prefers Mexican food.

- The person who likes music also likes history.

16

16

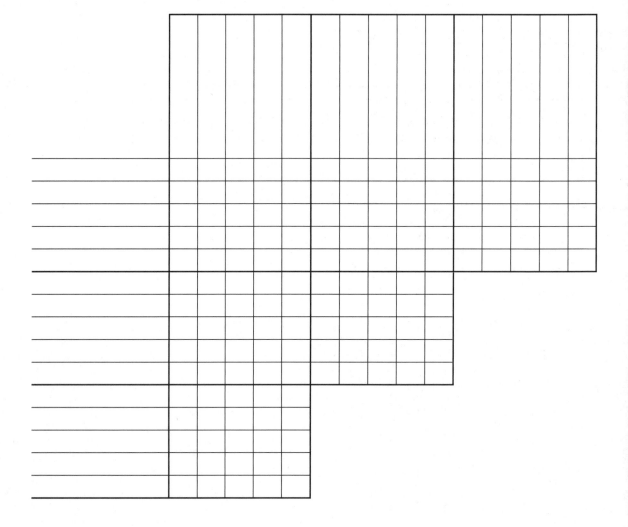

Name _____ Date _____

8. In Chambersville there are five parks (Spring, Center, Hill, Miller, and North). Each park has a unique sports area, number of picnic tables available, and special feature. The sports areas are a tennis court, volleyball court, baseball field, bike path, or basketball court. The numbers of picnic tables available are 2, 4, 8, 10, or 20. The special features are a pond, merry-go-round, pool, gazebo, and amphitheatre. Complete the grid and list each park name with its sports area, number of picnic tables, and special feature.

- You cannot play a team sport at Hill Park.

- Center Park has the most picnic tables.

- The amphitheatre is in the park with the basketball court.

- The park with a tennis court does not have a special feature with water.

- Fans attending the baseball games can ride the merry-go-round.

- North Park has half the number of picnic tables as Center Park, but it has plenty of seating in the amphitheatre.

- At one park you can feed the ducks from your bike, but there are only 2 tables for picnicking.

- There are 4 picnic tables around the gazebo.

- Swimming is not allowed at Hill Park, but Spring Park is open for swimming all summer.

16

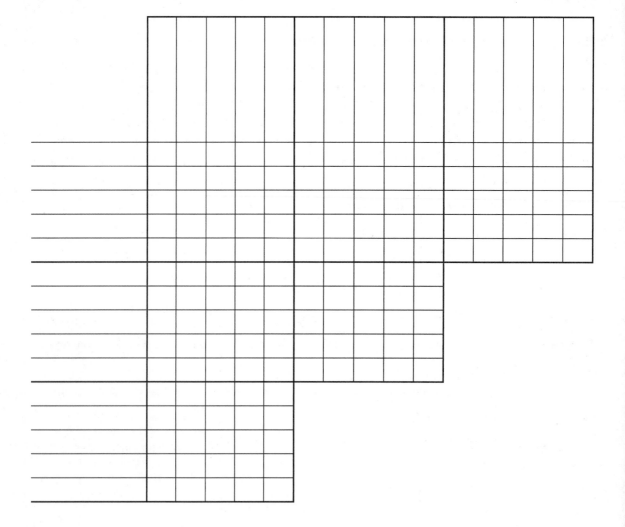

Odd-Numbered Answers

Chapter 1

LESSON 1.1

1. Independent quantity: time (hours) Dependent quantity: distance (miles)
3. Independent quantity: number of cups Dependent quantity: cost (dollars)
5. Independent quantity: time (hours) Dependent quantity: distance (miles)
7. Graph A
9. Graph B
11. Graph C

13.

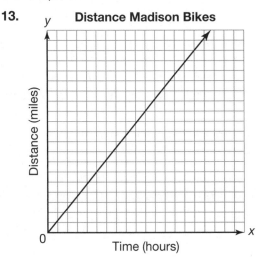

15.

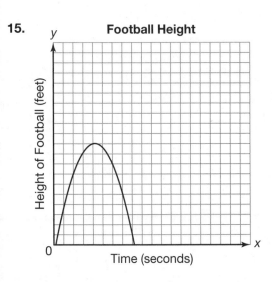

17.

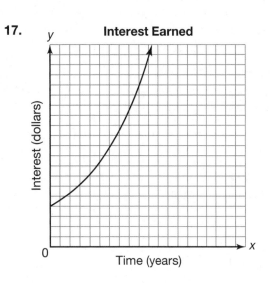

LESSON 1.2

1. Both graphs are always decreasing from left to right. Both graphs are functions. Both graphs are made up of straight lines.
3. Both graphs have an increasing and a decreasing interval. Both graphs have a minimum value. Both graphs are functions.
5. Both graphs are increasing from left to right. Both graphs are functions.
7. The graph is discrete.
9. The graph is continuous.
11. The graph is discrete.
13. Yes. The graph is a function.
15. No. The graph is not a function.
17. No. The graph is not a function.

LESSON 1.3

1. $f(x) = 3x - 8$
3. $P(x) = 3^x + 8$
5. $A(m) = -\frac{1}{2}m + 5$
7. Graph A
9. Graph B
11. Graph A

13. The graph represents an increasing function.

15. The graph represents a function with a combination of an increasing interval and a decreasing interval.

17. The graph represents a constant function.

19. The graph represents a function with an absolute minimum.

21. The graph represents a function with an absolute maximum.

23. The graph represents a function with an absolute maximum.

25. The graph represents an exponential function.

27. The graph represents a linear piecewise function.

29. The graph represents a constant function.

LESSON 1.4

11. $f(x) = x^2$

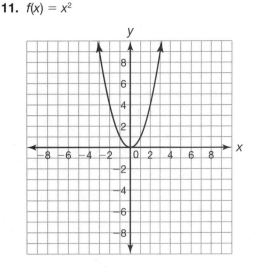

13. $f(x) = x^2$

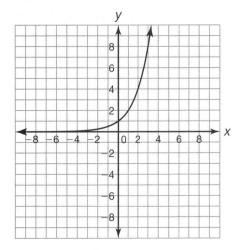

15. $f(x) = 3$

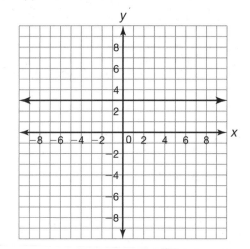

17. The graph represents a quadratic function.

19. The graph represents a linear absolute value function.

21. The graph represents a linear piecewise function.

Chapter 2

LESSON 2.1

1. The distance Nathan travels depends on the time. Distance, D, is the dependent quantity and time, t, is the independent quantity.

$D(t) = 6t$

3. The total number of envelopes Mario stuffs depends on the time. The total number of envelopes, E, is the dependent quantity and time, t, is the independent quantity.

$E(t) = 5t$

5. The amount of money the booster club earns depends on the number of cups sold. The amount of money, M, is the dependent quantity and the number of cups sold, c, is the independent quantity.

$M(c) = 2c$

7.

	Independent Quantity	Dependent Quantity
Quantity	Time	Distance
Units	hours	miles
Expression	t	7t
	0	0
	0.5	3.5
	1	7
	1.5	10.5
	2	14

(0.5, 3.5) and (1, 7)

$$\frac{7 - 3.5}{1 - 0.5} = \frac{3.5}{0.5}$$

$$= \frac{7}{1}$$

The unit rate of change is 7.

9. Noah is stuffing envelopes with invitations to the school's Harvest Festival. He stuffs 4 envelopes each minute.

	Independent Quantity	Dependent Quantity
Quantity	Time	Number of Envelopes
Units	minutes	envelopes
Expression	t	4t
	5	20
	10	40
	15	60
	20	80
	25	100

(5, 20) and (10, 40)

$$\frac{40 - 20}{10 - 5} = \frac{20}{5}$$

$$= \frac{4}{1}$$

The unit rate of change is 4.

11. The volleyball boosters sell bags of popcorn during the varsity matches to raise money for new uniforms. Each bag of popcorn costs $3.

	Independent Quantity	Dependent Quantity
Quantity	Number of bags of popcorn sold	Amount of money raised
Units	bags	dollars
Expression	b	$3b$
	5	15
	10	30
	15	45
	20	60
	25	75

(5, 15) and (10, 30)

$$\frac{30 - 15}{10 - 5} = \frac{15}{5}$$
$$= \frac{3}{1}$$

The unit rate of change is 3.

13. The input value is t.

The output value is $4t$.

The rate of change is 4.

15. The input value is e.

The output value is $15e$.

The rate of change is 15.

17. The input value is b.

The output value is $35b$.

The rate of change is 35.

19. Carmen earns $21 when she babysits for 3 hours.

21. Carmen earns $35 when she babysits for 5 hours.

23. Carmen earns $24.50 when she babysits for 3.5 hours.

25. $t = 3$

27. $t = 6$

29. $t = 2$

1.

	Independent Quantity	Dependent Quantity
Quantity	Time	Height
Units	minutes	feet
	0	1000
	2	1400
	4	1800
	6	2200
	8	2600
Expression	t	$200t + 1000$

3.

	Independent Quantity	Dependent Quantity
Quantity	Time	Height
Units	minutes	feet
	0	4125
	1	3575
	2	3025
	3	2475
	4	1925
Expression	t	$-550t + 4125$

Answers

5.

	Independent Quantity	Dependent Quantity
Quantity	Time	Depth
Units	minutes	feet
	0	−300
	2	−244
	4	−188
	6	−132
	8	−76
Expression	t	$28t - 300$

7. The input value is t, time in minutes. The output value is $f(t)$, height in feet.

The y-intercept is 130. The rate of change is 160.5.

9. The input value is t, time in minutes. The output value is $f(t)$, depth in feet.

The y-intercept is 0. The rate of change is −17.

11. The input value is t, time in minutes. The output value is $f(t)$, volume in gallons.

The y-intercept is 5. The rate of change is 4.25.

13.

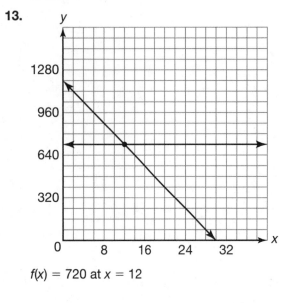

$f(x) = 720$ at $x = 12$

15.

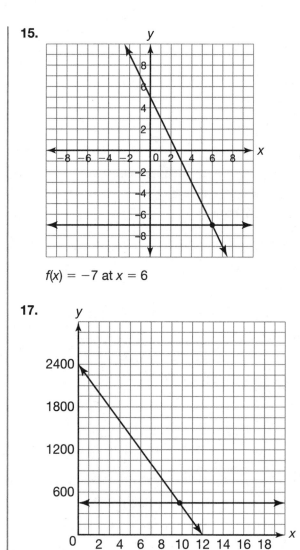

$f(x) = -7$ at $x = 6$

17.

$f(x) = 450$ at $x \approx 10$

19. $12 = x$

21. $6 = x$

23. $9.75 = x$

1. $x \geq 8$

3. $x < 3$

5. $x > 10$

7. Elena must sell at least 50 tickets. $x \geq 50$

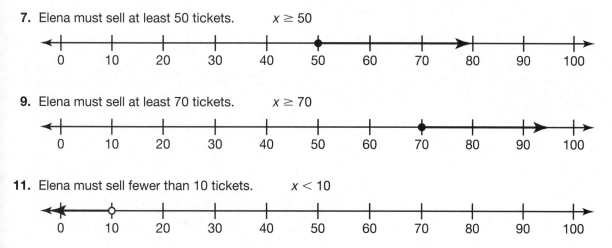

9. Elena must sell at least 70 tickets. $x \geq 70$

11. Elena must sell fewer than 10 tickets. $x < 10$

13. $5 \leq x$

Leon must play in 5 or more games to score at least 117 points.

15. $7 < x$

Leon must play in more than 7 games to score more than 143 points.

17. $2.54 > x$

Leon must play in 2 or fewer games to score fewer than 85 points.

19.

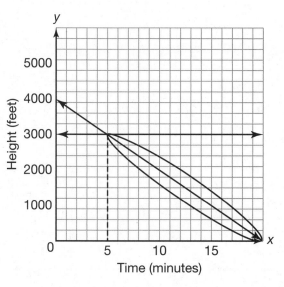

More than 5 minutes have passed if the balloon is below 3000 feet.

$x > 5$

21.

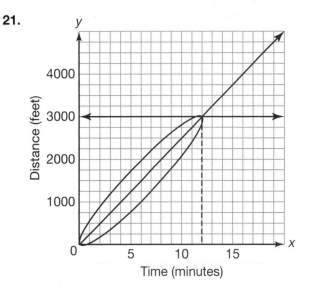

Less than 12 minutes have passed if Lea still has more than 2000 feet to walk.

$x < 12$

23.

At least 8 minutes have passed if the submarine is at least 160 feet below the surface.

$x \geq 8$

LESSON 2.4

7. $-8 < x \leq 11$

9. $7 < x < 25$

11. $-14 \leq x \leq 5$

1. $22 \geq x > -4$

3. $0 \leq x \leq 6$

5. $87 \geq x \geq 83$

13.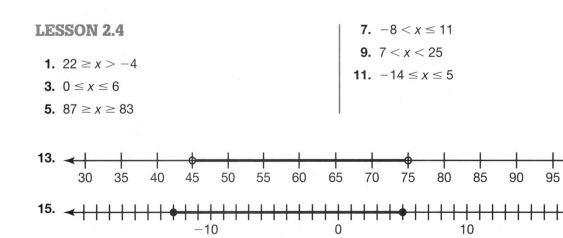

15.

17. $-35 \leq x \leq 50$

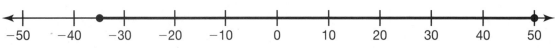

19. $x \geq 6$ or $x < 3$

21. $x > 31$ or $x \leq 26$

23. $x > 1000$ or $x < 10$

25.

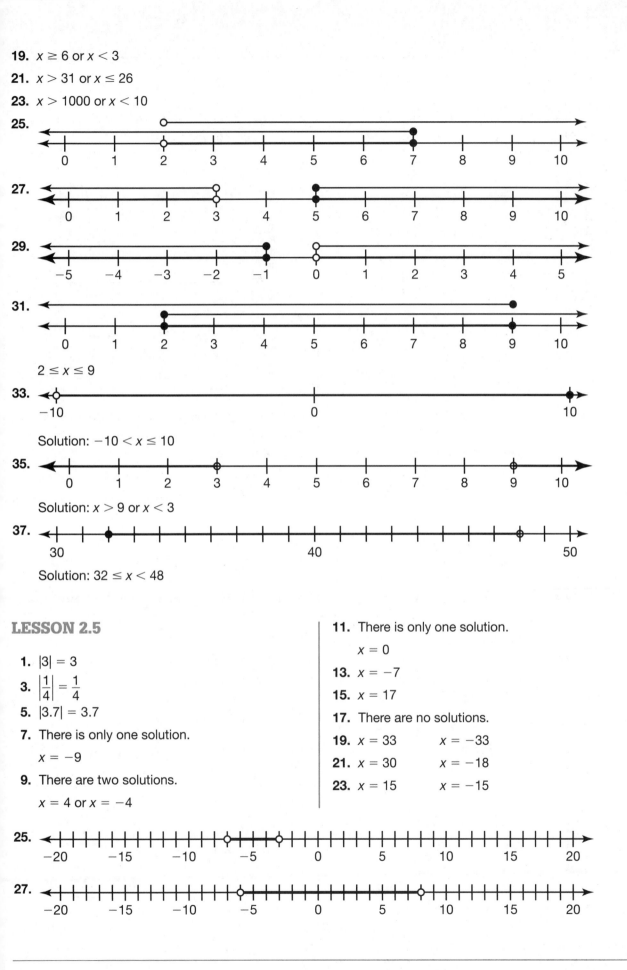

$2 \leq x \leq 9$

33.

Solution: $-10 < x \leq 10$

35.

Solution: $x > 9$ or $x < 3$

37.

Solution: $32 \leq x < 48$

LESSON 2.5

1. $|3| = 3$

3. $\left|\dfrac{1}{4}\right| = \dfrac{1}{4}$

5. $|3.7| = 3.7$

7. There is only one solution.

$x = -9$

9. There are two solutions.

$x = 4$ or $x = -4$

11. There is only one solution.

$x = 0$

13. $x = -7$

15. $x = 17$

17. There are no solutions.

19. $x = 33$ $x = -33$

21. $x = 30$ $x = -18$

23. $x = 15$ $x = -15$

25.

27.

29.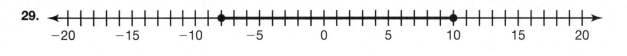

31. The necklaces can be between 15.5 and 16.5 inches long to meet the specifications.

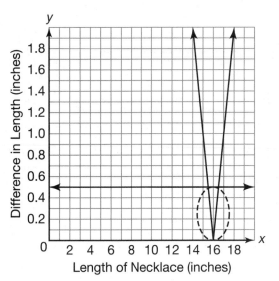

Length of Necklace (inches)

33. Each bag of chips can weigh between 7.75 ounces and 8.25 ounces.

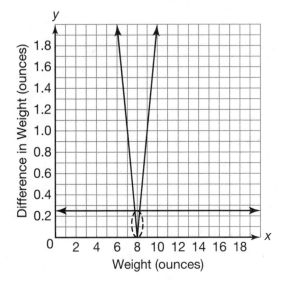

Weight (ounces)

35. A guess that is more than 270 or less than 250 will not win a prize.

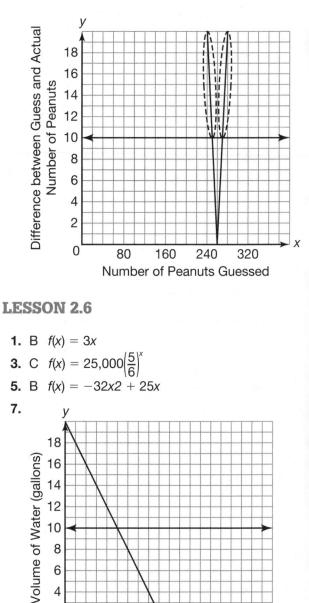

Number of Peanuts Guessed

LESSON 2.6

1. B $f(x) = 3x$
3. C $f(x) = 25{,}000\left(\dfrac{5}{6}\right)^x$
5. B $f(x) = -32x2 + 25x$
7.

Time (minutes)

After 2.5 minutes, half of the water in the tank (10 gallons) will be drained.

Answers

9.

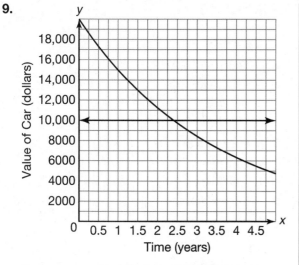

Ronna can own the car for almost 2.5 years before reselling and will still make at least $10,000.

11.

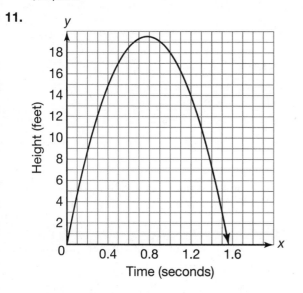

The softball is in the air for about 1.5 seconds.

Chapter 3
LESSON 3.1

1. The attendance during Game 9 will be 2620 people.

3. The average price of gas in August will be $3.44.

5. In 2014, Kata will travel 5623 miles.

1. a = pounds of apples

   b = pounds of oranges

   $0.75a + 0.89b$

3. m = matinee

   n = evening

   $7m + 10.5n$

5. d = daisies

   r = roses

   $8.99d + 15.99r$

7. c = carnations

   f = lilies

   $10.99c + 12.99f = 650$

9. q = pounds of oranges

   r = pounds of peaches

   $0.79q + 1.05r = 325$

11. d = DVDs

    b = Blu-ray discs

    $15.99d + 22.99b = 2000$

13. The booster club must sell 75 hot dogs to reach their goal.

15. The booster club must sell 360 hamburgers to reach their goal.

17. The booster club must sell 132 hot dogs to reach their goal.

19. The x-intercept is (12, 0) and the y-intercept is (0, 30).

21. The x-intercept is (−21, 0) and the y-intercept is (0, 168).

23. The x-intercept is approximately (24.43, 0) and the y-intercept is (0, 13.68).

Answers

25.

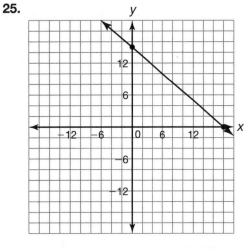

$x = 18$ $y = 15$

27.

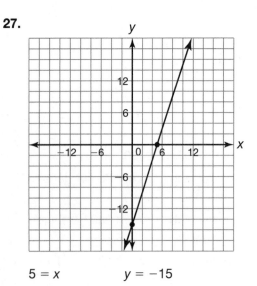

$5 = x$ $y = -15$

29.

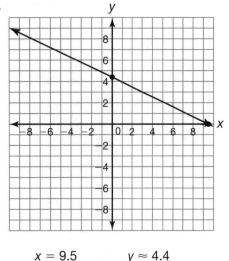

$x = 9.5$ $y \approx 4.4$

LESSON 3.3

1. $72°F \approx 22.22°C$

3. $102.6°F \approx 39.22°C$

5. $42°C = 107.6°F$

7. $y = -\frac{2}{3}x + 8$

9. $y = \frac{4}{9}x + 5$

11. $y = -\frac{1}{8}x - 12$

13. $-5x + y = 8$

15. $-2x + 3y = -18$

17. $5x + y = -13$

19. $\frac{2A}{b} = h$

21. $\sqrt{\frac{A}{\pi}} = r$

23. $\frac{3V}{lh} = w$

LESSON 3.4

1. $f(x) = 35x - 105$

3. $f(x) = 1.99x - 3.98$

5. $f(x) = 20x - 20$

7. The linear function $c(x) = \frac{5}{2}x - 24$ represents the total number of boxes that Line A and Line B can produce combined.

9. The linear function $f(x) = 2.16x - 12.44$ represents the total amount that Carlos and Hector can earn combined.

11. The linear function $c(x) = 47.75x - 279$ represents the total amount that Line A and Line B can make combined.

Chapter 4

LESSON 4.1

1. The second figure has 2 more squares than the first, the third figure has 3 more squares than the second, and the fourth figure has 4 more squares than the third.

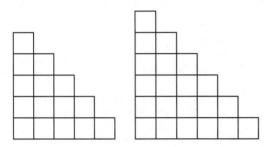

3. Each figure has 2 more circles than the previous figure.

5. Each figure has twice as many triangles as the previous figure.

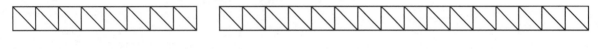

7. 1000, 995, 990, 985, 980, 975, 970

9. $40, $80, $120, $160, $200, $240

11. 1, 3, 7, 15, 31, 63, 127

13. 200, 225, 250, 275, 300, 325, 350

15. 50, 47, 44, 41, 38, 35, 32, 29

LESSON 4.2

1. $d = 5 - 1$

$d = 4$

3. $d = 13 - 10.5$

$d = 2.5$

5. $d = 91.5 - 95$

$d = -3.5$

7. $d = 1190 - 1250$

$d = -60$

9. $d = 9 - 8\frac{1}{2}$

$d = \frac{1}{2}$

11. $r = 10 \div 5$

$r = 2$

13. $r = -6 \div 3$

$r = -2$

15. $r = -30 \div 10$

$r = -3$

17. $r = 40 \div 5$

$r = 8$

19. $r = -1 \div 0.2$

$r = -5$

21. 8, 14, 20, 26, __32__, __38__, __44__, . . .

23. −24, −14, −4, 6, __16__, __26__, __36__, . . .

25. 20, 11, 2, −7, __−16__, __−25__, __−34__, . . .

27. −101, −112, −123, −134, __−145__, __−156__, __−167__, . . .

29. −500, −125, 250, 625, __1000__, __1375__, __1750__, . . .

31. 3, 9, 27, 81, __243__, __729__, __2187__, . . .

33. 5, −10, 20, −40, __80__, __−160__, __320__, . . .

35. 2, −2, 2, −2, __2__, __−2__, __2__, . . .

37. −8000, 4000, −2000, 1000, __−500__, __250__, __−125__, . . .

39. 156.25, 31.25, 6.25, 1.25, <u>0.25</u>, <u>0.05</u>, <u>0.01</u>, . . .

41. The sequence is arithmetic. The next 3 terms are 20, 24, and 28.

43. The sequence is geometric. The next 3 terms are 768, 3072, and 12,288.

45. The sequence is neither arithmetic nor geometric.

47. The sequence is arithmetic. The next 3 terms are 23.9, 28.0, and 32.1.

49. The sequence is geometric. The next 3 terms are 1280, −5120, and 20,480.

LESSON 4.3

1. $a_{20} = 58$

3. $a_{25} = 29.7$

5. $a_{42} = 104.50$

7. $a_{34} = 98.7$

9. $a_{57} = 0$

11. $g_{10} = 1536$

13. $g_{12} = 885{,}735$

15. $g_{20} = -65{,}536$

17. $g_{14} = 32{,}768$

19. $g_{12} \approx 46.57$

21. The sequence is geometric.

$g_5 = 64$

23. The sequence is geometric.

$g_4 = -54 \qquad g_6 = -486$

25. The sequence is arithmetic.

$a_4 = 590 \qquad a_5 = 680$

27. The sequence is arithmetic.

$a_4 = -113 \qquad a_5 = -128 \qquad a_6 = -143$

29. $a_{20} = 790$

31. $a_{30} = 248$

33. $a_{30} = 10{,}500$

35. $a_{24} = 68.9$

37. $a_{20} = 13{,}900$

LESSON 4.4

1.

Term Number (n)	Value of Term (a_n)
1	15
2	18
3	21
4	24
5	27
6	30
7	33
8	36
9	39
10	42

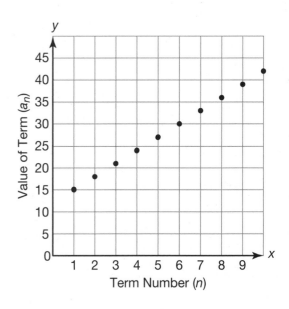

3.

Term Number (n)	Value of Term (a_n)
1	50
2	42
3	34
4	26
5	18
6	10
7	2
8	−6
9	−14
10	−22

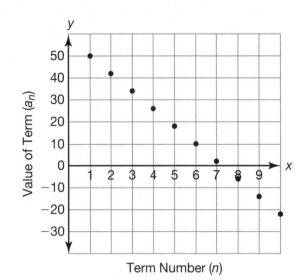

5.

Term Number (n)	Value of Term (a_n)
1	−24
2	−18
3	−12
4	−6
5	0
6	6
7	12
8	18
9	24
10	30

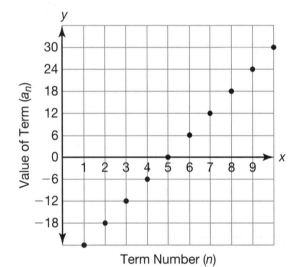

7.

Term Number (n)	Value of Term (a_n)
1	75
2	100
3	125
4	150
5	175
6	200
7	225
8	250
9	275
10	300

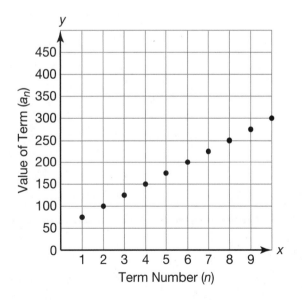

9.

Term Number (n)	Value of Term (a_n)
1	400
2	320
3	240
4	160
5	80
6	0
7	−80
8	−160
9	−240
10	−320

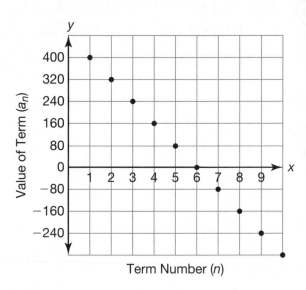

LESSON 4.5

1. $f(n) = 5n + 11$

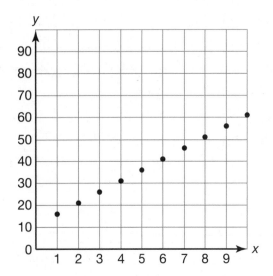

3. $f(n) = -20n + 120$

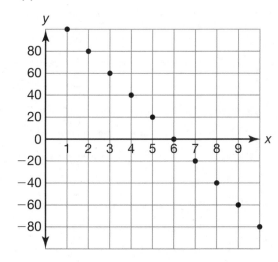

5. $f(n) = -50n + 600$

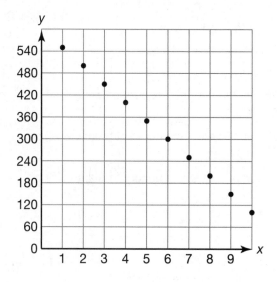

9. $f(n) = 8 \cdot 2.5^n$

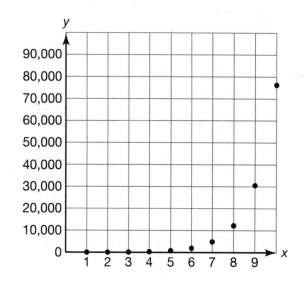

7. $f(n) = \dfrac{5}{2} \cdot 2^n$

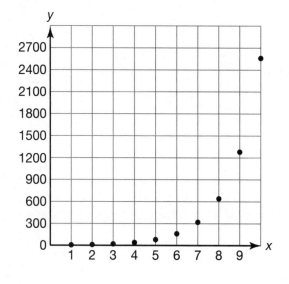

11. $f(n) = -0.25 \cdot 2^n$

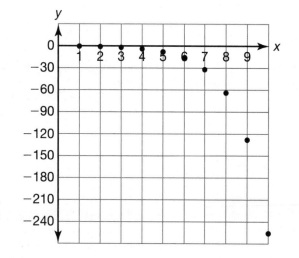

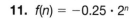

Chapter 5

LESSON 5.1

1. $P(t) = 500 + 15t$
3. $P(t) = 250 + 6.25t$
5. $P(t) = 175 + 7.4375t$
7. In 3 years, the account balance will be $556.25.
9. In 10 years, the account balance will be $687.50.
11. In 50 years, the account balance will be $1437.50.
13. It will take 5 years for the account balance to reach $505.
15. It will take 50 years for the account balance to reach $1450.

17. It will take about 19 years for the account balance to reach $800.
19. $P(t) = 500 \cdot 1.04$
21. $P(t) = 1200 \cdot 1.035^t$
23. $P(t) = 300 \cdot 1.0175^t$
25. In 2 years, the account balance will be $533.03.
27. In 15 years, the account balance will be $807.83.
29. In 50 years, the account balance will be 2474.42.
31. It will take about 8.3 years for the account balance to reach $1500.
33. It will take about 36.7 years for the account balance to reach $6000.
35. It will take about 14.2 years for the account balance to reach $2000.

37.

Quantity	Time	Simple Interest Balance	Compound Interest Balance
Units	years	dollars	dollars
Expression	t	$300 + 12t$	$300 \cdot 1.04t$
	0	300.00	300.00
	2	324.00	324.48
	6	372.00	379.60
	10	420.00	444.07

39.

Quantity	Time	Simple Interest Balance	Compound Interest Balance
Units	years	dollars	dollars
Expression	t	$1100 + 38.5t$	$1100 \cdot 1.035^t$
	0	1100.00	1100.00
	5	1292.50	1306.45
	10	1485.00	1551.66
	30	2255.00	3087.47

41.

Quantity	Time	Simple Interest Balance	Compound Interest Balance
Units	years	dollars	dollars
Expression	t	$2300 + 86.25t$	$2300 \cdot 1.0375^t$
	0	2300.00	2300.00
	2	2472.50	2475.73
	5	2731.25	2764.83
	15	3593.75	3995.30

LESSON 5.2

1. $P(t) = 7000 \cdot 1.014^t$
3. $P(t) = 8000 \cdot 0.9825^t$
5. $P(t) = 9500 \cdot 0.028^t$
7. The population after 1 year will be 16,240.
9. The population after 5 years will be about 17,237.

11. The population after 20 years will be about 21,550.
13. It will take about 4.7 years for the population to reach 17,000.
15. It will take about 57.4 years for the population to reach 9000.
17. The range of the function is all numbers greater than 0. The function never actually reaches 0.

19.

x	f(x)
−2	$\frac{1}{4}$
−1	$\frac{1}{2}$
0	1
1	2
2	4

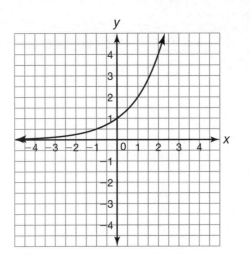

x-intercept: none

y-intercept: (0, 1)

asymptote: $y = 0$

domain: all real numbers

range: $y > 0$

interval(s) of increase or decrease: increasing over the entire domain

21.

x	f(x)
−2	9
−1	3
0	1
1	$\frac{1}{3}$
2	$\frac{1}{9}$

x-intercept: none

y-intercept: (0, 1)

asymptote: $y = 0$

domain: all real numbers

range: $y > 0$

interval(s) of increase or decrease: decreasing over the entire domain

23.

x	f(x)
−2	$-\dfrac{1}{2}$
−1	−1
0	−2
1	−4
2	−8

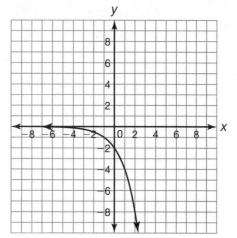

x-intercept: none

y-intercept: (0, −2)

asymptote: $y = 0$

domain: all real numbers

range: $y < 0$

interval(s) of increase or decrease: decreasing over the entire domain

LESSON 5.3

1. $g(x) = f(x) + 4$

3. $g(x) = f(x) - 8$

5. $g(x) = f(x) + 2$

7. $(x, y) \rightarrow (x, y + 8)$

9. $(x, y) \rightarrow (x, y - 4)$

11. $(x, y) \rightarrow (x, y + 6)$

13. $g(x) = 3^{(x + 1)} = f(x + 1)$

15. $g(x) = 2^{(x - 1)} = f(x - 1)$

17. $g(x) = 2(x - 3) = f(x - 3)$

19. $(x, y) \rightarrow (x + 2, y)$

21. $(x, y) \rightarrow (x - 1, y)$

23. $(x, y) \rightarrow (x + 1, y)$

25. The graph of $f(x)$ is b units below the graph of $h(x)$.

27. The graph of $f(x)$ is b units to the right of $h(x)$.

29. The graph of $f(x)$ is k units up from the graph of $h(x)$.

31.

33.

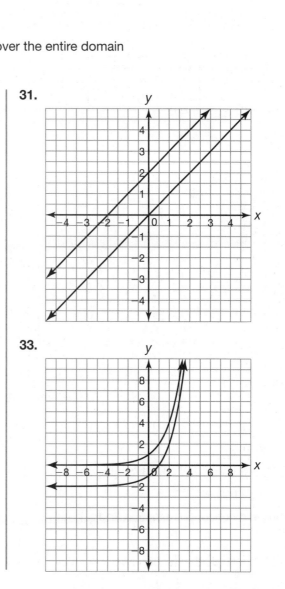

35.

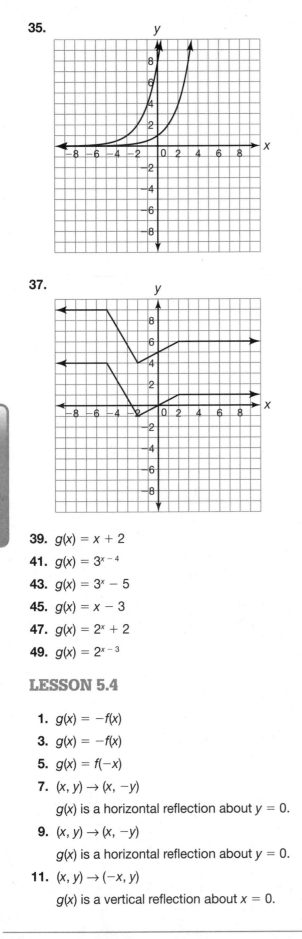

37.

39. $g(x) = x + 2$

41. $g(x) = 3^{x-4}$

43. $g(x) = 3^x - 5$

45. $g(x) = x - 3$

47. $g(x) = 2^x + 2$

49. $g(x) = 2^{x-3}$

LESSON 5.4

1. $g(x) = -f(x)$

3. $g(x) = -f(x)$

5. $g(x) = f(-x)$

7. $(x, y) \rightarrow (x, -y)$

$g(x)$ is a horizontal reflection about $y = 0$.

9. $(x, y) \rightarrow (x, -y)$

$g(x)$ is a horizontal reflection about $y = 0$.

11. $(x, y) \rightarrow (-x, y)$

$g(x)$ is a vertical reflection about $x = 0$.

13.

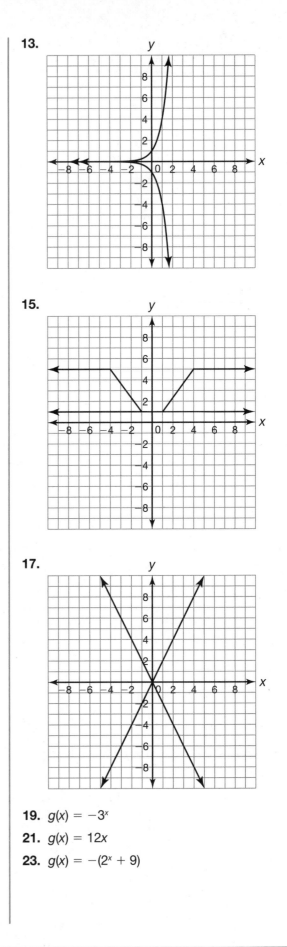

15.

17.

19. $g(x) = -3^x$

21. $g(x) = 12x$

23. $g(x) = -(2^x + 9)$

25. $g(x) = -5^x$

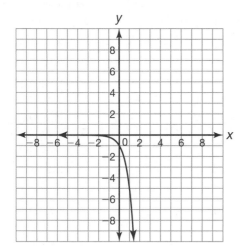

27. $g(x) = 3^x + 2$

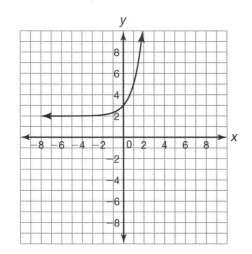

29. $g(x) = 4^x - 4$

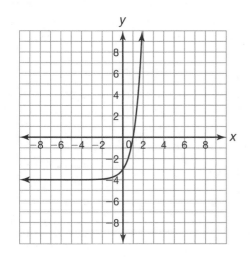

31. $g(x)$ is a reflection of $f(x)$ over the line $x = 0$.

33. $g(x)$ is a translation of $f(x)$ up 10 units or $g(x)$ is a translation of $f(x)$ left 5 units.

35. $g(x)$ is a translation of $f(x)$ right 4 units.

37. $g(x)$ is a reflection of $f(x)$ over the line $y = 0$.

39. $g(x)$ is a translation of $f(x)$ down 5 units.

41. $g(x)$ is a translation of $f(x)$ up 2 units.

LESSON 5.5

1. $\dfrac{10^5}{10^8} = 10^{5-8} = 10^{-3}$

3. $\dfrac{10^2}{10^5} = 10^{2-5} = 10^{-3}$

5. $\dfrac{5^3}{5^{10}} = 5^{3-10} = 5^{-7}$

7. $\sqrt[3]{216} = 6$

9. $\sqrt[3]{-125} = -5$

11. $\sqrt[3]{729} = 9$

13. $\sqrt[5]{32} = 2$

15. $\sqrt[6]{729} = 3$

17. $\sqrt[7]{-128} = -2$

19. $\sqrt[4]{15} = 15^{\frac{1}{4}}$

21. $\sqrt[4]{31} = 31^{\frac{1}{4}}$

23. $\sqrt[6]{y} = y^{\frac{1}{6}}$

25. $12^{\frac{1}{3}} = \sqrt[3]{12}$

27. $18^{\frac{1}{4}} = \sqrt[4]{18}$

29. $d^{\frac{1}{5}} = \sqrt[5]{d}$

31. $5^{\frac{2}{3}} = \sqrt[3]{5^2}$

33. $18^{\frac{3}{4}} = \sqrt[4]{18^3}$

35. $y^{\frac{4}{3}} = \sqrt[3]{y^4}$

37. $\sqrt[4]{6^3} = 6^{\frac{3}{4}}$

39. $\sqrt[3]{12^2} = 12^{\frac{2}{3}}$

41. $\sqrt[4]{p^7} = p^{\frac{7}{4}}$

1.

x	f(x)	Expression
0	1	3^0
1	3	3^1
2	9	3^2
3	27	3^3
4	81	3^4
5	243	3^5
x	3^x	-----

The exponents of the expressions in the third column equal x. So, $f(x) = 3x$.

3.

x	f(x)	Expression
0	−1	-2^0
1	−2	-2^1
2	−4	-2^2
3	−8	-2^3
4	−16	-2^4
5	−32	-2^5
x	-2^x	-----

The exponents of the expressions in the third column equal x. So, $f(x) = -2^x$.

5.

x	f(x)	Expression
0	$-\dfrac{1}{25}$	-5^{-2}
1	$-\dfrac{1}{5}$	-5^{-1}
2	−1	-5^0
3	−5	-5^1
4	−25	-5^2
5	−125	-5^3
x	-5^{x-2}	-----

The exponents of the expressions in the third column equal $x - 2$. So, $f(x) = -5^{x-2}$.

7.

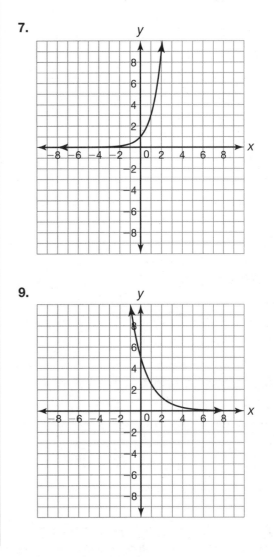

9.

11.

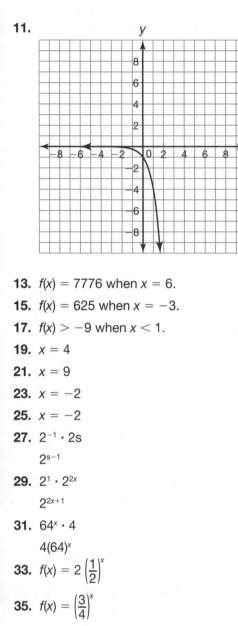

13. $f(x) = 7776$ when $x = 6$.

15. $f(x) = 625$ when $x = -3$.

17. $f(x) > -9$ when $x < 1$.

19. $x = 4$

21. $x = 9$

23. $x = -2$

25. $x = -2$

27. $2^{-1} \cdot 2s$

2^{s-1}

29. $2^1 \cdot 2^{2x}$

2^{2x+1}

31. $64^x \cdot 4$

$4(64)^x$

33. $f(x) = 2\left(\dfrac{1}{2}\right)^x$

35. $f(x) = \left(\dfrac{3}{4}\right)^x$

37. $f(x) = 3\left(\dfrac{1}{3}\right)^x$

Chapter 6

LESSON 6.1

1. The break-even point is between 6 and 7 model cars. Eric must sell more than 6 model cars to make a profit.

3. The break-even point is between 11 and 12 yards mowed. Chen must mow more than 11 yards to make a profit.

5. The break-even point is between 13 and 14 boxes of fruit. The Spanish Club must sell more than 13 boxes of fruit to make a profit.

7. $x + 3y = 8 \qquad 2x - y = 21$

9. $15x - 36 = 2y \qquad 2x + y = 9$

11. $2x - 4y = 20 \qquad -x - 5y = 11$

13. The solution is (4, 5). The system is consistent.

15. There is no solution. The system is inconsistent.

17. The solution is (2, 0.5). The system is consistent.

LESSON 6.2

1. $\begin{cases} 10x + 15y = 20 \\ 5x + 6y = 8.50 \end{cases}$

The solution is (0.5, 1). The band charges $0.50 for each apple and $1.00 for each orange.

3. $\begin{cases} 3x + 2y = 30 \\ 4x + 3y = 41 \end{cases}$

The solution is (8, 3). The Pizza Barn sells each pepperoni pizza for $8 and each order of breadsticks for $3.

5. $\begin{cases} 4x + 2y = 63.8 \\ 9x + 4y = 139.8 \end{cases}$

The solution is (12.2, 7.5). Each large block is 12.2 inches tall and each small block is 7.5 inches tall.

7. The solution is (6, −2).

9. The solution is (−3, −4).

11. The solution is (0, 7).

13. The solution is (2, −2).

LESSON 6.3

1. $\begin{cases} 4x + 10y = 200 \\ 6x + 5y = 200 \end{cases}$

The solution is (25, 10). Each large plate weighs 25 pounds. Each small plate weighs 10 pounds.

3. $\begin{cases} y = 0.25x + 2.50 \\ y = 0.50x + 1.50 \end{cases}$

The solution is (4, 3.50). Both vendors charge $3.50 for a sundae with 4 toppings. If Raja wants fewer than 4 toppings, then Colder & Creamier Sundaes is the better buy. If Raja wants more than 4 toppings, Cold & Creamy Sundaes is the better buy.

5. $\begin{cases} 10x + 6y = 193 \\ 8x + 10y = 183 \end{cases}$

The solution is (16, 5.5). Alicia charges $16 for each purse and $5.50 for each wallet.

LESSON 6.4

1. $\begin{cases} y = 0.02x + 20{,}000 \\ y = 0.01x + 25{,}000 \end{cases}$

The solution is (500,000, 30,000). Both real estate companies will pay Jun $30,000 per year for $500,000 in real estate sales. If Jun expects to sell less than $500,000 of real estate per year, then he should accept the offer from Amazing Homes. If Jun expects to sell more than $500,000 of real estate per year, then he should accept the offer from Dream Homes.

3. $\begin{cases} y = 25x + 15{,}000 \\ y = 21x + 18{,}000 \end{cases}$

The solution is (750, 33,750). Both companies will pay Renee $33,750 for selling 750 food processors. If Renee expects to sell fewer than 750 food processors in one year, then she should accept the offer from Puree Processors. If Renee expects to sell more than 750 food processors in one year, then she should accept the offer from Pro Process Processors.

5. $\begin{cases} y = 0.01x + 22{,}000 \\ y = 0.025x + 13{,}000 \end{cases}$

The solution is (600,000, 28,000). Both dealerships will pay Serena $28,000 for $600,000 in car sales. If Serena expects to have fewer than $600,000 in car sales in one year, then she should accept the offer from Classic Cars. If Serena expects to have more than $600,000 in car sales in one year, then she should accept the offer from Sweet Rides.

Chapter 7

LESSON 7.1

1. $x + y \geq 500$

3. $y > 6x + 20$

5. $7x + 3y > 28$

7. The line will be solid because the symbol is $\leq$.

9. The line will be dashed because the symbol is $<$.

11. The line will be solid because the symbol is $\geq$.

13. The line will be solid because the symbol is $\geq$.

15. The half-plane that includes (0, 0) should be shaded because the inequality is true for that point.

17. The half-plane that does not include (0, 0) should be shaded because the inequality is false for that point.

19. The half-plane that does not include (0, 0) should be shaded because the inequality is false for that point.

21.

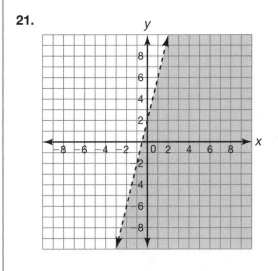

23.

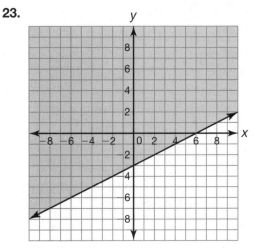

25.

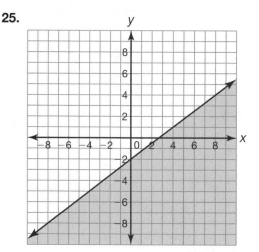

27. No. The ordered pair (6, 3) is not a solution to the inequality. It is not in the shaded half-plane.

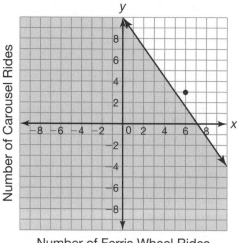

Number of Ferris Wheel Rides

29. No. The ordered pair (6, −1) is not a solution for the problem situation.

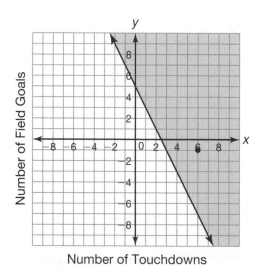

Number of Touchdowns

31. No. The ordered pair (−2, 4) is not a solution for the problem situation.

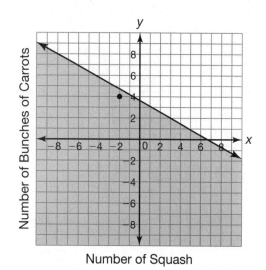

Number of Squash

LESSON 7.2

1. $\begin{cases} 3x + 2y \geq 24 \\ 200x + 100y \leq 1200 \end{cases}$

3. $\begin{cases} x + y \leq 15 \\ 200x + 100y \leq 3000 \end{cases}$

5. $\begin{cases} 10x + 25y \geq 200 \\ 15x + 45y \leq 480 \end{cases}$

7. The point (−2, −10) is a solution to the system of inequalities.

9. The point (3, 7) is not a solution to the system of inequalities.

11. The point (14, 8) is not a solution to the system of inequalities.

13. Answers will vary. (2, 3) and (6, 0)

15. Answers will vary. (1, 2) and (−2, 2)

17. Answers will vary. (−1, 6) and (1, 10)

LESSON 7.3

1. $\begin{cases} r \geq 65 \\ r \leq 180 \\ s \leq 0.65r \end{cases}$

3. $\begin{cases} r \geq 55 \\ r \leq 325 \\ c \leq 0.80r \\ c \geq 0.60r \end{cases}$

5. $\begin{cases} t \geq 5 \\ q \geq 5 \\ t + q \leq 20 \end{cases}$

7.

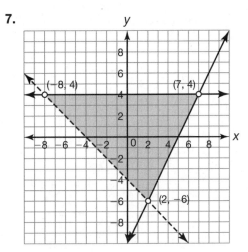

Answers will vary. A solution to the system of inequalities would be (0, 0).

9.

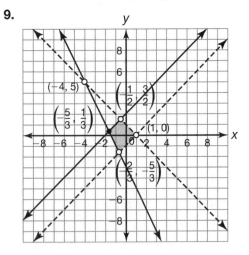

Answers will vary. A solution to the system of inequalities would be (0, 0).

11.

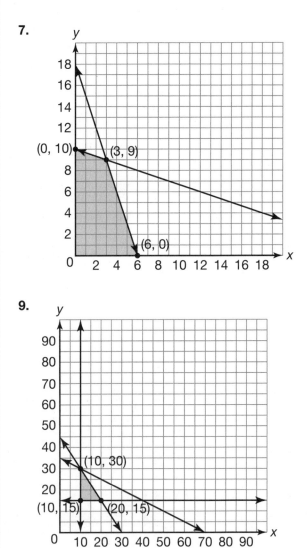

Answers will vary. A solution to the system of inequalities would be (−1, 1).

13. The most Pedro can save is $240 represented by the point (400, 240).

15. The most he will pay is $320.

17. The least he will pay is $160.

LESSON 7.4

1.
$$\begin{cases} t \geq 0 \\ f \geq 0 \\ t + f \leq 40 \\ t + 2f \leq 72 \end{cases}$$

3.
$$\begin{cases} t \geq 0 \\ p \geq 0 \\ t + p \leq 50 \\ 300t + 600p \leq 20{,}000 \end{cases}$$

5.
$$\begin{cases} i \geq 0 \\ a \geq 0 \\ 2i + 3a \leq 168 \\ 65i + 85a \leq 5000 \\ i + a \leq 65 \end{cases}$$

7.

9.

11.

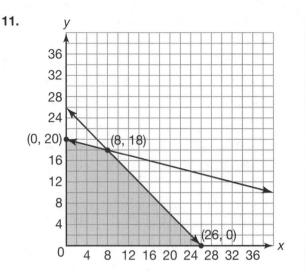

13. The minimum daily cost is $1080. To minimize their daily cost, the company should produce 3 basic models and 8 touch screen models.

15. The maximum profit is $960. To maximize their profit, the company should produce 12 basic models and 12 touch screen models.

17. The minimum number of work hours utilized is 60 hours per day. To minimize the number of work hours utilized per day, the company should produce 3 basic models and 8 touch screen models.

Chapter 8
LESSON 8.1

1.

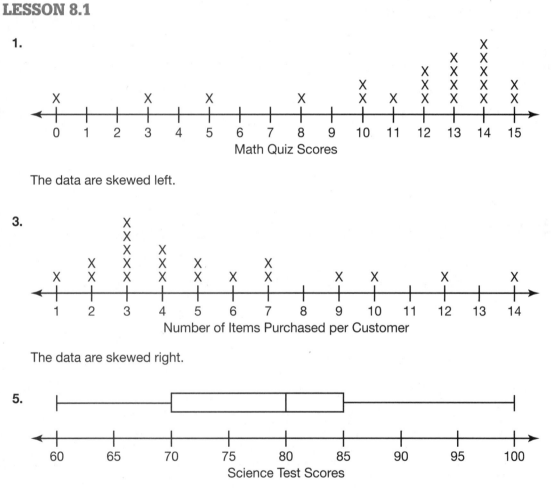

The data are skewed left.

3.

Number of Items Purchased per Customer

The data are skewed right.

5.

Science Test Scores

The data are symmetric.

7.

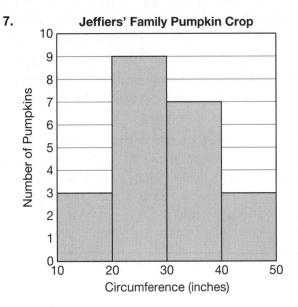

Jeffiers' Family Pumpkin Crop

The data are symmetric.

9. The data are skewed right, because a majority of the data values are on the left of the plot and only a few of the data values are on the right of the plot. This means that a majority of the players on the softball team hit a small number of home runs, while only a few players on the team hit a large number of home runs.

11. Five players hit more than 2 home runs.

13. Six players hit more than 1 and fewer than 9 home runs.

15. The middle 50 percent of the surveyed adults are at least 65 inches and at most 72 inches tall.

17. Fifty percent of the surveyed adults are 68 inches tall or shorter.

19. One hundred percent of the surveyed adults are at least 58 inches tall. Therefore, all 40 of the surveyed adults are at least 58 inches tall.

21. There are a total of 31 students represented by the histogram.

23. It is not possible to determine the number of students who scored exactly 25.

25. Twenty-six students had an ACT composite score less than 30.

LESSON 8.2

1.

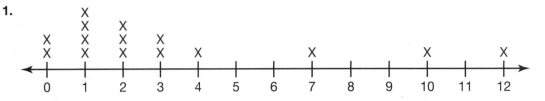

The mean is approximately 3.27 and the median is 2. The median is the best measure of center because the data are skewed right.

3.

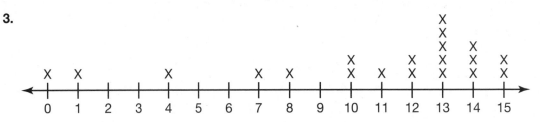

The mean is 10.6 and the median is 12.5. The median is the best measure of center because the data are skewed left.

5.

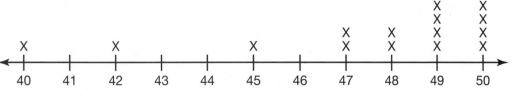

The mean is approximately 47.53 and the median is 49. The median is the best measure of center because the data are skewed left.

7. The mean is the best measure of center to describe the data because the data are symmetric. The mean and median cannot be determined because the data values are not given.

9. The median is the best measure of center to describe the data because the data are skewed right. The median number of movies watched last month is 6. The mean cannot be determined because the data values are not given.

11. The median is the best measure of center to describe the data because the data are skewed right. The mean number of fish caught is approximately 3.14 and the median number of fish caught is 2.

LESSON 8.3

1. IQR = Q3 − Q1

    = 14 − 5

    = 9

The value 30 is an outlier because it is greater than the upper fence.

3. IQR = Q3 − Q1

    = 40 − 28

    = 12

The value 9 is an outlier because it is less than the lower fence. The value 59 is an outlier because it is greater than the upper fence.

5. IQR = Q3 − Q1

    = 25 − 18.5

    = 6.5

The value 8 is an outlier because it is less than the lower fence.

7. IQR = Q3 − Q1

    = 10 − 7

    = 3

There is at least 1 outlier less than the lower fence because the minimum value of the data set is 1.

9. IQR = Q3 − Q1

    = 60 − 45

    = 15

There is at least 1 outlier less than the lower fence because the minimum value of the data set is 15. There is at least 1 outlier greater than the upper fence because the maximum value of the data set is 90.

11. IQR = Q3 − Q1

    = 550 − 350

    = 200

There is at least 1 outlier less than the lower fence because the minimum value of the data set is 0.

LESSON 8.4

1. The mean is 5. The standard deviation is approximately 3.16.

3. The mean is 13. The standard deviation is approximately 7.56.

5. The mean is 4. The standard deviation is approximately 1.15.

7. The mean is approximately 6.56. The standard deviation is approximately 3.34.

9. The mean is approximately 104.45. The standard deviation is approximately 1.44.

11. The mean is 7.9. The standard deviation is approximately 3.42.

LESSON 8.5

1.

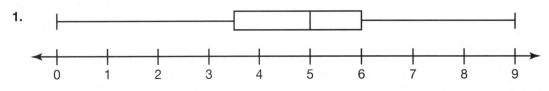

The most appropriate measure of center is the mean, and the most appropriate measure of spread is the standard deviation because the data are symmetric. The mean is 4.75 and the standard deviation is approximately 2.35.

3.

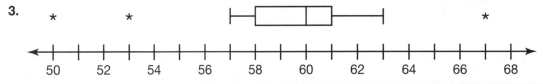

The most appropriate measure of center is the mean, and the most appropriate measure of spread is the standard deviation because the data are symmetric. The mean is 59.2 and the standard deviation is approximately 3.85.

5.

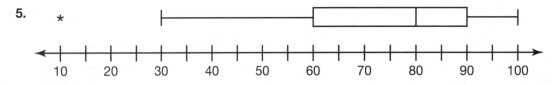

The most appropriate measure of center is the median, and the most appropriate measure of spread is the IQR because the data are skewed left. The median is 80 and the IQR is 30.

7. For each data set, the most appropriate measure of center is the median and the most appropriate measure of spread is the IQR, because the data are skewed right. For Data Set 1, the median is 11 and the IQR is 14. For Data Set 2, the median is 11 and the IQR is 15.

9. For Data Set 1, the most appropriate measure of center is the mean, and the most appropriate measure of spread is the standard deviation because the data are symmetric. For Data Set 1, the mean is 69.9 and the standard deviation is approximately 8.40. For Data Set 2, the most appropriate measure of center is the median, and the most appropriate measure of spread is the IQR because the data are skewed left. For Data Set 2, the median is 74 and the IQR is 16.5.

11. For Data Set 1, the most appropriate measure of center is the median, and the most appropriate measure of spread is the IQR because the data are skewed right. For Data Set 1, the median is 42 and the IQR is 11. For Data Set 2, the most appropriate measure of center is the mean, and the most appropriate measure of spread is the standard deviation because the data are symmetric. For Data Set 2, the mean is 49.5 and the standard deviation is approximately 7.98.

Chapter 9

LESSON 9.1

1. The least squares regression line for the points is $y = 1.13x - 1.02$.

3. The least squares regression line for the points is $y = -0.83x + 0.61$.

5. The least squares regression line for the points is $y = 1.00x + 1.25$.

7. The total number of T-shirts sold in 2008 should be about 143. The actual number of T-shirts sold was 175, so the predicted value is fairly close to the actual value.

9. The total number of T-shirts sold in 2012 should be about 371. The actual number of T-shirts sold was 375, so the predicted value is very close to the actual value.

11. The total number of T-shirts sold in 2020 should be about 829. The prediction is reasonable.

LESSON 9.2

1. These data have a positive correlation. Because of this the *r-value* must be positive. Also, the data are fairly close to forming a straight line, so $r = 0.8$ (A) would be the most accurate.

3. These data have no correlation. Because there is not a linear relationship in the data, the *r*-value will be close to 0, so $r = 0.01$ (A) would be the most accurate.

5. These data have a positive correlation. Because of this the *r*-value must be positive. Also, the data are fairly close to forming a straight line, so $r = 0.7$ (D) would be the most accurate.

7. The correlation coefficient of this data set is 0.8846.

9. The correlation coefficient of this data set is 0.9226.

11. The correlation coefficient of this data set is −0.4193.

13. $y = 34{,}571.4286x + 50{,}238.0952$

$r = 0.9571$

Because the *r*-value is close to 1, the linear regression equation is appropriate for the data set.

15. $y = -0.6286x + 20.2381$

$r = -0.0915$

Because the *r*-value is close to 0, the linear regression equation is not appropriate for the data set.

17. $y = -311.1429x + 9304.5238$

$r = -0.0857$

Because the *r*-value is close to 0, the linear regression equation is not appropriate for the data set.

LESSON 9.3

1.

x	y	Predicted Value	Residual Value
5	3	2.5	0.5
10	4	5	−1
15	9	7.5	1.5
20	7	10	−3
25	13	12.5	0.5
30	15	15	0

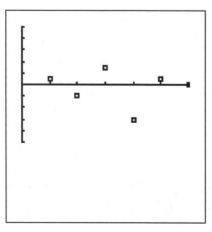

3.

x	y	Predicted Value	Residual Value
1	1.5	0.9	0.6
3	6.5	6.9	−0.4
5	12.5	12.9	−0.4
7	19.5	18.9	0.6
9	24.5	24.9	−0.4
11	31.5	30.9	0.6

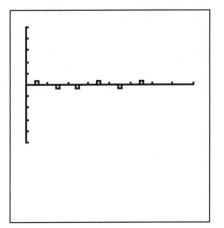

5.

x	y	Predicted Value	Residual Value
100	505	506.4	−1.4
90	460	457.4	2.6
80	415	408.4	6.6
70	360	359.4	0.6
60	305	310.4	−5.4
50	265	261.4	3.6

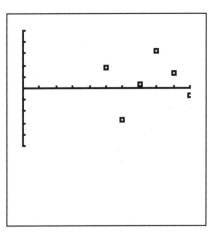

7. Based on the shape of the scatter plot and the correlation coefficient, a linear model appears to be appropriate for the data. Based on the residual plot, a linear model appears to be appropriate for the data.

9. Based on the shape of the scatter plot and the correlation coefficient, a linear model appears to be appropriate for the data. Based on the residual plot, there may be a more appropriate model than linear for the data.

11. Based on the shape of the scatter plot and the correlation coefficient, a linear model appears to be appropriate for the data. Based on the residual plot, a linear model appears to be appropriate for the data.

LESSON 9.4

1. Linear regression equation: $y = 24.98x + 100.86$, $r = 1.0000$

Scatter Plot & Line of Best Fit

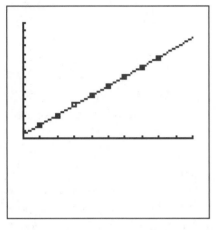

Residual Plot

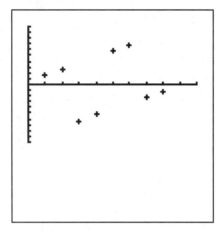

Based on the shape of the scatter plot and the correlation coefficient, a linear model appears to be appropriate for the data. Based on the residual plot, a linear model appears to be appropriate for the data.

3. Linear regression equation: $y = 16x - 42$, $r = 0.9701$

Scatter Plot & Line of Best Fit

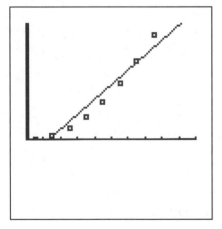

Residual Plot

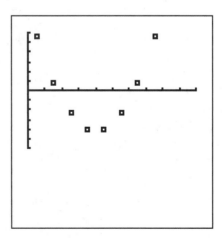

Based on the shape of the scatter plot and the correlation coefficient, a linear model may possibly be appropriate for the data. Based on the residual plot, there may be a more appropriate model than linear for the data.

5. Linear regression equation: $y = -2.51x + 40.18$, $r = -0.9993$

Scatter Plot & Line of Best Fit

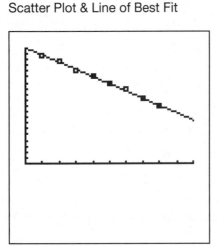

Residual Plot

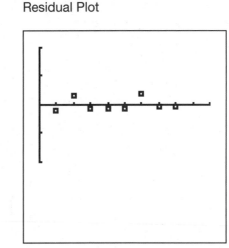

Based on the shape of the scatter plot and the correlation coefficient, a linear model appears to be appropriate for the data. Based on the residual plot, a linear model appears to be appropriate for the data.

LESSON 9.5

1. The correlation does not imply causation. There may be a correlation between ice cream sales and soup sales. For instance, ice cream sales may increase as soup sales decrease because ice cream sales typically increase in warmer weather and soup sales typically decrease in warmer weather. However, this trend does not mean that an increase in ice cream sales causes the soup sales to decrease.

3. The correlation does not imply causation. There may be a correlation between the amount of money spent on an education and a person's salary. For instance, someone who pays for 10 years of higher education to become a medical doctor may have a higher salary than someone who did not finish high school and is working at minimum wage. However, paying for more education does not cause one's salary to be higher. Other factors, such as available job positions, choice of career, and personal abilities impact the amount of annual salary a person receives.

5. The correlation does not imply causation. There may be a correlation between the number of hours a student plays video games per day and the grades a student receives at school. However, playing video games does not cause bad grades. There may be other factors such as poor study habits or a lack of attention that result in a student receiving bad grades.

7. a. Yes. It is very difficult for a student to perform well in school without a healthy breakfast.

   b. No. Not every student who eats breakfast every morning performs well at school.

9. a. No. It may be possible for there to be a large number of fatalities at a disaster site where there are not many paramedics.

   b. No. Not every disaster site that has a large number of paramedics in attendance also has a large number of fatalities.

11. a. No. It may be possible for a person to lose weight without reducing their caloric intake.

   b. Yes. Reducing caloric intake results in weight loss.

Chapter 10
LESSON 10.1

1. Two-way frequency table:

Favorite Color of Students

		Red	Blue	Purple	Green
Class	Class A	////	///	/	/
	Class B	/	////	///	///

Frequency marginal distribution:

Favorite Color of Students

		Red	Blue	Purple	Green	Total
Class	Class A	4	3	1	1	9
	Class B	1	4	3	3	11
	Total	5	7	4	4	20

3. Two-way frequency table:

Favorite Fruit of Students

		Apple	Banana	Grapes	Orange
Class	5th Grade	////	////	//	/
	6th Grade	///	//	/	///

Frequency marginal distribution:

Favorite Fruit of Students

		Apple	Banana	Grapes	Orange	Total
Class	5th Grade	4	4	2	1	11
	6th Grade	3	2	1	3	9
	Total	7	6	3	4	20

5. Two-way frequency table:

Favorite Sports Girls Play

		Soccer	Softball	Swimming	Basketball
Class	**Class A**	/	///	/	///
	Class B	///	/	//	
	Class C	/	/	/	///

Frequency marginal distribution:

Favorite Sports Girls Play

		Soccer	Softball	Swimming	Basketball	Total
Class	**Class A**	1	3	1	3	8
	Class B	3	1	2	0	6
	Class C	1	1	1	3	6
	Total	5	5	4	6	20

7.

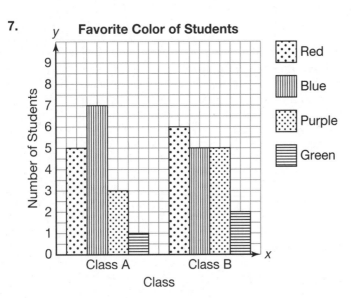

9.

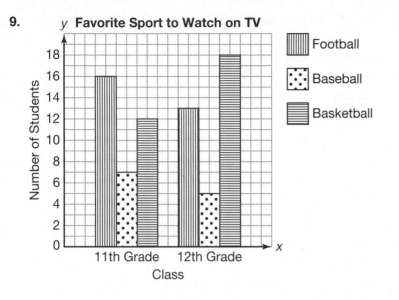

11.

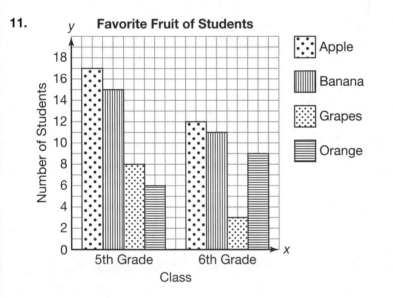

LESSON 10.2

1.

Favorite Music of Students

		Pop	Rap	Country	Rock	Total
Class	**Class A**	$\frac{15}{76} \approx 0.197$	$\frac{10}{76} \approx 0.132$	$\frac{4}{76} \approx 0.053$	$\frac{7}{76} \approx 0.092$	$\frac{36}{76} \approx 0.474$
	Class B	$\frac{12}{76} \approx 0.158$	$\frac{17}{76} \approx 0.224$	$\frac{6}{76} \approx 0.079$	$\frac{5}{76} \approx 0.066$	$\frac{40}{76} \approx 0.526$
	Total	$\frac{27}{76} \approx 0.355$	$\frac{27}{76} \approx 0.355$	$\frac{10}{76} \approx 0.132$	$\frac{12}{76} \approx 0.158$	$\frac{76}{76} = 1$

3.

Favorite Books of Students

Class	Comedy	Drama	Horror	Total
Class A	$\frac{20}{64} \approx 0.313$	$\frac{8}{64} \approx 0.125$	$\frac{3}{64} \approx 0.047$	$\frac{31}{64} \approx 0.484$
Class B	$\frac{18}{64} \approx 0.281$	$\frac{6}{64} \approx 0.094$	$\frac{9}{64} \approx 0.141$	$\frac{33}{64} \approx 0.516$
Total	$\frac{38}{64} \approx 0.594$	$\frac{14}{64} \approx 0.219$	$\frac{12}{64} \approx 0.188$	$\frac{64}{64} = 1$

5.

Favorite Vegetable of Students

Class	Green Beans	Broccoli	Carrots	Corn	Total
Class A	$\frac{9}{67} \approx 0.134$	$\frac{4}{67} \approx 0.060$	$\frac{12}{67} \approx 0.179$	$\frac{8}{67} \approx 0.119$	$\frac{33}{67} \approx 0.493$
Class B	$\frac{10}{67} \approx 0.149$	$\frac{7}{67} \approx 0.104$	$\frac{6}{67} \approx 0.090$	$\frac{11}{67} \approx 0.164$	$\frac{34}{67} \approx 0.507$
Total	$\frac{19}{67} \approx 0.284$	$\frac{11}{67} \approx 0.164$	$\frac{18}{67} \approx 0.269$	$\frac{19}{67} \approx 0.284$	$\frac{67}{67} = 1$

7.

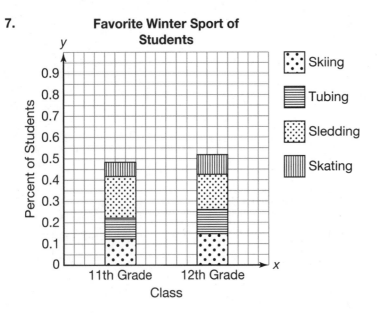

Favorite Winter Sport of Students

Skiing
Tubing
Sledding
Skating

9.

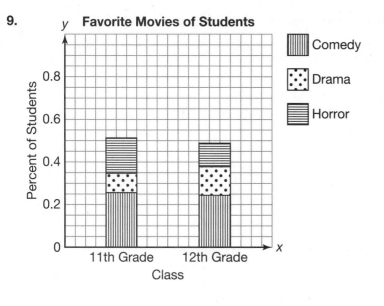

Favorite Movies of Students

11.

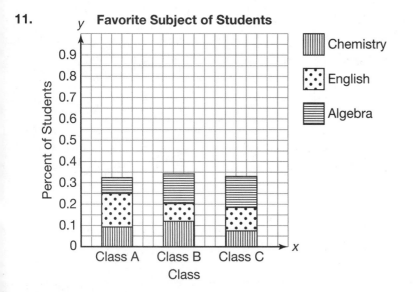

Favorite Subject of Students

LESSON 10.3

1.

Grades of Students

		A	B	C	D	F	Total
Class	**Algebra**	$\frac{6}{20} = 30\%$	$\frac{4}{20} = 20\%$	$\frac{8}{20} = 40\%$	$\frac{1}{20} = 5\%$	$\frac{1}{20} = 5\%$	$\frac{20}{20} = 100\%$
	Geometry	$\frac{6}{30} = 20\%$	$\frac{11}{30} \approx 36.7\%$	$\frac{9}{30} = 30\%$	$\frac{2}{30} \approx 6.7\%$	$\frac{2}{30} \approx 6.7\%$	$\frac{30}{30} = 100\%$
	Trigonometry	$\frac{3}{30} = 10\%$	$\frac{7}{30} \approx 23.3\%$	$\frac{12}{30} \approx 40\%$	$\frac{5}{30} \approx 16.7\%$	$\frac{3}{30} = 10\%$	$\frac{30}{30} = 100\%$

3.

Student's Choice of Shakespeare Play to Study

		Hamlet	Macbeth	King Lear	Othello
Class	**Class A**	$\frac{9}{23} \approx 39.1\%$	$\frac{10}{18} \approx 55.6\%$	$\frac{13}{20} = 65\%$	$\frac{5}{13} \approx 38.5\%$
	Class B	$\frac{14}{23} \approx 60.9\%$	$\frac{8}{18} \approx 44.4\%$	$\frac{7}{20} = 35\%$	$\frac{8}{13} \approx 61.5\%$
	Total	$\frac{23}{23} = 100\%$	$\frac{18}{18} = 100\%$	$\frac{20}{20} = 100\%$	$\frac{13}{13} = 100\%$

5.

Favorite Lunch Item of Students

		Pizza	Salad	Chicken	Burger	Total
Class	**Class A**	$\frac{12}{33} \approx 36.4\%$	$\frac{3}{33} \approx 9.1\%$	$\frac{10}{33} \approx 30.3\%$	$\frac{8}{33} \approx 24.2\%$	$\frac{33}{33} = 100\%$
	Class B	$\frac{9}{35} \approx 25.7\%$	$\frac{8}{35} \approx 22.9\%$	$\frac{13}{35} \approx 37.1\%$	$\frac{5}{35} \approx 14.3\%$	$\frac{35}{35} = 100\%$
	Class C	$\frac{7}{35} = 20\%$	$\frac{9}{35} \approx 25.7\%$	$\frac{7}{35} = 20\%$	$\frac{12}{35} \approx 34.3\%$	$\frac{35}{35} = 100\%$

7. Of the female students, 25.9% participate in track & field.

9. Among female students, swimming is the most popular sport with 36.5% of female students participating.

11. Among female students, soccer is the least popular sport with 16.5% of female students participating.

LESSON 10.4

1. Frequency marginal distribution table:

Favorite Senior Picnic Location of Students

		Beach	Amusement Park	Water Park	Total
Class	**Class A**	⌿⌿⌿⌿ //// 9	/// 2	// 2	13
	Class B	//// 4	// 2	⌿⌿⌿⌿ ⌿⌿⌿⌿ 10	16
	Class C	/// 3	⌿⌿⌿⌿ // 7	/// 3	13
	Total	16	11	15	42

The beach is the most popular location among all three classes.

3. Frequency marginal distribution table:

Favorite Senior Picnic Location of Students

		Beach	Amusement Park	Water Park	Total
Class	**Class A**	*####////* 9	*///* 2	*//* 2	13
	Class B	*////* 4	*//* 2	*#### ####* 10	16
	Class C	*///* 3	*####//* 7	*///* 3	13
	Total	16	11	15	42

In Class B, the water park is the most preferred location.

5. Relative frequency conditional distribution:

Favorite Senior Picnic Location of Students

		Beach	Amusement Park	Water Park	Total
Class	**Class A**	$\frac{9}{13} \approx 69.2\%$	$\frac{2}{13} \approx 15.4\%$	$\frac{2}{13} \approx 15.4\%$	$\frac{13}{13} = 100\%$
	Class B	$\frac{4}{16} = 25\%$	$\frac{2}{16} = 12.5\%$	$\frac{10}{16} = 62.5\%$	$\frac{16}{16} = 100\%$
	Class C	$\frac{3}{13} \approx 23.1\%$	$\frac{7}{13} \approx 53.8\%$	$\frac{3}{13} \approx 23.1\%$	$\frac{13}{13} = 100\%$

At 62.5%, Class B had the highest percentage of students choose the water park as their favorite senior picnic location.

7. Relative frequency conditional distribution:

Favorite Senior Picnic Location of Students

		Beach	Amusement Park	Water Park	Total
Class	**Class A**	$\frac{9}{13} \approx 69.2\%$	$\frac{2}{13} \approx 15.4\%$	$\frac{2}{13} \approx 15.4\%$	$\frac{13}{13} = 100\%$
	Class B	$\frac{4}{16} = 25\%$	$\frac{2}{16} = 12.5\%$	$\frac{10}{16} = 62.5\%$	$\frac{16}{16} = 100\%$
	Class C	$\frac{3}{13} \approx 23.1\%$	$\frac{7}{13} \approx 53.8\%$	$\frac{3}{13} \approx 23.1\%$	$\frac{13}{13} = 100\%$

Class A, with 69.2%, had the highest percentage of students within their class choose their preferred location, the beach.

9. Relative frequency conditional distribution:

Favorite Senior Picnic Location of Students

		Beach	Amusement Park	Water Park
Class	**Class A**	$\frac{9}{16} \approx 56.3\%$	$\frac{2}{11} \approx 18.2\%$	$\frac{2}{15} \approx 13.3\%$
	Class B	$\frac{4}{16} = 25\%$	$\frac{2}{11} \approx 18.2\%$	$\frac{10}{15} \approx 66.7\%$
	Class C	$\frac{3}{16} \approx 18.8\%$	$\frac{7}{11} \approx 63.6\%$	$\frac{3}{15} = 20\%$
	Total	$\frac{16}{16} = 100\%$	$\frac{11}{11} = 100\%$	$\frac{15}{15} = 100\%$

At 63.6%, Class C had the highest percent of students who supported the least popular overall location, the amusement park.

Chapter 11
LESSON 11.1

1. The domain is all times from 0 to 7 hours, which means the trip lasted 7 hours. The range is all distances from 0 to 3.5 miles, which means John went a maximum of 3.5 miles away from home. John traveled 1 mile in each of the first 2 hours. He rested for an hour, and then traveled 1.5 miles in the next hour. At this point he started back toward home. He traveled 1.5 miles in the next hour, and 1 mile in each of the following 2 hours, which brought him back home.

3. The domain is all times from 0 to 5 hours, which means the trip lasted 5 hours. The range is all distances from 0 to 4.5 miles, which means Alexandra's house is 4.5 miles from Tonya's house. Tonya traveled 1 mile in the first half hour, then turned around and traveled 1 mile back to her house in the second half hour. Leaving home again, she went 1.5 miles in the next hour, 1.5 miles the following half hour, half a mile the next half hour, and 1 mile the following half hour. She stayed half an hour at Alexandra's house then went back home, traveling 2 miles in the next half hour and 2.5 miles in the final half hour.

5. The domain is all times from 3:25 to 4:20 which means the trip lasts 55 minutes. The range is all distances from 0 to 1.9 miles which means the community center is 1.9 miles away from the school. Kurt jogged 1 mile in 10 minutes, and then stopped for 10 minutes. He then traveled the remaining 0.9 mile in the following 25 minutes.

7. The domain, which is from 0 to 10 hours, represents the time of Alicia's shift. The range, which is from 4 to 8°F, represents the temperature in the freezer.

9. The temperature is 5°F half an hour after the start of Alicia's shift and between 4 and 5 hours after the start of her shift.

11. The absolute maximum value is 8° and it occurs at 6 hours. This means that the freezer was at its warmest temperature 6 hours after Alicia's shift started.

The absolute minimum value is 4° and it occurs at 0 hours. This means that the freezer was at its coldest temperature when Alicia started her shift.

13. The relation is a function because at any time, the shark is exactly one depth. The function is a linear piecewise function.

Answers

15. The shark's depth is 2.5 meters one minute after the tracking device is installed.

17. The shark is swimming toward the surface between 5 and 8 minutes after the tracking device is installed.

19. Terrence is 2 miles from the car dealership after 7 minutes.

21. The absolute maximum value is 2 miles and it occurs between 6 and 8 minutes. This means that between 6 and 9 minutes, Terrence was farthest from the dealership.

The absolute minimum value is 0 miles and it occurs at 0 minutes and 10 minutes. This means that at 0 minutes and 10 minutes, Terrence was at the dealership.

23. Terrence is driving the fastest between 8 and 10 minutes after the start of his test drive. During this interval, Terrence is driving at a speed of 1 mile per minute.

LESSON 11.2

1.

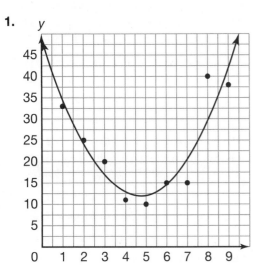

The function belongs to the quadratic function family.

3.

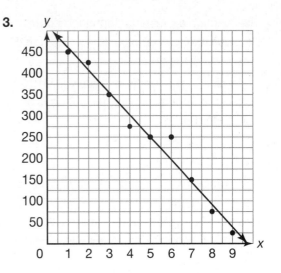

The function belongs to the linear function family.

5.

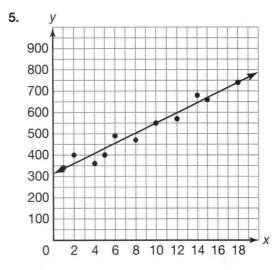

The function belongs to the linear function family.

7. The domain of the function is all real numbers. The range of the function is all real numbers.

9. My function represents continuous data, because data can exist for any time since 8 AM.

11. The total amount of snow accumulation at 6 PM is predicted to be approximately 3.9 inches.

13. This function has neither an absolute minimum nor an absolute maximum. However, in terms of the problem situation, the number of ants cannot be negative, so the function can never go below the x-axis.

15. The function represents continuous data, because the number of ants is a function of time and time is continuous.

17. According to the function, there will be 100 ants in the farm approximately 46 days after it was started.

19. The quadratic function family best represents the function.

21. The domain of the function is all real numbers. The range of the function is all real numbers less than or equal to approximately 8100. The domain of the problem situation is all real numbers greater than or equal to 0. The range of the problem situation is all real numbers greater than or equal to 0 and less than or equal to approximately 8100.

23. According to the function, the median price per acre of land will be approximately $3000 in the year 2015.

LESSON 11.3

1. $f(x) = 1.88(1.06)^x$

   $r \approx 0.98$

3. $f(x) = 6.91(1.07)^x$

   $r \approx 0.95$

5. $f(x) = 2101.58(0.25)^x$

   $r \approx -0.99$

7. 3.28

9. 1612.46

11. 439.24

13. 31.56

15. 479,377.65

17. $f(x) = 497.63(1.06)^x$

   $f(50) = 497.63(1.06)^{50}$

   ≈ 9166.42

   The account's value will be approximately $9166.42 in 2020.

19. $f(x) = 856.83(0.91)^x$

   $f(16) = 856.83(0.91)^{16}$

   ≈ 189.48

   There will be approximately 189 sunfish in the lake in his sixteenth year.

21. $f(x) = 14.75(2.74)^x$

   $f(7) = 14.75(2.74)^7$

   $\approx 17,101.96$

   There will be approximately 17,102 bacteria cells in the colony after 7 hours.

LESSON 11.4

1. $y = -0.5x^2 - 33.6x + 749.9$

   x represents the time in months the television has been for sale

   y represents the price in dollars of the television

3. $y = (885.8)(1.1)^x$

   x represents the time in months

   y represents the population of a town

5. $y = 0.06x^2 - 7x + 412.5$

   x represents the vehicle's mileage in thousands of miles

   y represents the cost for repairs in dollars

7. The exponential regression equation fits the data better than the quadratic regression equation. The exponential regression equation is closer to more points in the data set.

9. The quadratic regression equation fits the data better than the exponential regression equation. The quadratic regression equation is closer to more points in the data set.

11. The quadratic regression equation fits the data better than the exponential regression equation. The quadratic regression equation is closer to more points in the data set.

13. The height of the ball is 261 feet after 2 seconds.

15. The temperature reaches 152 degrees Fahrenheit about 27.7 minutes after the pot is removed from the stove.

17. The polar bear population is about 234 after 20 years.

19. The domain is all real numbers greater than or equal to 0, because the car did not have a value prior to the year of its manufacture. The range is all real numbers greater than or equal to approximately $1000, because the function's value starts at approximately $3685, and then drops to approximately $1000 before rising from that point onward.

21. The function has no *x*-intercepts, because it does not cross the *x*-axis. The function has a *y*-intercept of $3685.45, which represents the estimated value of the car in the year 1970 according to the function.

23. The intersection point is at about (40, 19,000) so the value of the car will be about $19,000 in 2010.

25. The function does not have a maximum value. Even though the given exponential function has no minimum value, the function as it relates to the problem has a minimum value of approximately 5 in the year 2005.

27. The function increases over the entire domain from the year 2005 to infinity.

29. The intersection point is at about (7, 200) so about 200 wild Burmese pythons will be captured in 2012.

Chapter 12

LESSON 12.1

1. $d = 5$

3. $d \approx 12.1$

5. $d = 10$

7. $d \approx 7.1$

9. $d \approx 9.2$

11. $d \approx 12.8$

13.

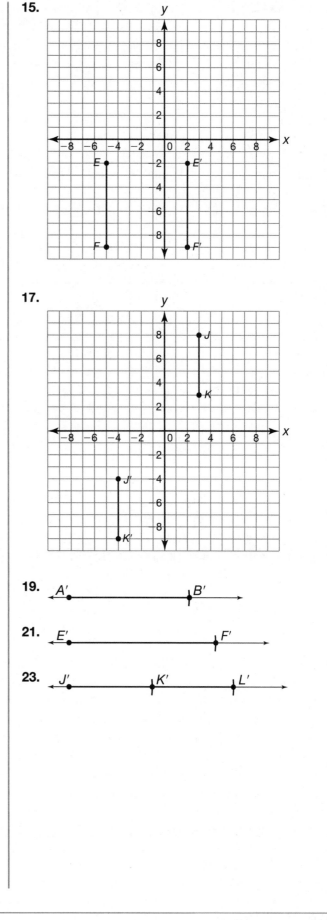

15.

17.

19. A' ———— B'

21. E' ———— F'

23. J' ——— K' ——— L'

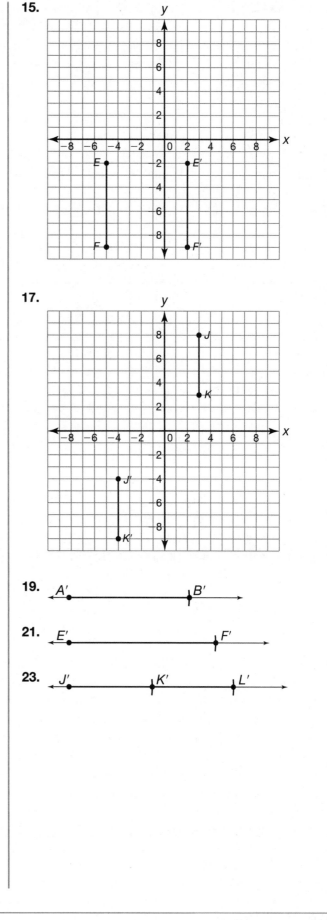

LESSON 12.2

1. (6, 3)
3. (−2, 4)
5. (−5, 1.5)
7. (5, 5)
9. (−1, 6)
11. (−4, −5.5)
13.

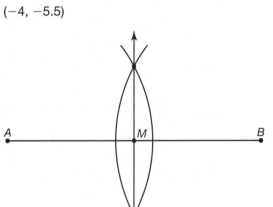

15.

17.

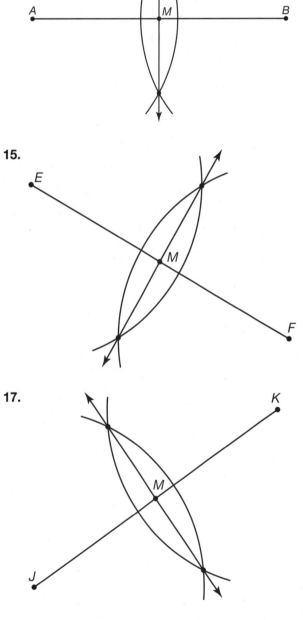

LESSON 12.3

1.

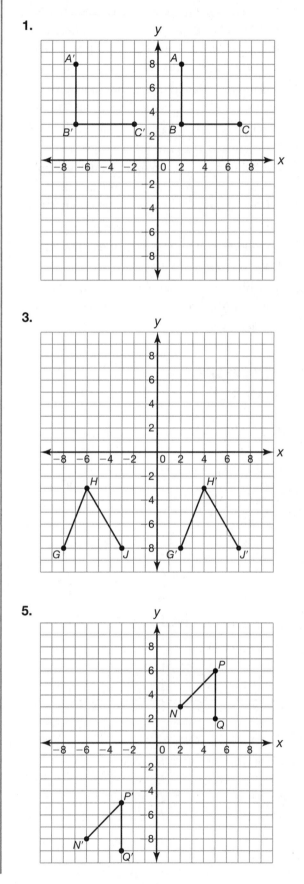

3.

5.

7.

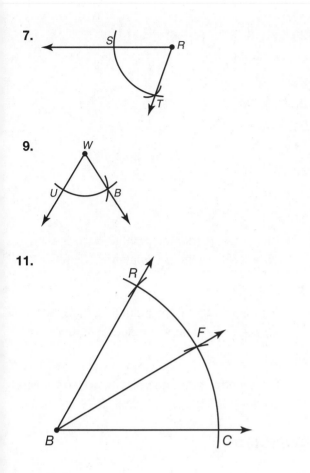

9.

11.

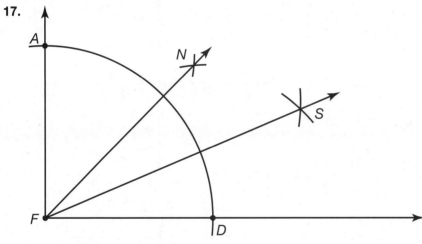

13.

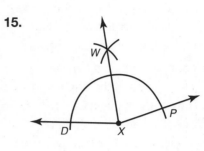

15.

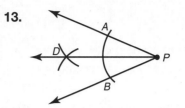

17.

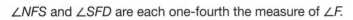

∠*NFS* and ∠*SFD* are each one-fourth the measure of ∠*F*.

1. Parallel. The slope of line n is -2, which is equal to the slope of line m, so the lines are parallel.

3. Perpendicular. The slope of line r is -5 and the slope of line s is $\frac{1}{5}$. The product of the slopes is $-5 \times \frac{1}{5} = -1$, so the slopes are negative reciprocals and the lines are perpendicular.

5. Neither. The equation for line p can be rewritten as $y = x + 4$, and the equation for line q can be rewritten as $y = -2x + 8$. The slope of line p is 1 and the slope of line q is -2. The slopes of the lines are not equal, so the lines are not parallel. The product of the slopes is $1 \times (-2) = -2 \neq -1$, so the lines are not perpendicular.

7. The lines are perpendicular. The slope of line p is $\frac{3}{2}$ and the slope of line q is $-\frac{2}{3}$. Because $\frac{3}{2}\left(-\frac{2}{3}\right) = -1$, the lines are perpendicular.

9. The lines are neither parallel or perpendicular. The slope of line t is $\frac{3}{2}$ and the slope of line u is 2. The slopes are not equal, so the lines are not parallel. The slopes are not negative reciprocals, so the lines are not perpendicular.

11. The lines are neither parallel or perpendicular. The slope of line s is $-\frac{4}{3}$ and the slope of line t is $-\frac{9}{7}$. The slopes are not equal, so the lines are not parallel. The slopes are not negative reciprocals, so the lines are not perpendicular.

13. $(y - 2) = \frac{4}{5}(x - 1)$
    $y = \frac{4}{5}x + \frac{6}{5}$

15. $(y + 2) = 7(x - 5)$
    $y = 7x - 37$

17. $(y - 8) = \frac{1}{3}(x - 9)$
    $y = \frac{1}{3}x + 5$

19. $(y - 4) = -\frac{1}{2}(x - 5)$
    $y = -\frac{1}{2}x + \frac{13}{2}$

21. $(y + 8) = \frac{5}{2}(x - 2)$
    $y = \frac{5}{2}x - 13$

23. $(y + 3) = -\frac{1}{6}(x - 6)$
    $y = -\frac{1}{6}x - 2$

25. $x = -2$

27. $x = 9$

29. $x = -5$

31. $y = 7$

33. $y = -3$

35. $y = 8$

37. $y = -\frac{1}{2}x + 4$.

    The distance from the point $(0, 4)$ to the line $f(x) = 2x - 3$ is approximately 3.13 units.

39. $y = -\frac{3}{2}x + 2$.

    The distance from the point $(-2, 5)$ to the line $f(x) = \frac{2}{3}x - \frac{1}{6}$ is approximately 5.41 units.

41. $y = -3x + 8$.

    The distance from the point $(3, -1)$ to the line $f(x) = \frac{1}{3}x - 6$ is approximately 3.79 units.

LESSON 12.5

1.

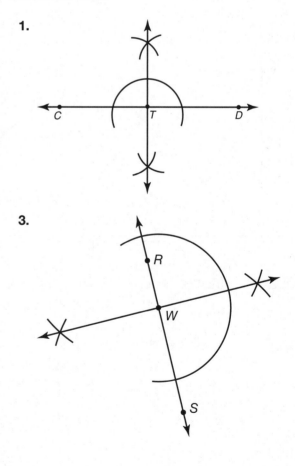

3.

5.

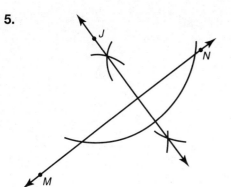

7.

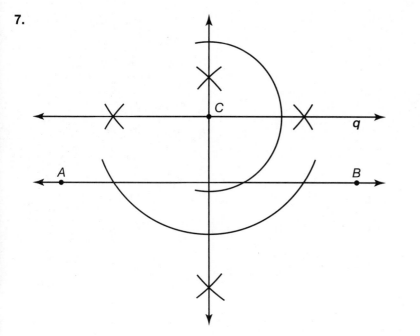

9.

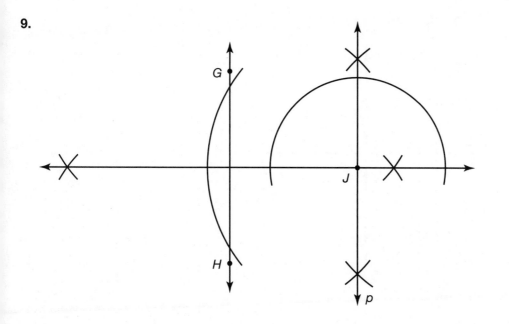

11.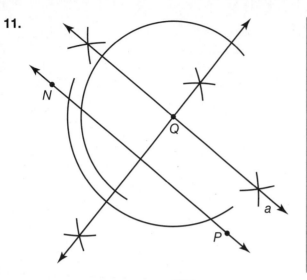

13.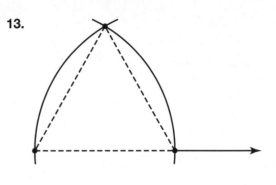

15.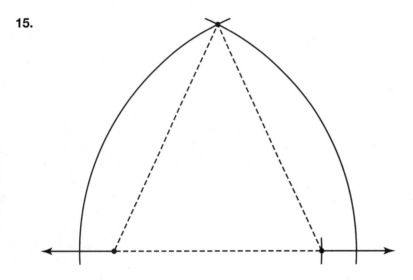

17.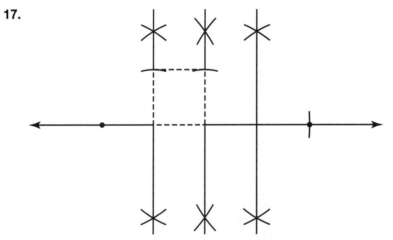

19.

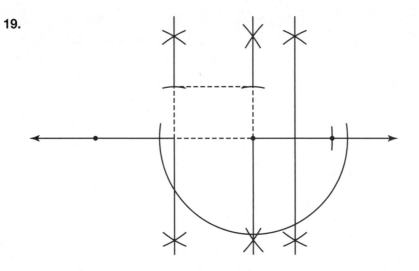

Chapter 13

LESSON 13.1

1.

3.

5.

7.

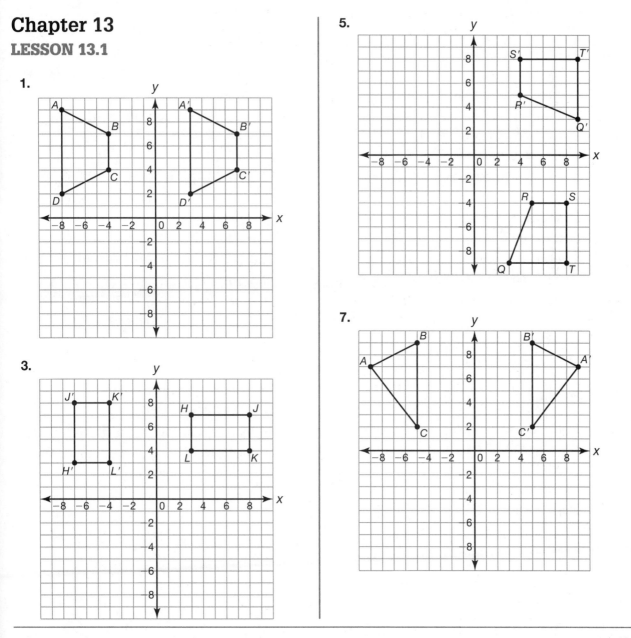

9.

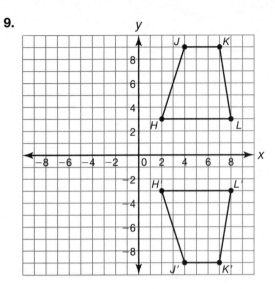

11. The vertices of triangle A′ B′ C′ are A′ (−1, 3), B′ (−4, 8), and C′ (−10, 5).

13. The vertices of parallelogram H′ J′ K′ L′ are H′ (2, 1), J′ (3, 6), K′ (7, 6), and L′ (6, 1).

15. The vertices of triangle R′ S′ T′ are R′ (−5, 6), S′ (−3, 10), and T′ (−2, 2).

17. The vertices of triangle A′ B′ C′ are A′ (−3, 5), B′ (−8, 2), and C′ (−5, −4).

19. The vertices of parallelogram H′ J′ K′ L′ are H′ (6, 2), J′ (1, 3), K′ (1, 7) and L′ (6, 6).

21. The vertices of triangle R′ S′ T′ are R′ (−3, 0), S′ (−7, 2), and T′ (1, 3).

23. The vertices of triangle A′ B′ C′ are A′ (5, −3), B′ (2, −8), and C′ (−4, −5).

25. The vertices of parallelogram H′ J′ K′ L′ are H′ (2, 6), J′ (3, 1), K′ (7, 1), and L′ (6, 6).

27. The vertices of triangle R′ S′ T′ are R′ (0, −3), S′ (2, −7), and T′ (3, 1).

LESSON 13.2

1. Triangle *BCA* was reflected over the *x*-axis to create triangle *XYZ*.
$\overline{BC} \cong \overline{XY}, \overline{CA} \cong \overline{YZ}$, and $\overline{BA} \cong \overline{XZ}$; $\angle B \cong \angle X$, $\angle C \cong \angle Y$, and $\angle A \cong \angle Z$.
$\triangle BCA \cong \triangle XYZ$

3. Triangle *MPT* was rotated 180° counterclockwise or clockwise about the origin to create triangle *XYZ*.
$\overline{MP} \cong \overline{XY}, \overline{PT} \cong \overline{YZ}$, and $\overline{MT} \cong \overline{XZ}$; $\angle M \cong \angle X$, $\angle P \cong \angle Y$, and $\angle T \cong \angle Z$.
$\triangle MPT \cong \triangle XYZ$

5. Triangle *AWF* was reflected over the *x*-axis to create triangle *XYZ*.
$\overline{AW} \cong \overline{XY}, \overline{WF} \cong \overline{YZ}$, and $\overline{AF} \cong \overline{XZ}$; $\angle A \cong \angle X$, $\angle W \cong \angle Y$, and $\angle F \cong \angle Z$.
$\triangle AWF \cong \triangle XYZ$

7. Triangle *GNR* was rotated 90° counterclockwise about the origin to create triangle *XYZ*.
$\overline{GN} \cong \overline{XY}, \overline{NR} \cong \overline{YZ}$, and $\overline{GR} \cong \overline{XZ}$; $\angle G \cong \angle X$, $\angle N \cong \angle Y$, and $\angle R \cong \angle Z$.
$\triangle GNR \cong \triangle XYZ$

9. Triangle *VTA* was reflected over the *y*-axis to create triangle *XYZ*.
$\overline{VT} \cong \overline{XY}, \overline{TA} \cong \overline{YZ}$, and $\overline{VA} \cong \overline{XZ}$; $\angle V \cong \angle X$, $\angle T \cong \angle Y$, and $\angle A \cong \angle Z$.
$\triangle VTA \cong \triangle XYZ$

11. $\overline{JP} \cong \overline{TR}, \overline{PM} \cong \overline{RW}$, and $\overline{JM} \cong \overline{TW}$; $\angle J \cong \angle T$, $\angle P \cong \angle R$, and $\angle M \cong \angle W$.

13. $\overline{LU} \cong \overline{MT}, \overline{UV} \cong \overline{TH}$, and $\overline{LV} \cong \overline{HM}$; $\angle L \cong \angle M$, $\angle U \cong \angle T$, and $\angle V \cong \angle H$.

15. $\overline{TO} \cong \overline{BE}, \overline{OM} \cong \overline{EN}$, and $\overline{TM} \cong \overline{BN}$; $\angle T \cong \angle B$, $\angle O \cong \angle E$, and $\angle M \cong \angle N$.

17. $\overline{CA} \cong \overline{SU}, \overline{AT} \cong \overline{UP}$, and $\overline{CT} \cong \overline{SP}$; $\angle C \cong \angle S$, $\angle A \cong \angle U$, and $\angle T \cong \angle P$.

LESSON 13.3

1. The triangles are congruent by the SSS Congruence Theorem.

3. The triangles are not congruent.

5. The triangles are congruent by the SSS Congruence Theorem.

7.

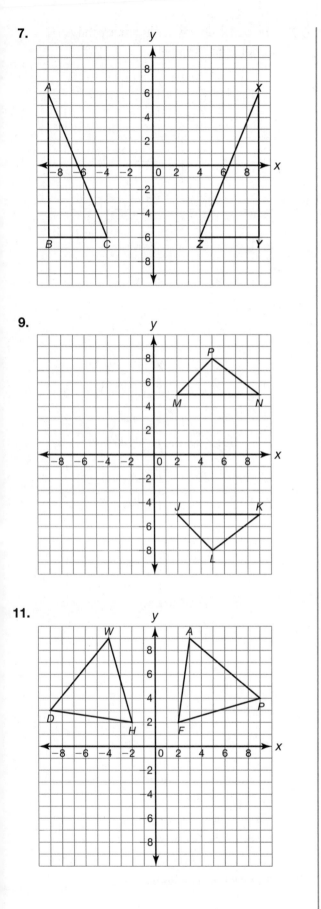

9.

11.

1. The triangles are congruent by the SAS Congruence Theorem.

3. The triangles are congruent by the SAS Congruence Theorem.

5. The triangles are congruent by the SAS Congruence Theorem.

7.

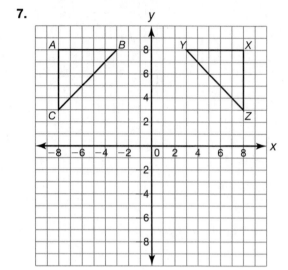

9.

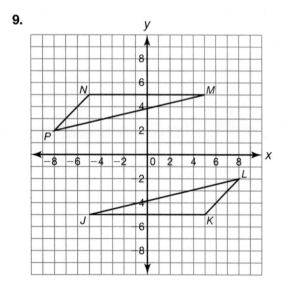

11.

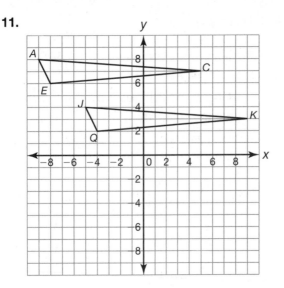

13. $SW = 8$

15. $MN = 2$

17. $m\angle D = 65°$

19. $m\angle T = 50°$

21. The triangles are congruent by SSS.

$\overline{MN} \cong \overline{PQ}$

$\overline{NP} \cong \overline{QM}$

$\overline{MP} \cong \overline{PM}$

23. The triangles are congruent by SAS.

$\overline{BE} \cong \overline{DF}$

$\angle BEC \cong \angle DFA$

$\overline{CE} \cong \overline{AF}$

25. The triangles are congruent by SSS.

$\overline{PQ} \cong \overline{ST}$

$\angle QPR \cong \angle TSW$

$\overline{PR} \cong \overline{SW}$

27. The triangles are congruent by SAS.

$\overline{BD} \cong \overline{BR}$

$\angle DBW \cong \angle RBN$

$\overline{BW} \cong \overline{BN}$

LESSON 13.5

1. The triangles are congruent by the ASA Congruence Theorem.

3. The triangles are not congruent.

5. The triangles are not congruent.

7. The triangles are congruent by the ASA Congruence Theorem.

9.

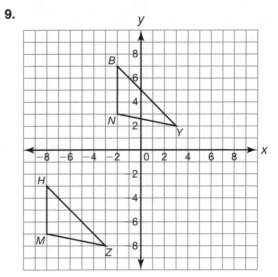

11.

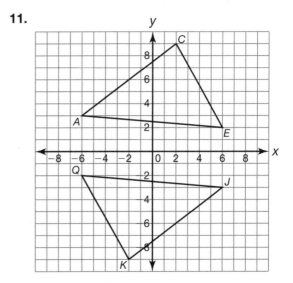

13. $m\angle B = 20°$

15. $m\angle R = 60°$

17. $m\angle T = 40°$

19. $m\angle G = 60°$

LESSON 13.6

1. The triangles are congruent by the AAS Congruence Theorem.

3. The triangles are congruent by the AAS Congruence Theorem.

5. The triangles are congruent by the AAS Congruence Theorem.

7.

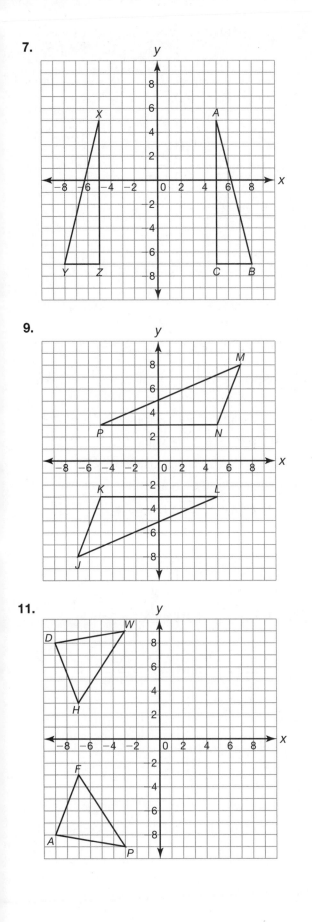

9.

11.

13. $m\angle B = 30°$

15. $m\angle G = 70°$

17. $m\angle Z = 70°$

19. $FR = 25$ m

21. The triangles are congruent by AAS.

$\angle BAD \cong \angle BCD$

$\angle ADB \cong \angle CDB$

$\overline{BD} \cong \overline{BD}$

23. The triangles are congruent by ASA.

$\angle MNQ \cong \angle PQN$

$\overline{NQ} \cong \overline{QN}$

$\angle MQN \cong \angle PNQ$

25. There is not enough information to determine whether the triangles are congruent by ASA or AAS.

27. The triangles are congruent by AAS.

$\angle DGF \cong \angle JTM$

$\angle DFG \cong \angle JMT$

$\overline{DF} \cong \overline{JM}$

Chapter 14

LESSON 14.1

1.

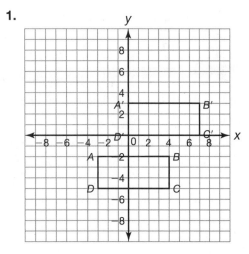

The perimeter of $A'B'C'D'$ is 20 units.

The area of $A'B'C'D'$ is 21 square units.

3.

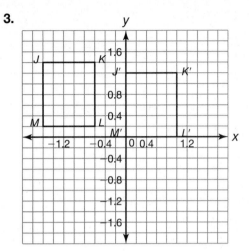

The perimeter of J'K'L'M' is 4.4 units.

The area of J'K'L'M' is 1.2 square units.

5.

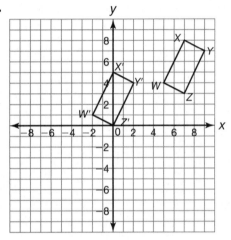

The perimeter of W'X'Y'Z' is approximately 13.42 units.

The area of W'X'Y'Z' is 10 square units.

7.

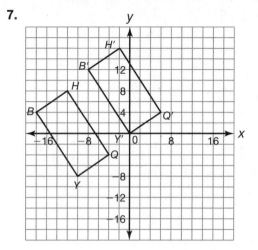

The perimeter of B'H'Q'Y' is approximately 43.27 units.

The area of B'H'Q'Y' is 104 square units.

LESSON 14.2

1. The perimeter is approximately 16.28 units.

3. The perimeter is 24 units.

5. The perimeter is approximately 35.9 units.

7. The area is 17.5 square units.

9. The area is 67.5 square units.

11. The area is 15 square units.

13.

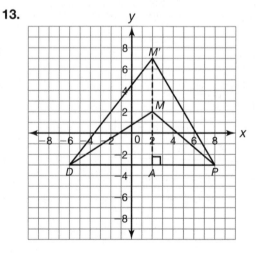

The area of triangle DMP is 35 square units.

The area of triangle DM'P is 70 square units.

15.

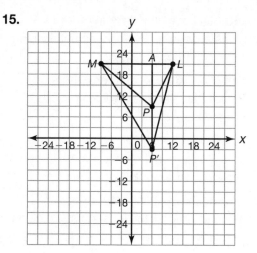

The area of triangle *MLP* is 126 units.

The area of triangle *MLP'* is 252 units.

17.

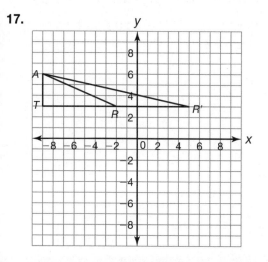

The area of triangle *ART* is 10.5 square units.

The area of triangle *AR'T* is 21 square units.

LESSON 14.3

1. The perimeter is 16 units.

3. The perimeter is 54 units.

5. The perimeter is approximately 4.83 units.

7. The area is 35 square units.

9. The area is 60 square units.

11. The area is 48 square units.

13.

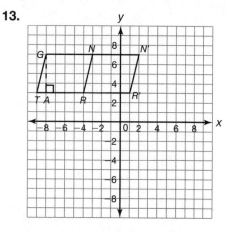

Area of parallelogram *GNRT*:

Area = *bh*

    = (5)(4)

    = 20

The area is 20 square units.

Area of parallelogram *GN'R'T*:

Area = *bh*

    = (10)(4)

    = 40

The area is 40 square units.

15.

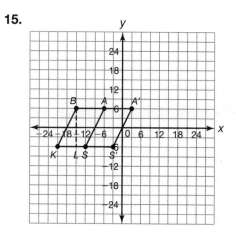

Area of parallelogram *BASK*

Area = *bh*

    = (9)(15)

    = 135

The area is 135 units.

Area of parallelogram *BA'S'K*

Area = *bh*

    = (18)(15)

    = 270

The area is 270 units.

17.

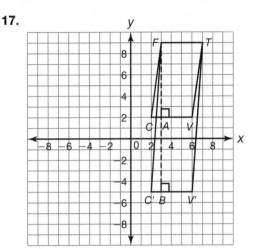

Area of parallelogram *CFTV*:

$Area = bh$

$= (4)(7)$

$= 28$

The area is 28 square units.

Area of parallelogram *C'FTV'*:

$A = bh$

$= (4)(14)$

$= 56$

The area is 56 square units.

LESSON 14.4

1. The perimeter is approximately 19.83 units.
3. The perimeter is approximately 19.21 units.
5. The perimeter is 60 units.
7. The area is 40 square units.
9. The area is 70 square units.
11. The total area is 42 square units.

Chapter 15
LESSON 15.1

1. Point *C* can have an infinite number of locations as long as the location satisfies one of the following conditions:

   • Point *C* could be located anywhere on line $y = 3$ except where $x = 2$.

   • Point *C* could be located anywhere on line $y = -3$ except where $x = 2$.

3. Point *C* can have an infinite number of locations as long as the location satisfies one of the following conditions:

   • Point *C* could be located anywhere on Circle *A* between the *y*-values of 3 and 9 except where $x = 2$.

   • Point *C* could be located anywhere on Circle *B* between the *y*-values of -3 and -9 except where $x = 2$.

5. Point *C* can have an infinite number of locations as long as the location satisfies one of the following conditions:

   • Point *C* could be located anywhere on line $y = 0$ except where $x = 2$.

   • Point *C* could be located anywhere on Circle *A* except where $x = 2$.

   • Point *C* could be located anywhere on Circle *B* except where $x = 2$.

7.

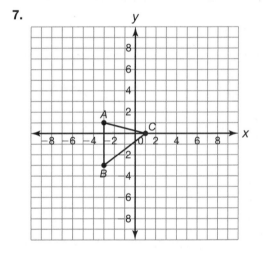

Because each of the side lengths are different, triangle *ABC* is scalene.

9.

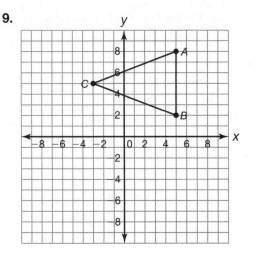

Because sides *AC* and *BC* are equal, triangle *ABC* is isosceles.

11.

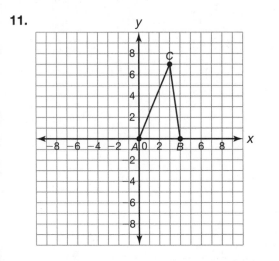

Because each of the side lengths are different, triangle *ABC* is scalene.

13.

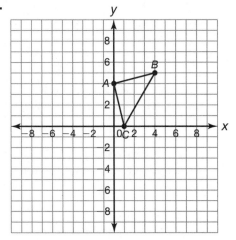

The slope of line segments *AB* and *AC* are negative reciprocals and therefore form a right angle. Triangle *ABC* is a right triangle.

15.

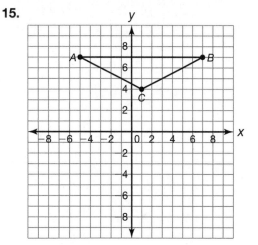

Triangle *ABC* is not a right triangle. Because one angle is greater than 90°, triangle *ABC* is an obtuse triangle.

17.

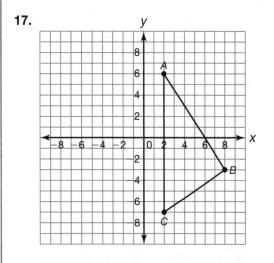

The slope of line segments *AB* and *BC* are negative reciprocals and therefore form a right angle. Triangle *ABC* is a right triangle.

LESSON 15.2

1. The coordinates of point *D* are (7, 4).

3. Point *D* can lie anywhere on the line $y = 2x + 1$ where $x > -1$ and $y > -1$, except at the point (1, 3). Point *D* can lie anywhere on the line $y = -\frac{1}{2}x + \frac{7}{2}$ where $x > -3$ and $y < 5$, except at the point (1, 3).

5. The coordinates of point *D* are (6, −4).

7.

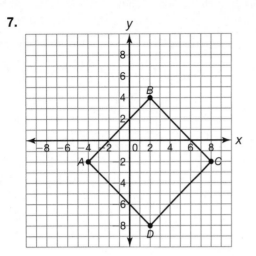

Quadrilateral *ABCD* can best be described as a square.

9.

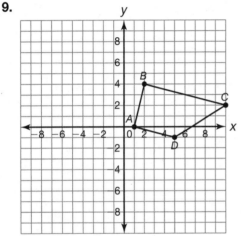

parallel. Quadrilateral *ABCD* can best be described as a trapezoid.

LESSON 15.3

1. The length of segment *AB* is the same length as the radius of circle *A*. Therefore point *B* must lie on circle *A*.

3. The length of segment *AB* is the same length as the radius of circle *A*. Therefore point *B* must lie on circle *A*.

5. The length of segment *AB* is not the same length as the radius of circle *A*. Therefore point *B* does not lie on circle *A*.

7. The length of segment *AB* is the same length as the radius of circle *A*. Therefore point *B* must lie on circle *A*.

9. The length of segment *AB* is not the same length as the radius of circle *A*. Therefore point *B* does not lie on circle *A*.

11. The length of segment *AB* is not the same length as the radius of circle *A*. Therefore point *B* does not lie on circle *A*.

13. The length of segment *A′B* is the same length as the radius of circle *A′*. Therefore point *B* must lie on circle *A′*.

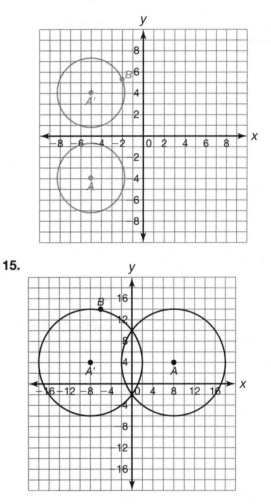

15.

The length of segment *A′B* is not the same length as the radius of circle *A′*. Therefore point *B* does not lie on circle *A′*.

17.

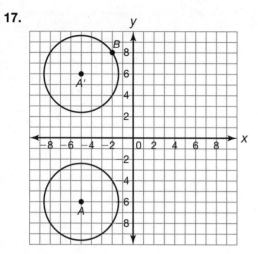

The length of segment $A'B$ is the same length as the radius of circle A'. Therefore point B must lie on circle A'.

LESSON 15.4

1.

Radius of circle A	x-intercepts	y-intercepts	Point in Quadrant I
13	(13, 0)	(0, 13)	(12, 5)
	(−13, 0)	(0, −13)	

3.

Radius of circle A	x-intercepts	y-intercepts	Point in Quadrant III
2.5	(2.5, 0)	(0, 2.5)	(−2, −1.5)
	(−2.5, 0)	(0, −2.5)	

5.

Radius of circle A	x-intercepts	y-intercepts	Point in Quadrant I
6.5	(6.5, 0)	(0, 6.5)	(6, 2.5)
	(−6.5, 0)	(0, −6.5)	

7.

Center	Radius	Points Above & Below Center	Points Right & Left of Center	Point B	Point C
(3, 2)	5	(3, 7)	(8, 2)	(6, 6)	(0, 6)
		(3, −3)	(−2, 2)		

9.

Center	Radius	Points Above & Below Center	Points Right & Left of Center	Point B	Point C
(3, 4)	$3\sqrt{2}$	$(3, 4 + 3\sqrt{2})$ $(3, 4 - 3\sqrt{2})$	$(3 - 3\sqrt{2}, 4)$ $(3 + 3\sqrt{2}, 4)$	(6, 7)	(6, 1)

11.

Center	Radius	Points Above & Below Center	Points Right & Left of Center	Point B	Point C
(8, −6)	10	(8, 4) (8, −16)	(18, −6) (−2, −6)	(16, −12)	(0, −12)

Chapter 16
LESSON 16.1

1. Specific information: Your father has a lot of fat in his diet.

   General information: High-fat diets increase the risk of heart disease.

   Conclusion: Your father is at higher risk of heart disease.

3. Specific information: There have been a lot of people at the mall when Janice has been there.

   General information: The problem does not include any general information.

   Conclusion: It's always crowded at the mall.

5. Specific information: Mario watched 3 parades this summer with each having a fire truck in the lead.

   General information: The problem does not have any general information.

   Conclusion: A fire truck always leads a parade.

7. It is inductive reasoning because he has observed specific examples of a phenomenon—the color of school buses—and come up with a general rule based on those specific examples.

   The conclusion is not necessarily true. It may be the case, for example, that all or most of the school buses in this school district are yellow, while another school district may have orange school buses.

9. It is deductive reasoning because she has taken a general rule about lightning and applied it to this particular situation.

   Her conclusion is not correct because she was given incorrect information. It is a myth that lightning never strikes twice in the same place.

11. It is inductive reasoning because she has observed specific examples of a phenomenon—the color of fire trucks—and come up with a general rule based on those specific examples.

    The conclusion is not necessarily true. It may be the case, for example, that all or most fire trucks are red, but other communities may have orange or yellow fire trucks.

13. Madison used inductive reasoning to conclude that the Johnsons were paying her at a rate of $15 per hour. From that general rule, Jennifer used deductive reasoning to conclude that 4 hours of babysitting should result in a payment of $60. The inductive reasoning looks at evidence and creates a general rule from the evidence. By contrast, the deductive reasoning starts with a general rule and makes a prediction or deduction about what will happen in a particular instance.

15. Tamika used inductive reasoning to conclude that the coin flipping was following a pattern of heads, then tails, then heads, etc. Then Javon used deductive reasoning to conclude that the next flip would land tails. Inductive reasoning looks at specific examples and creates a general rule from the evidence. Because of the limited number of specific examples it is easy to create an incorrect rule. Because deductive reasoning makes a prediction based on given general rule the accuracy of the prediction is dependent on the rule being correct.

17. Vance used inductive reasoning to conclude that he was paid $12 per lawn by the Greenvalley Homeowners Association. From that general rule, Sherwin used deductive reasoning to conclude that mowing 7 lawns should result in a payment of $84. The inductive reasoning looks at evidence and creates a general rule from the evidence. By contrast, the deductive reasoning starts with a general rule and makes a prediction or deduction about what will happen in a particular instance.

LESSON 16.2

1. Statement: I am not 15 now.

2. Statement: It is raining today.

3. Statement: I did read the notice.

5. Statement: The sun is not shining today.

7. If <u>it is sunny tomorrow</u>, <u>we will go to the beach</u>.

9. If <u>a and b are real numbers</u>, then <u>$a^2 + b^2$ is greater than or equal to 0</u>.

11. If <u>I get a raise</u>, then <u>I will buy a new car</u>.

13.

p	q	p → q
T	T	T
T	F	F
F	T	T
F	F	T

Row 1: If p is true, then I can play the violin. If q is true, then I can join the orchestra. It is true that if I can play the violin, I can join the orchestra, so the truth value of the conditional statement is true.

Row 2: If p is true, then I can play the violin. If q is false, then I cannot join the orchestra. It is false that if I can play the violin, I cannot join the orchestra, so the truth value of the conditional statement is false.

Row 3: If p is false, then I cannot play the violin. If q is true, then I can join the orchestra. It could be true that if I cannot play the violin, I can join the orchestra, so the truth value of the conditional statement in this case is true. (For instance, if I play another instrument.)

Row 4: If p is false, then I cannot play the violin. If q is false, then I cannot join the orchestra. It could be true that if I cannot play the violin, I cannot join the orchestra, so the truth value of the conditional statement in this case is true.

15.

p	q	p → q
T	T	T
T	F	F
F	T	T
F	F	T

Row 1: If p is true, then a plant is an oak. If q is true, then that plant is a tree. It is true that if a plant is an oak, then that plant is a tree, so the truth value of the conditional statement is true.

Row 2: If p is true, then a plant is an oak. If q is false, then that plant is not a tree. It is false that if a plant is an oak, then it is not a tree, so the truth value of the conditional statement is false.

Row 3: If p is false, then a plant is not an oak. If q is true, then the plant is a tree. It could be true that a plant that is not an oak is a tree, so the truth value of the conditional statement in this case is true.

Row 4: If p is false, then a plant is not an oak. If q is false, then the plant is not a tree. It could be true that if a plant is not an oak, then it is not a tree, so the truth value of the conditional statement in this case is true.

17.

p	q	p → q
T	T	T
T	F	F
F	T	T
F	F	T

Row 1: If p is true, then the traffic light is red. If q is true, then the car is stopped. It is true that if the traffic light is red, the car is stopped. The truth value of the conditional statement is true.

Row 2: If p is true, then the traffic light is red. If q is false, then the car is not stopped. It is false that if the traffic light is red the car is not stopped. The truth value of the conditional statement is false.

Row 3: If p is false the traffic light is not red. If q is true, then the car is stopped. It could be true that if the traffic light is not red, the car is stopped. The truth value of the conditional statement is true.

Row 4: If p is false, then the traffic light is not red. If q is false, then the car is not stopped. It is true that if the traffic light is not red, the car is not stopped. The truth value of the conditional statement is true.

19. If Janis has a piano lesson after school, then today is Tuesday.

21. If he was crazy, then he would believe that the sky is green.

23. If it is a rose, then the flower is red.

25. If you do not go to the grocery store on Saturday, then there will not be very long lines.

27. If the bus arrives on time, then Milo will not be late for work.

29. If the figure does not have 3 sides, then the figure is not a triangle.

31. If the sides of a triangle are not all equal, then the triangle is not an equilateral triangle.

33. If this classroom is not too crowded, there are not more than 30 students in it.

35. If a figure is not a decagon, then the figure does not have 10 sides.

37. If the last digit in N is 0, then N is divisible by 10. True.

Biconditional statement: N is divisible by 10 if and only if the last digit in N is 0.

39. If N is divisible by 5, then the last digit in N is 5.

The converse is not true by counterexample: 10 is divisible by 5, but its last digit is not 5. So a true biconditional statement cannot be written.

41. If a triangle is scalene, then the triangle has no equal sides. True.

Biconditional statement: A triangle has no equal sides if and only if the triangle is scalene.

LESSON 16.3

1. Associative property of addition

3. Inverse property of multiplication

5. Identity property of multiplication

7. Associative property of multiplication

9. $12(6 + 10) = 12(6) + 12(10) = 72 + 120 = 192$

11. $4(x + y) = 4x + 4y$

13. $mn - mp = m(n - p)$

15. $a(b + c) = b(a + c) + ac$

$ab + ac = ba + bc + ac$	Distributive property
$ab + ac = ab + bc + ac$	Commutative property of multiplication
$ab + ac - ac = ab + bc + ac - ac$	Subtraction law of equality
$ab = ab + bc$	Inverse property of addition
$ab - ab = ab + bc - ab$	Subtraction property of equality
$0 = bc + ab - ab$	Commutative property
$0 = bc$	Additive inverse
$b = 0$ or $c = 0$ (or both)	If a product is equal to zero, at least 1 factor in the product is equal to zero.

17. $(x + a)(x + b) = x^2 + ab$

$x^2 + bx + ax + ab = x^2 + ab$	Distributive property
$x^2 + bx + ax + ab - ab = x^2 + ab - ab$	Subtraction property of equality
$x^2 + bx + ax = x^2$	Inverse property of addition
$x^2 - x^2 + bx + ax = x^2 - x^2$	Subtraction property of equality
$bx + ax = 0$	Inverse property of addition
$x(b + a) = 0$	Distributive property
Either $x = 0$ or $a + b = 0$	
$a = -b$	

Even though the statement works for $x = 0$, the statement must be true for all x and $a = -b$ is a counterexample, so the statement is false.

19. Let $a = 3$ and $b = 4$. Then

$a(b + 2) = ab + 2$

$3(4 + 2) = (3)(4) + 2$

$3(6) = 12 + 2$

$18 \neq 14$

This is false, so by counterexample, the conditional statement is false.

LESSON 16.4

1. So, Shelia's birthday is March 12, 1972.

3. 10 coins in his pocket, pennies cannot be the third coin. So, there must be one quarter, one dime, and three nickels in his pocket.

5. the far right either. So, the brown frame is in the middle, the silver frame is on the right, and the black frame is on the left. The tree photo is to the left of the brown frame, so it is in the black frame. The flower photo is to the right of the bird photo, so the bird must be in the brown frame in the middle and the flower in the silver frame on the right.

7. Math Club is advised by Mr. Juarez and meets in Room 10.

   Yearbook is advised by Mrs. Aiello and meets in Room 6.

   Jazz Band is advised by Mr. Dalton and meets in Room 9.

9. Ella took first place with her Physics experiment.

   Hector took second place with his Biology experiment.

   Mitsu took third place with her Chemistry experiment.

11. John has a nylon duffle bag.

    Yasmine has a canvas messenger bag.

    Zach has a leather backpack.

LESSON 16.5

1. Farmer Gray grows cotton on 500 acres.

   Farmer White grows soy on 750 acres.

   Farmer Brown grows corn on 250 acres.

   Farmer Green grows wheat on 400 acres.

3. The round blue bin holds aluminum.

   The square gray bin holds paper.

   The octagonal green bin holds glass.

   The rectangular yellow bin holds plastic.

5. The Bryants live in a farmhouse at 425.

   The Levines live in a brick house at 427.

   The Smiths live in a modern house at 431.

   The Fogartys live in a Victorian house at 433.

   The Singhs live in a Tudor house at 429.

7. Ty likes history, pizza, and listening to music.

   Maddie likes art, tacos, and riding a bike.

   Eva likes math, spaghetti, and reading.

   Ben likes science, turkey subs, and playing on the computer.

   Zoe likes drama, salad, and walking the dog.